The Philosophy of
Gadamer

Continental European Philosophy

This series provides accessible and stimulating introductions to the ideas of continental thinkers who have shaped the fundamentals of European philosophical thought. Powerful and radical, the ideas of these philosophers have often been contested, but they remain key to understanding current philosophical thinking as well as the current direction of disciplines such as political science, literary theory, comparative literature, art history, and cultural studies. Each book seeks to combine clarity with depth, introducing fresh insights and wider perspectives while also providing a comprehensive survey of each thinker's philosophical ideas.

The Philosophy of Gadamer
Jean Grondin

The Philosophy of Merleau-Ponty
Eric Matthews

Forthcoming titles include

The Philosophy of Deleuze Peter Sedgwick	*The Philosophy of Husserl* Burt Hopkins
The Philosophy of Derrida Mark Dooley	*The Philosophy of Kant* Jim O'Shea
The Philosophy of Habermas Andrew Edgar	*The Philosophy of Kierkegaard* George Pattison
The Philosophy of Hegel Allen Speight	*The Philosophy of Nietzsche* Rex Welshon
The Philosophy of Heidegger Jeff Malpas	*The Philosophy of Sartre* Anthony Hatzimoysis

The Philosophy of Schopenhauer
Dale Jacquette

The Philosophy of Gadamer

Jean Grondin

Translated by Kathryn Plant

McGill-Queen's University Press
Montreal & Kingston • Ithaca

English language translation © Kathryn Plant, 2003

ISBN 0-7735-2469-X (hardcover)
ISBN 0-7735-2470-3 (paperback)

Legal deposit second quarter 2003
Bibliothèque nationale du Québec

First published in French as *Introduction à Hans-Georg Gadamer* by
Les Editions du Cerf, Paris, 1999.

Published simultaneously outside North America
by Acumen Publishing Limited

McGill-Queen's University Press acknowledges the financial support of
the Government of Canada through the Book Publishing Development
Program (BPIDP) for its activities.

National Library of Canada Cataloguing in Publication Data

Grondin, Jean
    The philosophy of Gadamer / Jean Grondin ; translated by Kathryn Plant.

Includes bibliographical references and index.
ISBN 0-7735-2469-X (bound).—ISBN 0-7735-2470-3 (pbk.)

    1. Gadamer, Hans Georg, 1900- I. Plant, Kathryn II. Title.

B3248.G34G77 2003   193   C2002-904562-2

Designed and typeset by Kate Williams, Abergavenny.
Printed and bound by Biddles Ltd., Guildford and King's Lynn.

Contents

Abbreviations

AC Hans-Georg Gadamer, *L'Art de Comprendre. Ecrits I: Herméneutique et Tradition Philosophique,* trans. M. Simon (Paris: Aubier-Montaigne, 1982). *L'Art de Comprendre. Ecrits II: Herméneutique et Champs de l'Expérience Humaine,* trans. I. Julien-Deygout, P. Forget, P. Fruchon, J. Grondin and J. Schouwey (Paris: Aubier, 1991).

GA Martin Heidegger, *Gesamtausgabe* (Frankfurt: Klostermann, 1975–).

GW Hans-Georg Gadamer, *Gesammelte Werke,* vols 1–10 (Tübingen: Mohr, 1985–95).

LV Hans-Georg Gadamer, *Langage et Vérité,* trans. J.-C. Gens (Paris: Gallimard, 1995).

PCH Hans-Georg Gadamer, *Le Problème de la Conscience Historique,* ed. P. Fruchon (Paris: Editions du Seuil, 1966).

PH Hans-Georg Gadamer, *La Philosophie Herméneutique,* trans. J. Grondin (Paris: PUF, 1996).

SZ Martin Heidegger, *Sein und Zeit* (1927), (Tübingen: Niemeyer, 1977, fourteenth edition). Cited with the original pagination followed in all translations.

TM Hans-Georg Gadamer, *Truth and Method,* trans. W. Glen-Doepel (London: Sheed and Ward, 1975), second edition, 1989, translation revised by Joel Weinsheimer and Donald G. Marshall.

TPHGG *The Philosophy of Hans-Georg Gadamer,* The Library of Living Philosophers, volume XXIV, ed. L. E. Hahn (Chicago and La Salle, IL: Open Court, 1997).

WM Hans-Georg Gadamer, *Wahrheit und Methode* (1960), cited following the edition of *GW* 1.

Translator's Note

The quotes in the text are taken from *Truth and Method*, second edition (London: Sheed and Ward, 1989). I have added explanatory footnotes where applicable and these are indicated by [trans] at the end of the footnote.

Kathryn Plant

Introduction

1900

Hans-Georg Gadamer was born in Marburg, Germany on 11 February 1900. By chance, he was born, to the exact day, 250 years after Descartes's death. There are coincidences in the calendar! Indeed, it is difficult not to draw a further parallel with Descartes in the very title of Gadamer's major work, *Truth and Method*.

Descartes is the originator of the idea of method that forms the basis of the scientific project of modern times, or quite simply the modern method. For Descartes, the whole edifice of certain and indubitable knowledge, that of science, must be methodologically reviewed and made secure: knowledge founded on prejudice and tradition is from the beginning under suspicion, because its ultimate foundation does not enjoy absolute certainty: it is not resistant to all possible doubt. Descartes finds the foundation and model of this certainty in the evidence of the *cogito*, of the "I think" which is true each time I am aware of thinking, even when I take the trouble to doubt it, and even if an evil genius exerts himself in deceiving me when I am convinced of its certainty.

Modern knowledge is what wishes to eliminate the traditional because its ultimate foundation is not secure, and it promises to begin everything anew, starting with an unbreakable certainty – that of thought which is aware of its own thought. I cannot doubt that I am thinking when I think: I am, and at first I am only, a thinking thing. All other knowledge, following the example of geometry, can be deduced by the same method of certainty, and by virtue of the same clarity. Based on the evidence of the "I think", methodological knowledge is still not that which is dependent on each individual subject. Rather, methodological knowledge is that in which all stages are made secure and which can be verified by others, provided that they follow the rational order, or in other words the natural train of

1

thought. With this method, knowledge is no longer based on fixed opinion, whether prejudice or tradition. From now on, only evidence and the clarity of rightly ordered thought count. If the first resting-place of this knowledge is not found in the external world, for example in the evidence of the senses, which Descartes judges to be dubitable, it is so much the worse for it. The evidence is found first of all in the consciousness of the subject, but it extends to the whole universe of mathematical and geometrical truths which share in the same certainty and find their true basis in the certainty of the "I think". It only remains to extend this type of methodological certainty to the other sciences, beginning with physics, astronomy (which Galileo, a contemporary of Descartes, had made mathematical) and medicine, as the human body is a machine. Metaphysics will eventually be ordered in the same rigorous way, following the same methodological clarity. This was the dream of Descartes, who published his *Meditations* in 1641, four years after the *Discourse on Method*. It was also the dream of Kant, who in 1783 wrote his own *Prolegomena of a Future Metaphysics*. Any method which tries to turn philosophy into a purely methodological enterprise, and additionally all philosophy which considers the indubitable evidence of science to be the only model of knowledge have their great precursor in Descartes and in his idea of method.

But we can certainly say about Gadamer that his whole enterprise stems from a doubt centred on this universal applicability of the idea of method taken as a unique means of access (and doubtless it remains a privileged means of access) to the truth. A quarter of a millennium after Descartes's death and the beginning of the modern scientific and philosophical method, the philosopher who showed its limits and difficulties was born. Gadamer questioned two crucial elements of the Cartesian theory of method. Descartes's scepticism, the decision to adhere to what is certain and indubitable, arises from an act of modesty about human consciousness which does credit to Descartes. But do we not give up this modesty first in thinking that we can find a certain and indubitable knowledge in all its variations, and secondly in wishing to look for this keystone only in the evidence of thinking about our own thoughts? Against these two "claims", and the word is valuable here, Gadamer's philosophy points out that human knowledge and more crucially human practice depend much more on the input of tradition and its prejudices than is generally supposed under the influence of Cartesianism. In support of this view, the conventions of a living language are chiefly invoked, but it can be noted that the transparency of consciousness is anything but a certain and incontestable point of departure. Gadamer here implicitly follows Nietzsche, the master of suspicion, who died in 1900, and Freud, whose seminal work

The Interpretation of Dreams also appeared in 1900.[1] Far from being the most obvious thing in the world, or even prior to our knowledge of the world, knowledge of oneself is perhaps the most problematic of all (for Nietzsche and Freud, it is even illusive). It is in any case anything but a point of departure which is certain of itself.

In both cases, it is human finitude that Gadamer, following his teacher Heidegger, invokes against illusions and flights of consciousness, and also against the prospect of a philosophy which despairs because it is not yet a science. To wish to turn subjective certainty into an absolute, and to wish to reduce the knowledge and the practice of humankind into a series of geometrical deductions, is to ignore this finitude.

From this point on, it would be tempting to turn Gadamer into a "postmodern" thinker, because he throws into question the whole of the evidence of "modernity". But to speak of postmodernism is still to remain on Cartesian soil. Even the term "postmodern" in fact suggests the idea of a new departure, of a *tabula rasa*, which is never the case for Gadamer's thought. In their philosophy of history, the postmoderns are unwitting Cartesians. Their questioning of the idea of method includes their rejection of the idea of Cartesian truth. For postmodernism, criticism of the infatuation with method and with scientific certainty ends in questioning all truth, all notion of the adequacy of consciousness and of reality. For the postmoderns, there are therefore only interpretations or perspectives, interchangeable and equivalent. In Gadamer's view, the great misunderstanding of postmodernism lies here. It still follows Descartes in making knowledge and truth dependent on the idea of method.

What Gadamer takes issue with is not the link between truth and method. The dependence of truth on method is so obvious that it would be useless to try to repeat it once more.[2] What he criticizes is the method's attempt to exercise a monopoly on the notion of truth. This is the modernist Cartesian assumption, which remains that of postmodernism. It stems not only from not taking finitude into consideration, but also from a disregard of the real possibilities of human consciousness. Gadamer's hermeneutics serves as a reminder.

The work

The whole of Gadamer's thought centred around one great work, *Truth and Method*, which appeared in 1960 when Gadamer was already sixty. This was certainly a mature work, meticulously researched, but if we take account of Gadamer's longevity and also of his prodigious output after

1960, it can almost be seen as a youthful publication. He was only twenty-two when he wrote his doctoral thesis, *The Essence of Pleasure in Plato's Dialogues*, which he produced under the benevolent supervision of the famous neo-Kantian Paul Natorp (1854–1924), as one of his last students. Natorp was an eminent historian of philosophy and a first-rate thinker, whose interests included psychology and education. Today he is best known as the author of a work typical of the time, *Platons Ideenlehre* (*The Doctrine of Plato's Forms*), which is notorious for a Kantian approach to Plato's works, even though Natorp tried to minimize the influence of Kant in a postscript to the second edition which appeared in 1921. At the beginning of the twentieth century, Kant was an obligatory point of reference because he was considered to have been the gravedigger of metaphysics and to have replaced it with the royal road to a theory of scientific knowledge.

The framework in which Gadamer received his early philosophical training, whether in Breslau where he studied with the neo-Kantian Richard Hönigswald in 1918–19,[3] or in Marburg where he continued his studies with Natorp and Nicolai Hartmann from 1919, were those of Kant's critical philosophy. The Kantian philosophy then taught was mainly dependent on the rise of the natural sciences in the positivist nineteenth century, which seemed to imply that philosophy was deprived of its objects. Philosophy could no longer be anything other than epistemology or theory of knowledge, even when it took an ethical form: Kantian ethical theory was simply one which sought to make explicit the universally presupposed law to which all human activity should conform, as if it were (the analogy is already Kantian) a law of nature. Within the framework of neo-Kantianism, this "objectivist" moral theory was expressed above all in the objectivism of values.

But the young Gadamer did not entirely endorse the neo-Kantian presuppositions, which regarded philosophical thought as dependent on science. The chief sign of his uncertainty was that, from the time of his doctoral thesis, he was interested in Plato. Ever since he was a schoolboy, Gadamer had been fascinated by poetry, especially that of Stefan George. Gadamer knew that poetry was a means of communication, even though it could not be treated according to the categories of a theory of knowledge centred on the sciences. Worse still, epistemology tends to exclude all poetry and all art from the domain of knowledge: in short, it excludes everything that does not conform to its ideal of systematic knowledge. Gadamer regarded this as a great mistake, and the whole of his hermeneutics tried to correct it.

Besides, Gadamer entered philosophy through poetry. He was attracted by literature, poetry and drama, and in April 1919 he enrolled at the

University of Breslau, where his father was Professor of Pharmaceutical Chemistry, to study "Germanistik", or German literature. Almost immediately he was disappointed in his German studies, thinking that his lecturers were perhaps too preoccupied by issues in formal linguistics. Gadamer realized that what interested him was not so much the formal structure of language, but whether language was a means of understanding.[4] So Gadamer, who had always been interested in all the social sciences, eventually preferred philosophy to purely literary studies, even if philosophy, and the tendency of construction and abstraction that characterize it, were poorly regarded at the time by the intellectuals close to Stefan George's circle. Some of these intellectuals exerted an important influence over Gadamer during the early years of his apprenticeship, including the economist Friedrich Wolters; the two great specialists in classical antiquity, Paul Friedlaender and Karl Reinhardt; the literary critics Ernst Robert Curtius and Max Kommerell; and the poet Oskar Schürer.[5] Under their influence, the young Gadamer continued to immerse himself in writers who doubted the self-sufficiency of modern science and belief in progress: Dostoyevski, Tagore, Theodor Lessing, Thomas Mann and Søren Kierkegaard, whose works enraptured the whole of Germany, and so planted the seeds of German existentialism.

But these authors were not wholeheartedly welcomed by the inner chamber of mainstream philosophy, in thrall to its Kantian lordship. However, Gadamer was seduced by the clandestine interest which Natorp, in later life, paid to mysticism, music and poetry.[6] It is therefore not surprising that Gadamer very soon turned to Plato, whose philosophy still retained a poetic element, because it revealed truth through dialogue. But the young Gadamer's thesis, *The Essence of Pleasure in Plato's Dialogues*, remains a modest university work, which can be compared to an MA thesis today (the thesis is composed of 116 pages of careless typing, with only five notes). Gadamer was then only twenty-two years old, and his strictly philosophical formation, as he soon realized, was still to be undertaken. He therefore did not publish his thesis, although Natorp appeared to be highly satisfied with it.[7] Its non-publication could also have been due to the economic and political crisis which overwhelmed Germany in 1922–3.

This was not the only misfortune to afflict Gadamer. Immediately after he had submitted a copy of his thesis, at the end of the summer of 1922, Gadamer became a victim of the polio epidemic which was raging in Marburg. For a long time he hovered between life and death, and modern medicine could do nothing. He was confined to bed for many months, and during this time he read voraciously (Husserl's *Logical Investigations* amongst other texts) and thought about his future, after his prematurely submitted doctoral thesis. A stroke of destiny changed his life. During the long months of his convalescence, Paul Natorp sent him a manuscript which one of Husserl's young associates at Freiburg, Martin Heidegger, had just submitted to support his application for the post of lecturer at Marburg University. Natorp was enthusiastic about it. Solely on the basis of this manuscript, which remained unpublished until 1989, he succeeded in obtaining for Heidegger (who had not yet published anything of importance) the post of "extraordinary" (or "non-permanent", and so less than "ordinary") lecturer at Marburg from the autumn of 1923. Heidegger had for a long time been thought of as the rising star of phenomenology, and this manuscript, which promised further research and publications on Aristotle, confirmed his talent and even more his genius. The manuscript was entitled *Phenomenological Interpretations of Aristotle* (*Indication of the Situation in Hermeneutics*[8]), but we know today that it contained the seeds of *Being and Time*, which would become one of the great works of the twentieth century. Heidegger must have known this himself, as he did not publish his original manuscript, so certain was he that his thought would soon emerge in a major publication. He did not keep a copy of his manuscript, but instead sent it to Georg Misch in Göttingen, where at the same time he had applied for another post. Unlike Natorp, Misch was somewhat discouraged by the text, which he found to be rather radical, even though it did not appear lacking in promise. Eventually it was Moritz Geiger, a more orthodox representative of phenomenology from Munich, who obtained the post in Göttingen. But Misch did not keep the precious manuscript either. Forty years later, he gave it as a birthday present to his student Joseph König, and it was found by chance amongst König's papers in 1989 (it had long been thought that this famous manuscript had been destroyed forever, because Gadamer had lost it in the bombing during the war).

Like Natorp, Gadamer was spellbound by the manuscript. He had the feeling that he had found in Heidegger what he had been looking for for a long time. Heidegger's electrifying eloquence recalled George's poetry, and he recognized his own philosophical approach in the Heideggerian critique of epistemology that underlay the phenomenological treatment of Aristotle, which made it possible for the first time to see the phenomena of which Aristotle spoke. With Heidegger, what has always fascinated Gadamer is the "immediacy of showing" which is a characteristic of phenomenology. There is something of the poetic in this capacity for visualization, and Heidegger possessed its secret. Gadamer well understood that it was accompanied by a destruction of the traditional categories of Aristotelianism, and also by the neo-Kantian bible of epistemology; idealism, realism, etc., are so many categories which prevent access to the understanding of Aristotle's thought. This gives a revolutionary cast to Heideggerian thought, which corresponds to the attempts of a whole generation of students disillusioned by scholarly philosophy and by the traumatic experiences of the First World War. Such experiences brought about the crumbling of faith in progress and in science that still darkened university philosophy, because the crucial assumption, the point of departure for all philosohical enquiry, remained the province of science. Heidegger was to overturn it all.

As soon as his health allowed, in the summer semester of 1923, Gadamer decided to pursue his studies in Freiburg, above all with Heidegger, but also with Husserl, and Richard Kroner who was then working on his book *From Kant to Hegel*. That semester, by chance, Heidegger was giving his famous course, "The Hermeneutics of Facticity", which is for us one of the most powerful testimonies of the thought of the young Heidegger, on his way to *Being and Time*. The first encounter between Gadamer and Heidegger therefore took place under the sign of hermeneutics, of which Gadamer was later to become the great theorist. But above all, Gadamer was seduced by the seminar that Heidgegger gave on Aristotle's ethics. In numerous autobiographical accounts, Gadamer has always spoken only of this seminar, and never of the hermeneutics course itself.[9] He was everlastingly fascinated by the Heideggerian approach to Aristotle's practical knowledge, by the *phronesis* which has traditionally been translated as "prudence". This is the knowledge of a situation concerning me directly in my own being, but which is nonetheless a source of truth. Knowledge is not solely a matter of detachment and systematic control; it has its roots in a concern for existence for its own sake. As long ago as 1930, Gadamer devoted a groundbreaking essay to this issue of "practical wisdom".[10]

Heidegger of course endorsed an analogous concept in his 1923 summer course on the hermeneutics of facticity. Throughout this semester in Freiburg, although he did not know it was his last, Gadamer followed everything that Heidegger did; besides the seminar on Book VI of Aristotle's *Nichomachean Ethics*, he attended another seminar for beginners on Aristotle, and then the seminar which he taught with Julius Ebbinghaus under the title, "Religion Within the Limits of Common Reason". Both Gadamer and Heidegger also participated in Husserl's seminars. In total, Gadamer went to no less than five of Heidegger's courses during this fateful semester.[11] But that was not all. Doubtless because he understood that the young Gadamer was passionately interested in the Greeks, Heidegger invited him to a private tutorial of one hour a week to go through Aristotle's *Metaphysics*.[12] At the end of the summer semester, Heidegger invited him to spend four weeks in the tiny cabin which he had just had built at Todnauberg.

The exchange was reciprocal: Gadamer could initiate his teacher, who had never really lived outside the little world of Freiburg, into the environment of Marburg where Heidegger had just been appointed "extraordinary lecturer". Heidegger later wrote to Jaspers that he presented himself there a few weeks later with a "militia" of sixteen faithful followers, as he had promised himself to give his fellow-candidate, Nicolai Hartmann, a fright.[13]

Already familiar with Heidegger's world of thought, Gadamer published his first two articles at the end of 1923. In a contribution to a *Festschrift* for Paul Natorp's seventieth birthday, he threw into doubt the claim that the idea of a philosophical system was absolutely relevant, as he suspected that such a system yielded a distortion of historicity and of openness essential to philosophical debate.[14] It was his mentor and friend Nicolai Hartmann who had paid him the honour of inviting him to contribute to such a prestigious collection of articles. The second essay was a long review of the work which Nicolai Hartmann had just published, the *Metaphysics of Knowledge*, but Gadamer's discussion of it took a critical stance. Although Gadamer praised Hartmann's openness to phenomenology, he took him to task for lacking a radical approach and for remaining in thrall to the neo-Kantian fief of epistemology that he nevertheless sought to unravel. Gadamer betrayed his Heideggerian origins, but did not cite Heidegger in claiming that he had undertaken a "critical destruction of traditional philosophy".[15] His reason for not citing Heidegger was that Heidegger had not published any of his research (it is certainly an issue of *Destruktion* in the manuscript which he sent to Natorp). In his review, Gadamer was perhaps the first to use Heideggerian terminology in a publication. He was therefore not only an early Heideggerian, but he was in advance of Heidegger himself. The gesture was nonetheless daring, and later, Gadamer saw in his youthful articles nothing but "impertinent chatter".[16] This does not prevent us from finding, in his criticism of the notion of a system and of the paradigm of epistemology, one of the essential threads of his later hermeneutics, which sprang from his view that the understanding should be placed in its historical framework.

In the winter semester of 1923–4, Gadamer followed Heidegger to Marburg, where he became his assistant. As he had at last been appointed lecturer, Heidegger also became more autonomous and more sure of himself. From his very first course, he indulged in a formal analysis of Husserl, which he had not dared to do in public whilst he was still at Freiburg.[17] The future of phenomenology, and even of philosophy, lay with him. In Marburg, Heidegger engaged in teaching of great power, which cast a spell over a whole generation of students. Like others, Gadamer was dazzled but also crushed by the force of Heidegger's thought. Following a severe letter from Heidegger, he began to have doubts about his capacities and his future in philosophy. He thus decided to devote himself to a series of courses on the ancient world which ended in a state examination in 1927. If Gadamer were never to become an academic, at least he could become a teacher of Greek and Latin in a secondary school. He therefore studied the important classical works in poetry, tragedy and rhetoric, and of course continued to read the "two greats", Aristotle and Plato. In Marburg, Gadamer had the opportunity to work with the great philologist Paul Friedlaender, who was concentrating on editing his most important work, the three volumes on Plato. In Friedlaender's seminar, Gadamer presented for the first time his important interpretation of Aristotle's *Protrepticus*, where he contrasted with great adroitness the framework which yielded the genetic interpretation of Aristotelian ethics proposed by Werner Jaeger.[18] Jaeger wanted to establish that the *Protrepticus* was one of Aristotle's early works, because he could still recognize in it a Platonic concept of philosophy and of *phronesis*, understood as universal wisdom, whereas the later Aristotle limited *phronesis* to practical wisdom. Gadamer charged Jaeger with not taking account of the literary genre of protreptic (or "provocative") writings, where the defence of a particular concept of philosophy and the importance paid to differences between the various schools of philosophy were not at issue, but the defence and promotion of philosophy itself were. It thus comes as no surprise that the Aristotle of the *Protrepticus* ranged himself alongside the most Platonic conception of *phronesis* and of philosophy in the context of such a work. The young Gadamer's critique already revealed his hermeneutic instincts: against the textual obsession of the philologists who stayed with the literal meaning of the text, he effectively took into account the context and the spirit of the writings. Gadamer is still very proud of this first scholarly incursion into the domain of classical philology, which remains one of his great passions. Once again, Gadamer's long criticism was bold, because Jaeger was the undisputed authority of ancient studies in Germany. His work on the development of Aristotle represented without any doubt the biggest breakthrough in Aristotelian research in the twentieth century, and the new educational humanism that Jaeger found amongst the Greeks (a theme elaborated in his great work *Paideia*) acted as a beacon to the whole philological fraternity of the ancient world. Despite his critics, Gadamer himself was profoundly influenced by that humanism.[19]

His studies in classical philology enabled Gadamer to acquire a certain autonomy from Heidegger. But Gadamer was still under Heidegger's influential patronage (he had just published *Being and Nothingness*) when in 1928 he wrote his thesis of certification, equivalent to a State-awarded doctorate, in which he set out a phenomenological interpretation of

Plato's *Philebus*, which still used much Heideggerian terminology, even though Gadamer developed a notion of philosophical dialogue which already represented the first important distance between himself and Heidegger. In 1931 he developed his thesis into a book, *Plato's Dialectical Ethic*, which for a long time, in fact until *Truth and Method*, remained his only true book.

There were several reasons for Gadamer's lengthy silence. His university thesis of 1928 enabled him to teach at the University of Marburg, where he became Privatdozent (lecturer) at about the same time as Heidegger went back to Freiburg to succeed his mentor Husserl. Gadamer thus became more autonomous, just like his colleagues and friends Karl Löwith and Gerhard Krüger who, with him, made up a redoubtable trio of teachers who carried on in Marburg the critical inheritance of Heidegger's thought. Gadamer devoted all his time to his teaching activities. Then came the Nazis and their reign of terror. We cannot truly say that the Nazis prevented Gadamer from publishing, but they at least made him cautious, which has always been one of his most important characteristics. Like his friends from Marburg, Krüger, Löwith and Erich Frank (who had succeeded Heidegger there), Gadamer had been afraid of Heidegger's political involvement, and so had seen him very little since his departure for Freiburg. Although he was able to sympathize, like every ordinary German, with the need for a German national recovery after the humiliation of Versailles, Gadamer could never subscribe to the Nazi Party's petit-bourgeois resentment. In contrast with Heidegger, his much more liberal upbringing caused him rather to despise the Nazis. Why should he take seriously a party which had turned anti-Semitism into a political tool? Furthermore, almost all of Gadamer's close friends in Marburg were Jews: Karl Löwith, Erich Frank, Jakob Klein, Leo Strauss, Eric Auerbach and Richard Kroner, to say nothing of his mentors Paul Friedlaender (who had gone to Halle), the archaeologist Paul Jacobsthal, and many others. Like them, he did not take the Nazis seriously, and hoped that, in a few months, after the self-destruction of the Weimar governments had done its work, the nightmare would disappear. After 30 June 1934, it was too late. In assassinating Röhm and Schleicher and in brutally liquidating the SA, Hitler suppressed all forms of dissidence and did not leave any doubt about the criminal nature of his regime. Every intellectual who respected himself, and who was not suicidal, had to remain silent. This was what Gadamer did.[20] With him, prying minds did not find direct criticisms of National Socialism, but neither did he truly adopt a compromising position, which is to his credit. Forced into silence, in the Nazi reign he concentrated on his teaching activities, contenting himself with intermittent publications, almost all of which focused on

Greek philosophy. Thus there were conferences entitled, respectively, "Plato and the Poets" (1934) and "Education and the State in Plato" (1942). Gadamer became one of the rare specialists in Greek philosophy in Germany. He was even offered a post in classical philology in Halle, which he refused, preferring in 1939 to accept a post in philosophy at Leipzig, the most independent university in the Reich, where he was in addition the only true philosophy lecturer. He therefore had to extend his teaching to the whole of the philosophical tradition, which forced him to delay any important publication.

In 1945 National Socialism at last collapsed and reconstruction began. As he had not compromised himself politically, Gadamer became Rector of the University of Leipzig, with the authorization of the Soviet army of occupation. As an administrator under a new ideological and totalitarian yoke, he tried to preserve the independence of the university, but the longed-for unity between East and West Germany did not happen. Like the majority of his colleagues, he hoped to obtain a post in West Germany. In September 1947, he was appointed Professor in Frankfurt, where he had as colleagues Max Horkheimer and Theodor Adorno.

None of these convulsions were conducive to the preparation of ground-breaking publications. During his twenty months in the post of Rector, he was content with suggesting interpretations of the poems of Rilke, Goethe, Hölderlin, Hesse and Karl Immermann (since collected together in volume 9 of his *Gesammelte Werke*). Poetry represented the only refuge which he could offer himself besides his administrative tasks.

During the postwar years, he also took to heart the need for a German spiritual reconstruction. He arranged several public conferences, as the German people needed focus and were thirsty for philosophy, in the original sense of knowledge and wisdom. He published these conference proceedings in two small monographs of 1947 and 1948.[21] To Gadamer, it appeared crucial to defend the autonomy of both philosophy and science at a time when they were both threatened by new ideological diktats, certainly in the East, and also in Frankfurt.

He did not stay in Frankfurt for very long, as in 1949 he went to Heidelberg to succeed the illustrious Karl Jaspers. In Heidelberg, Gadamer continued to devote his whole energy to the pedagogical imperatives of the time. He published a second edition of Dilthey's useful work on the history of philosophy,[22] translated Book XII of Aristotle's *Metaphysics*, and in 1949 published at great risk a *Festschrift* to commemorate Heidegger's sixtieth birthday. He ensured that Karl Löwith returned to Heidelberg after a long exile in Italy, Japan and New York. In 1953 he founded a philosophical review, the *Philosophische Rundschau*, which was devoted exclusively to the discussion of philosophical articles. Several brilliant young thinkers, including Jürgen Habermas, Dieter Heinrich, Walter Schulz, Ernst Tugendhat and Rüdiger Bubner, attracted attention in the review and received strong encouragement from Gadamer, even if their thoughts were in complete opposition to his own, because Gadamer always valued philosophical talent more than doctrinal fidelity. Just as with the *Protreptic*, what was essential for him was not to defend subtle philosophical positions, but to defend philosophy itself, to practise dialogue, which is its crucial component.

Still, all this does not constitute a work. Gadamer was urged on all sides to produce something substantial. But his purpose was not to set up systems of thought. He was essentially a Platonic dialectician. The truth is reached not through abstract constructions, but through dialogue. He therefore preferred to engage in dialogue with the greats of the philosophical tradition. He was also conscious of his mentor's shadow, which he confessed in an important philosophical text: "Writing, for me, has been for a long time a real torment. I always have the damned feeling that Heidegger is looking over my shoulder."[23]

But his students encouraged him to present that concept of philosophy which owed everything to the practice of philosophical dialogue. There is no better name to use for that method of philosophizing than hermeneutics. For Gadamer, it is always a matter of interpreting and carrying on a dialogue with texts, because everyone is a being with the duty of interpretation, just as he had learnt hermeneutics from the facticity of the young Heidegger. But his hermeneutics also went back to Dilthey, who linked philosophy with the social sciences, and to Husserl, who, like himself, distrusted abstract constructions. The philosophy which he proposed, and which above all he practised, was thus a hermeneutics of philosophy. He dared not speak of a philosophy of hermeneutics,[24] as Heidegger would have wished, because he did not want to claim for himself the ambitious title of philosopher. Philosophy for him could be nothing other than an attribute;[25] he therefore developed a hermeneutics which included a philosophical dimension because it had a universal significance. To interpret, to understand, is not only a process which is practised in the social sciences, but implies yet more fundamentally the whole existence of a human being.

During the 1950s he devoted himself to the great task of hermeneutics. Like Kant and Heidegger, he maintained a complete silence for ten years, but the great force of his thoughts welled up from his formative years in Marburg, where he associated with Heidegger and Bultmann. He discussed many of his thoughts in the Protestant theological circles close to Rudolf Bultmann,[26] obviously more directly concerned with the problems of hermeneutics to which Bultmann had devoted an illuminating article perhaps of inspiration to Gadamer.[27]

Gadamer eventually completed a voluminous manuscript of five hundred pages in which his whole dialogical nature was reflected. Everyone expected a "hermeneutics" from him. He put forward a more modest title, *Major Themes of Philosophical Hermeneutics*, as if a more systematic hermeneutics would one day follow (the Italian jurist Emilio Betti published a yet more voluminous *General Theory of Interpretation* in 1955). The publisher Mohr, who also published Bultmann, accepted this long manuscript, but thought the title strange. Who knew what hermeneutics was in 1960? It was suggested to Gadamer that he should think of a more memorable title. At first, Gadamer thought of *Verstehen und Geschehen*, which in German forms an evocative coupling, but is lost in English (*Understanding and Event*), but the title was too close to Bultmann's *Glauben und Verstehen*, which rhymes very well in German; *Faith and Event* is insipid in the extreme. Gadamer finally proposed *Wahrheit und Methode*, which this time was reminiscent of Goethe (*Wahrheit und Dichtung – Truth and Poetry*). The title was inspired – vague, evocative, mysterious and striking. *Grundzüge einer Philosophischen Hermeneutik* (*Great Themes of Philosophical Hermeneutics*) remained the subtitle, as if to act as a reminder that it was a great systematic work.

It was a great book, by all accounts the most important to come out of German philosophy since *Being and Time*. It represented the outcome of Gadamer's progress. All his previous thoughts led there. The work forms volume 1 of *Gesammelte Werke*, which were published from 1985 onwards. In the finished collection, Gadamer ensured that volumes 5 and 6, devoted to the Greeks, were published before the first volume, as if to remind us that he came to philosophy through the Greeks, and Plato above all. The publication of *Gesammelte Werke* in 1986 was the fifth edition of *Truth and Method*, and was enriched by a very important Preface and Afterword to draw the editions together. But there was a little surprise – the title *Truth and Method* this time covered the first two volumes of the *Gesammelte Werke*, with the second being preparatory and complementary works devoted to hermeneutics before *Truth and Method*. Gadamer seemed to want to say that they were also part of the work itself, as they were all part of the process of which *Truth and Method* was only an extract. The first volume reverted to its initial theme, covering only the "Great Themes of Philosophical Hermeneutics", with the important Preface and Afterword being relegated to the second volume. Gadamer's work was thus a model of the dialogue which it had opened.

The whole of Gadamer's philosophy after *Truth and Method* held to the dialogue form. Gadamer never held back from the need to present a new and systematic version of his thought. Certainly, new emphases in the final edition could easily be noted, and these were put down to the debates arising from the work, but Gadamer spoke only of extensions or complements. *Truth and Method* is nothing other than the defence of a conception, or more, of a practice in philosophical hermeneutics which the later Gadamer singlemindedly carried out. How could he have a *Kehre,* a "turning", as Heidegger and Wittgenstein did, with such an approach?

Gadamer's thought has evolved a long way. It has now become more precise and has been applied to new areas, of which the complete edition in ten volumes, which he himself supervised, gives a thematic glimpse. Volumes 3 and 4 are devoted to interpretations of modern philosophy, and in particular of the three Hs: Hegel, Husserl and Heidegger, whose successor Gadamer has more and more clearly become. Volumes 5, 6 and 7 bring together studies devoted to the Greeks. Volume 7, *Plato in Dialogue,* is the most brilliant and the most refreshing, since it represents the great work on Plato which Heidegger was always expecting from Gadamer. But Gadamer has once again been patient, only publishing this work at the biblical age of ninety-one. Here we discover Gadamer at the height of his wisdom, and we are tempted to compare him, physically as well, with Socrates. Volumes 8 and 9 are given over to poetry and aesthetics, which are the departure-point and the culmination of the complete work. There is also a volume 10, neccessarily retrospective (as is indicated by the title, *Hermeneutik im Rückblick, Hermeneutics in Retrospective*), where Gadamer looked back on his formation, beginning as he had to with the young Heidegger, in recent decades once more accessible in his much more ambitious *Complete Works* (Part 1, *Heidegger im Rückblick*). Gadamer has already devoted an important collection of articles to the work *Heideggers Wege,* which appeared in 1983, and which is taken up and amplified in volume 3. In volume 10, he completed this return to Heidegger by documenting what he justly called the "hermeneutic turning" (Part 2, *Die Hermeneutische Wende*) of twentieth-century philosophy; essays on the exemplary importance of practical philosophy (Part 3, *Hermeneutik und die Praktische Philosophie*); the place of philosophy in society (Part 4, *Die Stellung der Philosophie in der Gesellschaft*), a protreptic theme recurring in Gadamer's work; then a survey of his philosophical encounters with his friends and mentors (Part 5, *Philosophische Begegnungen*), which completes his autobiography published in 1977, where he talked less of himself than of his mentors.

The 300-page bibliography of all Gadamer's publications drawn up by Etsuro Makita in 1994 shows that these ten volumes contain only the thematic quintessence of Gadamer's work. Numerous interpretations of historical and poetic works have been left out, just as have several incidental articles. After he retired in 1968, Gadamer effectively became an itinerant professor and was invited to speak at courses and conferences throughout the world, particularly in the United States and in Italy. From these conferences, often given unprepared, emerged several manuscripts, some of which were gathered together in collections published by Suhrkamp: *Reason in the Age of Science* (1976), *In Praise of Theory* (1983), *The European Heritage* (1989), and *The Enigma of Health* (1994). To these collections have been added great interpretations of poetry, such as that of the cycle by Paul Celan, *Cristaux de Souffle, Qui suis-je et qui es-tu?* (Suhrkamp, 1970, which also forms volume 9 of *Gesammelte Werke*), and a series of conferences on *The Relevance of the Beautiful*. A work which was originally modest thus became gigantic, and no friend of hermeneutic thought will complain.

The unoriginal approach of this present introduction is that *Truth and Method* represents a privileged access to Gadamer's thought. This is Gadamer's obvious purpose: the book is after all the first volume of the *Gesammelte Werke*.[28] What is proposed is a major reading of this critical work,[29] but one which, following the example of Gadamer himself, takes into account the complement furnished by the whole of his work, which allows us to appreciate its full details.

CHAPTER ONE

The Problem of Method and the Project of a Hermeneutics of the Human Sciences

The problem of the beginning according to Rilke: where does our power to live in a world come from?

Gadamer's work opens with one of Rilke's poems, which does not fail to capture the reader's attention. It is also an issue of capture: "as long as you follow and capture only that which you yourself have initiated, it is nothing but competence and venial gain". These words also remind us of Descartes and of his ideal of a method of knowledge thanks to which we will become the "masters and possessors of nature". But who are we, Rilke seems to reply, to hope to master what has always captured us until now? Does true power not come from elsewhere?

> Only if you suddenly capture the ball which an eternal playfellow
> has thrown to you alone, in the core of your being, in a fair throw,
> in one of the arches of God's great bridges, then only then will the
> ability to capture become power, but it will not be your power, it
> will be that of the world.

But who is this "eternal playfellow"? If only we knew! But to think we know is to become masters of our destiny once more and, eventually, to have as playfellows only ourselves, in a reflexive turning back of the *cogito* on itself, so that it always considers only its own thoughts. No, says Gadamer: to understand, to be able to live in a world, comes to us from an "elsewhere" over which we do not have total control. The poetic metaphors of throwing, of a game and of the world with which we are familiar evokes the Heideggerian idea of a *Geworfenheit*, our being which has been "cast" or "projected" into existence, in a kind of dereliction which for Heidegger is a source of *Angst*.[1] This "projected being" is very well understood in Gadamer and Rilke,[2] but there is also the Other, the "eternal playfellow". The projection is never an anonymous outpouring; it comes from the Other who throws the ball, "to me alone, to the core of my being". There is thus a dialogue, a "being-together", a game in which we are involved.

And it is in the midst of this game, which Rilke boldly associates with the arch in God's great bridge, that our own ability to capture and to have power is deployed. It is never just our own, but always that of a world in which we live, which contains us. To speak of God's bridges is less to give ourselves up to a concrete theology than to set boundaries to our capture. The Greek gods first of all appeared in the position of the predicate.[3] *Theos* is always the quality of something which we do not understand: storms which blow up at sea, wars which break out, love which transports us – none of these events can be explained in terms of human control. This is why the gods were often called the *kreittones* in Homer: the "superiors", the "greater", which are both terms of comparison. The gods were not primarily subjects or substances, but were attributes of everything which is produced without our agency. To speak more positively of the gods would probably be to place ourselves on the same level as them, which would be a contradiction if indeed the gods were *kreittones*, up there somewhere, but at the same time everywhere. So there are God's great bridges in Rilke. But it is *we* who take and catch the ball, it is we who are in the game and are capable of being part of the world. This capacity is a reception, in the sense of *pathos*, rather than an activity, and is called "understanding", of which hermeneutics is the philosophical explanation. But it also asks, "what do we really understand?" Because do we not succumb to a share of illusion when we are determined to control the understanding at any price by imposing on it rules and a sure and certain method, which is above all sure of itself? And when we understand, do we really understand ourselves? Do we not reinforce the mystery which passes all understanding? Does the understanding always know where it comes from and what it is? This dimension, this great mystery, which the understanding is to itself, is the issue that Gadamer raises in the crucial preface to the second edition of *Truth and Method* (unfortunately not translated in the recent complete edition): "Do we need a foundation for what has supported us up to now?"[4] Is the understanding always a foundation, and can we give foundations to the understanding itself?

Even though Gadamer raises these questions, he is not "antifoundation-alist". Unlike the postmodernists, he does not reject the whole idea of a foundation. It could be that his thought restores to this issue, crucial for philosophy and for existence, what is most central to it: a foundation so fundamental that it escapes the whole search for a foundation. The fundamental is not always what we think it is. We certainly cannot say that

Gadamer is hostile to foundations. Rather, he is opposed to an easy fundamentalist solution, to foundations that are too convenient, that can be tamed or explained, because to explain foundations is to cut them off from their essential dimension, or the basis from which everything else flows. Gadamer thus denounces the evasions of foundationalism. The idea of a method of understanding is a good example. There is nothing reprehensible in proposing rules for understanding, but can we then get to the bottom of the understanding? Perhaps even the idea of a methodology, in proposing that it can be technically controlled, deprives the understanding of its fundamental element. The issue of foundations is not a technical matter. In offering, or rather imposing, a hold over phenomena, the technical perhaps does not yield their foundation.

Understanding and event: being rather than consciousness

Hermeneutics looks to understand what the understanding is, over and above the ease of a purely technical control of it. This is perhaps what hermeneutics wanted to be, as far as the art of understanding goes (*Kunstlehre des Verstehens, ars interpretandi*). This art presumes to subject the understanding to rules that are the exclusive guarantors of truth. Does the experience of the truth of understanding truly allow itself to be reduced to rules? In all acts of understanding, is there not the aspect of an event, a happening which is not truly dependent on a methodology? We remember that Gadamer thought of entitling his work *Understanding and Event*, *Verstehen und Geschehen*.[5] We can now see why. What is at issue, again as he says in the Preface to the second edition, "is not so much what we should do, but what happens outside our wishes and our acts"[6] when we understand and live in a world.

The experience of truth to which Gadamer appeals is found to depend less on epistemology, or the theory of knowledge in the strict sense, than on a "grounding", or we can also call it a well, which is at one and the same time the soil, source and water of life, but which is not knowledge in the strict sense. Perhaps this aspect of Gadamer's hermeneutics is the most important, and also the most misunderstood. If it is misunderstood, it is because Gadamer in *Truth and Method* sometimes has a tendency, as he himself later recognized, to take an epistemological approach to the problem in talking of "knowledge" and of "assumptions" that would be the conditions of understanding. It could be, in fact it is certain, that he was here the victim of too epistemological a connection with the problem of understanding that he wanted to unsettle. Besides, this is why he placed less emphasis in his later works on the roots of his thoughts in the human sciences, still an issue of epistemology, than on his debt with regard to the experience of art, where epistemology has no place at all. We are here reminded of the essay from 1992, "The Word and the Image: So Much Truth, So Much Being".[7]

If the understanding (and the term is still almost too epistemological) is a matter of event, we do not really know how, nor from where, it comes. It is produced, it rocks and nourishes us, it is the element in which we bathe and which allows us properly to understand ourselves and to share in common experiences. Gadamer draws on the crucial term "experience" in *Truth and Method*. It is not, of course, the experiment which the scientist undertakes in his laboratory, but experience understood in the way meant by Aeschylus (*pathei mathos*: we learn through suffering): experience which strikes us and becomes part of us, more deeply than any syllogism or analytic argument. Our understanding, our experience, are dependent on such a "grounding". The great enticement of modern methodology is to persist in making us forget it. It is like an instumentalist conception of the understanding which hides its essential unavailability. Fundamentally, Gadamer questions this instrumentalism. To understand is not to control, but is a little like breathing or loving: we do not know what sustains us, nor where the wind which gives us life comes from, but we know that everything depends on it and that we do not control anything. We must be there to know what it is, and to know that it is being rather than knowing. To speak of criteria, of norms, of foundations, as happens in contemporary philosophical literature, is to give an instrumentalist conception of the understanding which perhaps misses what is essential. A similar mistake is to think again that Gadamer stands against method and instrumentalism. But this is not the case at all: we must follow a method if we want to build a bridge, solve a mathematical problem or try to find a cure for AIDS. Gadamer has never tried to deny it: instead, he has learnt a lot from the methodologies of understanding, for which he has the highest praise. For him, they are evidence and gain. He never challenges science, but only the fascination which emanates from it[8] and which threatens to reduce the understanding to an instrumental process. He therefore writes, in an important autobiographical work, that hermeneutics perhaps had "fewer things to learn from modern scientific theory than from ancient traditions which should be remembered".[9] Gadamer was thinking here of traditions in rhetoric and practical philosophy that were pushed aside by modern science precisely because they did not subscribe to a strictly instrumentalist conception of the understanding. To say that hemeneutics has "less" to learn from modern science is to recognize that it owes it a lot, but the empire of science is today so obvious, so universally recognized, that perhaps it is more urgent to appeal to traditions which point out the limits of science.

It is thus the easy instrumentalism of epistemology that seems too brief to Gadamer. It is obvious that *Truth and Method* tends to give too objective and intellectual a slant to the hermeneutic experience of understanding, as it speaks of "assumptions" and of the formulation of a proper historical "consciousness" from their subterranean determination. Gadamer recognized that he was here the son of his time, but the transcendence of the wholly epistemological and instrumental consideration was his main concern. Heidegger disliked Gadamer's reference to consciousness here.[10] Gadamer only settled on this term because it is also used in ordinary language to refer to an experience, an awakening or a "crisis of consciousness" which is not reducible to scientific objectivity. After *Truth and Method* Gadamer found a more fortunate turn of phrase, which exploited the sonority of the term in German, as Marx had already done in another context, in saying that the consciousness (*Bewusstsein*) to which he was referring was "Being rather than consciousness".[11] Perhaps the whole of Gadamer is found in that formulation. Not everything is a matter of consciousness, including consciousness itself. To recognize that thought has limits is not to silence it, but to allow it to better apprehend itself and to open itself more easily to dialogue. Its absolute autonomy and its pride are found to be shaken but, knowing itself to be determined, "grounded", thought develops a sharper consciousness from its determination and its historical sources.

Heidegger had previously liberated the notion of understanding from its epistemological straitjacket on listening to the German phrase, *sich auf etwas verstehen*, which refers to a skill more practical than theoretical, an activity rather than reflective knowledge. We say the same in English: "to be skilled at something", to mean that we are on top of something, that we can get something done, that we are capable of doing it.[12] Understanding is always power, power-to-be, force, as in Rilke's poem. But is this "power" always to do with knowing and controlling? There is always a lack of control and a lack of understanding in all understanding. All power conceals impotence. The phrase "to be on top of something", to be capable, already hints at it. It indicates that we are only just on top, that we are scarcely capable, that if need be we can just manage. But what we understand, or are able to do, can at any moment topple into an incapacity, a lack of understanding. To be capable of something is to know that we are never completely capable of it. There is thus an element of mystery in the arising of the understanding. Heidegger also recognized this dimension in his concept of truth, because the Greek term is *a-letheia*, where the initial alpha denotes a lack, a lifting of the veil, an unveiling. But in the experience of truth, which each time is a discovery, the veiling is present, like that to which all truth is deaf.

This experience of truth is central to Gadamer's hermeneutics, a truth which is not really "knowledge", but power and a discovery which does not forget that it cannot discover everything, and that something of the truth essentially remains hidden. The understanding does not always know how it operates, nor from where it comes, but it is nonetheless the source of truth. It is this hermeneutic experience of the truth that interested and intrigued Gadamer. The truth does not only, and perhaps not even primarily, rely on what has an absolutely firm foundation, as scientific methodology insists. The primary role of Gadamer's hermeneutics is to value experiences of truth, of "knowledge", which go beyond the infinitely restricting limits of what allows itself to be objectified in a method of knowledge. The great anamnetic effort of his thought is to recall that the truth is not only, nor even initially, what can be guaranteed by a method.

Gadamer discovered this experience of truth in valuable forgotten traditions that were rediscovered mainly through his own philosophy: in the legacy of rhetoric, where the truth is a matter of belief, integrity and probability, but the certainty or ultimate foundation is lacking, or, it could be added, is still missing; then in practical philosophy, where the truth is always what concerns me directly, without being a matter of technique (like applied ethics, which is so widespread nowadays); in legal and theological hermeneutics because understanding is still and always a matter of application to a particular situation. But the privileged witness of the mystery of this understanding which comes to us from a source of equal mystery is found by Gadamer in the experience of art. This is the departure-point of *Truth and Method*.

The destruction of aesthetics in the name of the humanist tradition

Before the reconquest of this experience of art, this buried truth, we must undo what prevents us from perceiving it. Even if he does so without recognizing it, or by instinct, it is clear that Gadamer follows the method of his master Heidegger in his great confrontations with the history of ideas: to have access to phenomena, we must first of all destroy the "evidence" that hides them. In a word, paradoxically, it is a case of destroying aesthetics. We must destroy the aesthetic consciousness if we want to have access to the truth of art.

What is aesthetic consciousness? As a tautology this time, it is consciousness which considers works of art only as aesthetic objects, in taking away from them their moral or cognitive overtones. It is clear that ignoring the moral and cognitive dimensions has led to the rise of the autonomy of art in modernism, and that contemporary art is unthinkable without them. But this autonomy comes at a price: it cuts off works of art from their aspiration to the truth, from what can be called their "message" (*Aussage*). The autonomous appreciation of aesthetics has its claims, and the aesthete in Gadamer easily recognizes them, but it forgets that a work of art is above all participation in an experience of truth. *King Lear* teaches us what ingratitude is,[13] just as Frans Hals revealed to us who Descartes was. It was imperative for Gadamer to reinstate this experience of truth, for several reasons: first, to free the concept of truth from the web imposed by modern science; next, to counteract the pernicious effects of the contemporary reductionism of the human sciences (and of philosophy) to a simple matter of "aesthetics", understood as arbitrary and deprived of seriousness, in order to arrive at last at a better understanding of the relationship between truth and art, when the former is freed from its aesthetic pseudo-liberation. This experience of truth should allow us to understand better the understanding which is used in the human sciences. If we wish to disengage (*freilegen* also means "to free", "to allow to breathe") the question of truth from the experience of art, as the title of the first section of *Truth and Method* indicates, we must "go beyond the realm of aesthetics". In the course of an analysis of great richness, Gadamer shows that even if the aesthetic consciousness appears to oppose it, it is really the direct product of the methodological consciousness.

Gadamer starts from the problem that is raised by the methodology of the human sciences. Obviously the problem has existed only since the division of knowledge between the exact and the human sciences, which took place in the nineteenth century. And the problem is truly only raised because of the inferiority complex that haunts the human sciences in the face of the launch and explosive success of the exact sciences. Gadamer recalls that all the debates in epistemology raised by the challenge of a proper understanding of the human sciences have been dominated by the problem of method and its ideal of a knowledge of uniformities, regularities and laws,[14] from which is excluded all intervention of contingent factors concerning the observer himself. There are then two possibilities for the human sciences: either to adopt or purely and simply to imitate the method which has (or will have) guaranteed the success of the exact sciences, an attempt which we can associate with positivism, and which ultimately abolishes the distinction between the exact and the human sciences to the profit of *unified science* (positivism which ordinary judgement follows by reserving the term "science" for the pure and hard sciences); or the demarcation of an autonomous methodology for the human sciences. This latter possibility was very largely the approach taken by Dilthey and was that of the methodologists who took care to preserve the threatened autonomy of the human sciences. This autonomy in method could, for its part, be founded either on the *object* of investigation (the wish to grasp the particular as opposed to investigating general laws), or on the *mode of understanding*, with the scientific *explanation* of phenomena being distinguished from the *understanding* which would constitute the components of the human sciences. But if this understanding wishes to be scientific, it must itself be carried out according to method. So was born the great project of a methodology of understanding (which hermeneutics could be, in so far as it is *ars interpretandi*), capable of ensuring and defending the scientism of the human sciences. Gadamer's question here is simple but revolutionary: can we adequately grasp the mode of understanding proper to the human sciences with the help of method? Are we not still, despite our best intentions, allowing ourselves to be dazzled by the model of scientific method? This glare could in fact make us ignore what is proper to the human sciences.

Gadamer's iconoclastic question doubles as a suggestion and as a memory: instead of adopting a methodological paradigm, as if it were the only mode of knowledge, would it not be possible to come closer to the truth of the human sciences by starting from the tradition of humanism, where the *Geisteswissenschaften* (human sciences) continue the legacy? But this humanist tradition has lost its influence, as far as we are concerned. Even Heidegger is amongst those who have distanced themselves from it, to such an extent that it is today often not recognized as a rejected tradition. Gadamer courageously teaches that this rejection is perhaps also the effect of modern science, which is so concerned to limit the term "science" to purely methodological knowledge. In the first chapters of his work, Gadamer devotes himself to recalling what constitutes knowledge for the humanist tradition. Here he starts with Herder and his concept of formation (*Bildung*).[15] For Herder, a human being is a historical being to the extent to which he is called upon to form himself. The term "*Bildung*", used since the time of Goethe and the novels of education (*Bildungsroman*), has several meanings in German, so that it is impossible to give one single equivalent in translation: formation, culture, education. In addition, the term first means in German a natural formation, for example the form of a chain of mountains. Formation is thus not opposed to nature, but is its natural and organic development. In human culture, *Bildung* means the uniquely human way of developing inherent dispositions.[16] According to Gadamer, this concept of formation, education or culture has always been the natural element of the human sciences. The truths of the human sciences are the truths of formation, which form us in all senses of the term: they are stamped on us, they constitute us, and they transform us.

But we would be wrong to consider Gadamer's rehabilitation of the term *Bildung* as a prejudice towards the accumulation of cultural knowledge, which is most often the exclusive preserve of an elite. Gadamer maintains that what is cultivated, "formed", *gebildet*, is not what has factual knowledge, nor displays brilliant cultural knowledge. Those who have a fund of factual knowledge are often called pedants, and they are not proposed as a model to the human sciences. This is not culture. Cultivated people are those who can adopt a position of detachment, a distance in relationship to all of the items of knowledge that characterize the pedant. Here it is permissible to give a long quote from Gadamer's lecture at a conference of 1995, which confirms that this issue had preoccupied him for a long time:

> To be cultured is obviously to cultivate a particular form of distance. Hegel already wondered what constituted a cultured person. The cultured person is the one who is ready to admit as plausible (literally, to value) the thoughts of others. I say that we discover here a remarkable description of the uncultured person: it is typically the person who maintains in all possible circumstances and all possible contexts and with a dictatorial assurance whatever wisdom he has picked up by chance. On the contrary, to leave something undecided is what constitutes the essence of those who can ask questions. The person who is not equal to recognising his own ignorance and, for that reason, to keeping the open character of some decisions precisely in order to find the right solution, will never be what is called a cultured person. The cultured person is not the one who displays superior knowledge, but only the one who, to take an expression from Socrates, has not forgotten the knowledge of his ignorance.[17]

Such is the ideal of culture which has always been that of the human sciences, and indeed that of the human condition. It is a matter of knowing limitations and humility. The essential is not to store items of knowledge, but to realize one's own ignorance when in contact with historical, literary, linguistic and philosophical knowledge. By this hold of self-awareness, one is raised to a certain universality. Gadamer was inspired here by Hegel's pedagogic texts: if the essence of culture or of formation is to raise us to universality, it is because we are taught to open ourselves to other approaches, to other and more general perspectives.[18] To be able to adopt a distance with respect to particularity, beginning with one's own, is what constitutes essential knowledge, that of culture and formation, because it transforms us.

But how do we describe this type of knowledge? Certain scientists, including Helmholtz, clearly realized that it was not a case of inductive knowledge, as in the exact sciences. This is why Helmholtz talked of a certain "feel", a nimbleness which is acquired and which concerns more than memory and a certain sensitivity. The problem with this description is that it risks being taken in a simplistically psychological way, as if it were a case of cultivating the faculties. But Gadamer is quite sympathetic to Helmholtz's description and willingly takes up the idea of "feel" because it fortunately evokes a *je ne sais quoi* that has nothing to do with method: "Does not what is scientific about the human sciences lie rather [in this feeling] than in their methodology?"[19] We must avoid psychologizing these notions because they are less about a way of doing, a method, than about a being.

Gadamer talks here of knowledge by acquaintance because he is a bringer of truth, but we would be wrong again to interpret this term in a strictly epistemological or instrumental sense. It is perhaps better to talk here of a "sense", not a mysterious sixth sense, but a "common sense"[20] which is a capacity to understand the universal. The concept of *Bildung* contributes to that of "common sense", which in turn is Gadamer's second great borrowing from the humanist tradition. Gadamer must obviously guard against a depreciation of "common sense", probably more pronounced in the German Enlightenment than in its French or English counterparts, where "common sense" retains elements of wisdom. But the pejorative connotation of the term is recognized in the idea of "common places",[21] negatively regarded today, but which used to be advantageous to the extent that they made communication possible, as rhetoric has always known. We are reminded here of the doctrine of Melanchthon's *loci communes*.[22] The struggle against "common places" and "common sense" goes back to Descartes, who saw in them a doubtful collection of pseudo-truths, *because* they were not built on a clear and distinct foundation. Whence the Cartesian concept of a new method that would make a *tabula rasa* of the ill-founded truths of tradition and common sense. But are the truths of common sense amenable to an ultimate foundation? In contrast with the truths of the natural sciences, which rest on data favourable to a method of distance, "common sense" is above all concerned with moral, historical and political truths. Here objective method is more problematic because our own being is involved: the human sciences are about our very being. What history as *memoria vitae* gives us is not knowledge of method, but wisdom in life.

26

What is formed here is thus a capacity for judgement, or taste, but this concept no longer has anything other than a trivially aesthetic sense. But Gadamer reminds us that taste was originally primarily a moral, not an aesthetic, term. For humanism, taste still meant a mode of knowledge or a "sense" that was not just learned, but which was formed and was essential to social life and human culture. It was also a sense of what was fitting, of a standard, and also of fairness. Gadamer often noted that we see it clearly in the negative example of a person who has no taste or no tact. It is not a question of the lack of a universal rule, but of a faulty judgement in a particular case which extends beyond the case in question.

Gadamer already associates the nature of this historical knowledge with the Aristotelian idea of practical wisdom (*phronesis*, often translated as the fine term "prudence", understood in its original sense[23]). Several crucial elements are common to these types of knowledge: as is indicated by the Aristotelian distinction (often forgotten in contemporary ethics) between the practical and the technical, it is not a matter of learning rules, but of a wisdom in life; further, this virtue is not taught, it is formed or cultivated; this wisdom has no particular content and is not dogmatic, but rather consists of a capacity to adapt itself to particular situations. It is a matter of knowledge, or better, of a sense, or better, of a common sense since it allows us to transcend particularity. Science seeks the universal in the form of laws, but we must recognize, with Aristotle, that we are here talking about knowledge of another sort.

It would thus appear natural to found the human sciences on this type of knowledge, which can be termed hermeneutics:

> There is something immediately evident about grounding philo-logical and historical studies and the ways the human sciences work on this concept of the *sensus communis*. For their object, the moral and historical existence of humanity, as it takes shape in our words and deeds, is itself decisively determined by the *sensus communis*.[24]

But this evidence of common sense is the least shared in today's world. Why? Essentially because it is not, or is no longer, a matter of knowledge. In a way, this is not false. We have always known that formation, common sense, judgement and taste are not concerned with knowledge in the purely epistemological or theoretical sense of the term. But is this a reason for excluding this way of knowing from the field of knowledge or, worse still, for reducing it to a function that is purely aesthetic, cosmetic or trivial? Gadamer accurately recognizes that this would be an enormous loss, because we would be deprived of the driving concepts of the humanist tradition, a human conception of human knowledge, which has been sacrificed on the altar of exact knowledge according to the method of the pure sciences.

The Kantian turning-point

The great thinker responsible for this change was Kant. It should not be said that he is to blame, because according to Gadamer, Kant was still nourished by the humanist tradition. We can read between the lines of the *Critique of Pure Reason* that he calls lack of judgement "stupidity", for which he has no cure. We can also see it in the "knowledge" which he mysteriously reserves for the use of practical reason, and also in the eminently moral, if not metaphysical, weight which he gives to aesthetic and teleological judgement in his third *Critique*. But by his interrogation and his success, Kant succeeds in making the humanist tradition invisible and obsolete.

Kant's initial question has in the first place nothing to do with the humanist tradition. As everyone knows, it is concerned with the possibility of metaphysics as a science, the driving issue of the *Critique of Pure Reason* of 1781. Kant's enquiry is in principle favourable to metaphysics. It sets out to help metaphysics to become at last a rigorous science, as is suggested by the famous title of 1783, *Prolegomena and Metaphysical Foundations of Natural Science*. But Kant adopts a hard, proud tone that announces his intentions are to bring about a change: convinced that his own critical assumptions are well founded, he appears to institute an intractable case against previous metaphysics, which seems to be condemned without recourse to appeal, and he appears to be inspired by Newton when he talks of science. The criticism is so pitiless that Kant's positive intentions are forgotten (except, it should be noted, in German idealism, where there was an attempt to complete the idealist metaphysics promised by Kant, but in so ambitious or pretentious a way, in terms of knowledge, that it cast nothing less than total discredit on all knowledge that did not conform to the criteria applied to pure science). Science was henceforth embodied in methodological and verifiable knowledge of the natural experimental sciences of which Kant had ensured the foundations. We should pass over the fact that Kant almost never concerned himself with the "methods" of the exact sciences, but the case instituted against the unverifiable ephemera of metaphysics and his reference to Newton were enough to make of Kant a positivist in the exact sciences.

But it was a fatal development for the human sciences, which were not at first obviously implicated in this debate. In fact, it was only after Kant that the human sciences as such began to exist, but in a way through him.[25] It was the celebration and the success of the natural sciences which placed the human sciences in a separate field of knowledge, which did not, or not then, conform to the rigorous norms of methodological scientific guarantees. From this point of view, the human sciences have suffered from a deficit in methodology from the start. But if the human sciences are implicated in the Kantian turning-point, it is because all of the humanist tradition is discredited by its non-methodological knowledge. Cultural knowledge, which cannot be reduced to an apprenticeship of content and of strict method, but which only makes a more successful contribution to the formation of judgement, of common sense and of taste, is not science. But as it is nothing, to what order does it belong? The reply, which is prefigured in Kant, but which his successors have radicalized, is to aesthetics. The "culture" of good taste has become what it is today, a purely aesthetic matter. But that has made us lose sight of the cognitive aspects of the humanist sense of culture.

If we must have science in the cultural domain, it is a case of knowledge which conforms to rigorous methods, the very ones which have ensured the success of the exact sciences. No longer can anything be left to the exercise of judgement. Suddenly there were methodological analyses, mathematical and statistical ones in politics and in economics, which we are now so used to, and also of literature and history. We are assured that all the rest belongs to aesthetics, or is nothing but a matter of taste, in the sense which recognizes no credible scientific aspect to the judgement of taste.

If this development is fatal for the human sciences, it is because it cuts them off from what is crucial in the humanist tradition from which they originated:

> The importance of this cannot be easily overestimated, for what was here surrendered was the element in which philological and historical studies lived, and when they sought to ground themselves methodologically under the name of "human sciences" side by side with the natural sciences, it was the only possible source of their full self-understanding.[26]

Not only did human sciences find themselves exiled from their original territory, but they were restricted to understanding their own scientific contribution from the only epistemological method available, that of the method of the natural sciences, where objectivity reigned supreme: "In discrediting any kind of theoretical knowledge except that of natural science, it compelled the human sciences to rely on the methodology of the natural sciences in conceptualizing themselves"; the Kantian turning-point thus "pushed the sciences of the mind into leaning on the method developed for the natural sciences".[27]

The human sciences were thus placed before the deadly alternative: method or aesthetics? If the human sciences could often repel the methodological model, so foreign to their discipline, they have not always succeeded in avoiding the rocks of aestheticism. Gadamer has taught us to see it even where it is not clearly a matter of art or aesthetics, notably in historicism. From the nineteenth century, when the human sciences had barely become autonomous, they veered more and more towards history. Gadamer would be the last to put into question the gains, if not the faults, of historicism, but he noted that the project of understanding all phenomena from their context resulted in a degree of aestheticization. Works of art, of culture and even of philosophy were seen more and more as "expressions" which had to be understood in their era, in the lives of their authors, etc. Once again, this has become natural, but we end up by losing sight of the truth, which is tested in encounter and which is still waiting for philosopical legitimation. Is to understand really only to know that such-and-such a "creation" is the expression of its era or of its author? Is it not to take part in a hermeneutic truth, a truth of formation which forms and transforms us?

Gadamer battles on two fronts, those of historicism and the aesthetic, but against a common enemy. In both cases, it is a matter of the same reductionism of truth which has its source in the monopoly that the modern method claims over all issues of knowledge. And the subtlety of Gadamer's analysis shows that reductionism operates even in the very disciplines thought to be completely opposed to modern science, for example in the aestheticism of "art for art's sake", a *sui generis* aesthetic movement, anti-methodological or anarchic, but one which secretly participates in the reductionism that it tries to combat by celebrating the autonomy of art and therefore by proclaiming its separation or independence with regard to all questions of truth, which are left to science and to pure knowledge.

It is clear that for a hermeneutics like Gadamer's, which is embedded in the tradition of a hermeneutics of the human sciences, flowing from Dilthey, the principal adversary is found on the side of historicism. For Gadamer, to consider historical knowledge in terms of expression and of method is to fail to encapsulate the specificity of sciences still called "human". But Gadamer attacks aestheticizing historicism only in the second part of his work. First, he settles his account with aesthetic consciousness, because everything begins there, and also because we can redeem from the experience of art a concept of truth that is adapted to hermeneutic understanding in a wide sense. Gadamer thus seems to play the game of the consciousness of method in beginning with art and the aesthetic to understand the human sciences. But his intention is to show that a purely aesthetic understanding of art is an abstraction caused by the monopoly of the methodological consciousness. And what is taken from art is a concept, or rather an *experience* of truth, which allows us not only better to grasp what art is, but also what are the human sciences and, still more fundamentally, what we are ourselves in so far as we are beings who understand.

The direction of Gadamer's argument is thus fully mapped out. It seems to start off with a limited question, that of truth in a work of art, but its implications are vast: "But is it right to reserve the concept of truth for conceptual knowledge? Must we also not acknowledge that the work of art possesses truth? We shall see that acknowledging this places not only the phenomenon of art but also that of history in a new light."[28] Despite its traditional association with the human sciences, hermeneutics starts from art, in order to denounce aestheticism and to find in art a better concept of *truth*, before coming back to the human sciences. But hermeneutics will end by transcending this limited and still epistemological horizon, as it will discover a concept of truth that will burst the framework of the human sciences. The hermeneutic experience will become universal.

From the aesthetics of taste to that of genius

We know that Kant was the great thinker responsible for the aestheticization of the experience of "truth" which does not meet the norms of the exact sciences. This is for several reasons: first, for his successors, he seemed to have raised methodological knowledge in the exact sciences into an absolute norm (but here he followed Cartesian modernism, as well as Hume's empiricism), and to have downgraded the other sorts of knowledge to mere opinion or non-knowledge. But Kant, in his *Critique of Judgement* of 1790, also established the foundations of aesthetics by giving them an autonomous sphere outside knowledge (the object of the first *Critique* of 1781), and outside ethics (the object of the second *Critique* of 1788). And when Kant was forced to circumscribe this autonomy of aesthetics, he did so with the help of the driving concepts of humanism, those of taste, of common sense, and of course of judgement. It was a sign that the humanist tradition was still home territory for Kant and for the whole of pre-Kantian aesthetics, but these concepts remained unacknowledged after Kant.

The field of aesthetics had previously arisen from the critique of taste (*Geschmack*) in the wider sense which, before Kant, included ethics and politics. Kantian reductionism here was so effective that we no longer even talk of taste in these disciplines. But we can understand what was meant by the term "taste" here, from what we still call common sense, or good sense, or sociability. It is not a case of knowledge in the sense of the sciences, but we could say of a way of being in which culture matters, so essential is it to public life and political life in general. But how do we justify taste's pretensions to validity? Doubtless this was already Kant's question, but to state it in these terms already betrays the dominance of the epistemological model. We could say that the question itself is biased, because it is clear that the validity – or universality – of the judgement of taste is not that of science. We cannot here speak of objective validity, nor probably of knowledge. But what sort of validity is it? In his *Critique of Judgement*, Kant made heroic efforts to define this non-objective validity. Objective universality was reserved for science, but Kant went as far as speaking of a validity or "subjective universality", as taste was dependent on an interplay of our faculties of knowledge, a game that would be the origin of aesthetic pleasure. The rich, intricate details of the Kantian analysis are not of interest to us here, but it is clear that the Kantian foundation for aesthetics has pretensions to scientific objectivity as its backcloth. Aesthetics must be something else if it wants to be autonomous.

Gadamer's examination of the Kantian aesthetic starts from a relatively minor distinction in the structure of the third *Critique*, but he considers that it is symptomatic of Kant's whole effort, and of the whole question of the autonomy of aesthetics. It is about the Kantian distinction between free and bound beauty. According to Kant, free beauty is that which comes from a pure judgement of taste, without any involvement of the intellect. The exemplars here are arabesques, instrumental music and ornamental flowers, which are "beautiful" only in the sense that their beauty is an end. But we are concerned with a less free and less pure beauty when it is subsumed under a concept. Bound beauty is found where the end, or finality, is not only aesthetic. We think here of works of architecture that have a useful function, or of works of art that have a moral dimension. Here, beauty is not pure because it is bound by a concept which makes it beautiful.

This is a secondary consideration for Kant, but Gadamer brings it up at the beginning of his analysis because he considers it "absolutely fatal" for the understanding of art.[29] Above all, it reveals Kant's intentions, because real beauty from that time onwards is what is beautiful alone; that is to say, which alone is aesthetic. The aesthetic is thus defined in opposition to ethics and science.

But Gadamer also knows that Kant only prepares for this view of aesthetics. He recognizes that Kant considers beauty to be a "symbol of morality" (according to the title of § 59 of the *Critique of the Faculty of Judgement*). But it is a symbol of a highly specific type, which Kant's system alone clearly allows. What astonishes Kant in aesthetic judgement is that nature itself seems to want us to have aesthetic pleasure, in the play of faculties, which perhaps has no objective aspects, but which nevertheless is the source of a pure, universally communicable, aesthetic feeling. We are tempted to say that nature wishes us well, on account of the aesthetic pleasure which she arouses in us. In Kant's mind, here similar to Leibniz's, it confirms in a way that we are the last end of creation: "noting the unintentional harmony between nature and disinterested delight (the interest which we take in the agreeable in nature) turns attention to us as the last end of creation, to our 'moral destiny'".[30]

It is in this precise and exclusively Kantian sense that aesthetics contains a moral finality. And we then understand why Kant prefers natural beauty to that of works of art. In art, this appeal to our intelligible destiny is intended: the work of art is already a language for the mind: "But the products of art exist only in order to address us in this way – natural objects, however, do not exist to address us in this way."[31] Again Gadamer writes, "Natural beauty does not deliver any determinate language." But it is more eloquent, more sublime, because the delight which only we can appreciate reminds us of our vocation as understanding beings. It is not by chance that Kant addresses the issue of aesthetic judgement in a work in which the whole of the second part is given over to teleological judgement, to the finality of nature. Even if the Kantian foundation wishes to be autonomous, it is secretly unthinkable without a theology of creation.

It was obviously this metaphysical aspect that stopped being a constraint on Kant's successors. It appeared precisely to compromise the autonomy of aesthetics which Kant took so much trouble to establish. Post-Kantian aesthetics, beginning with Schiller, tried in its way to be more Kantian than Kant, in radicalizing the autonomy of aesthetics which Kant's third *Critique* had only prepared. The humanist legacy became still more unrecognizable. Kant was still a descendant of that tradition in addressing the issues of taste and of natural beauty within the more or less hidden framework of an ethico-theological metaphysics, which showed that its links with the theory of knowledge and ethical theory had not finally been cut. So Romanticism came to replace the issue of natural beauty by that of artistic or creative beauty, and to replace the perspective of taste with that of genius. These were intricate adjustments, which nevertheless constituted a system. But if aesthetics carved out an autonomous sphere, separate from those of knowledge and ethics, which concerned only the free exercise of our subjectivity, it had to give priority to the subjective point of view which at its most pure is expressed in the artistic creation of genius. The issue of genius came to replace that of taste, because they are in a way antinomous: taste has a levelling function which often prevents it from placing proper value on the creations of genius, because these creations consciously and rightly strike a blow at the standards of "good taste". The Kantian priority given to natural beauty and taste would break down, because in the end they are opposed to the full autonomy of aesthetics.

In this way, the concepts of genius and artistic creation were imposed on aesthetics in the nineteenth century. Gadamer rightly talks of an apotheosis of creative genius which became the equivalent of a universal axiom throughout the whole of the nineteenth century.[32] It was of course accompanied by a certain cult of unconscious production and of irrationalism, which contributed only to the greater separation of the world of art from those of knowledge and ethics where the cold laws of reason held sway.

Other than Schiller, the great inspiration for this aesthetic vision of the world came from Goethe and Rousseau. Both of them linked their poetic creations to their personal experiences, as if art were mixed with biography. We think of the long biography, *Dichtung und Wahrheit* (*Poetry and Truth*), or of the many versions of Rousseau's *Confessions*. Focused on the notions of genius, artistic production and personal experience, notions that remain obvious to us, the whole of nineteenth-century aesthetics bears the imprint of Goethe. As a margin to the scientific monopoly of knowledge, aesthetic experience resorted to the order of lived experience, of *Erlebnis*. Dilthey became the theoretician of this aesthetic vision of the world when in 1905 he published his greatest success, *Das Erlebnis und die Dichtung*.[33] For Gadamer, it is not inconsequential that Dilthey is amongst those who have directly contributed to the spread of this concept of *Erlebnis*, of lived experience of creation, which is recreated in oneself when one comes to understand. This notion also operates in the hermeneutics of the human sciences, which Dilthey defends. But this hermeneutics of *Erlebnis* is tacitly understood as more or less following the recognized model of aesthetics, conceived as a sphere of creative expression at the margins of knowledge proper. In his treatment of Dilthey, Gadamer was opposed to this reductionism. But he is already so in the first section, when he recalls that the concept of "lived experience" comes from the realm of aesthetics, defined in opposition to that of knowledge. Is understanding, even in art, the recreation in oneself of the creative *Erlebnis* of the artist?

In fact, the notion of lived experience in the nineteenth century stems from two contradictory tendencies, which both reveal the atmosphere of positivism: on the one hand, *Erlebnis* is believed to be the ultimate gift, comparable to the achievements of the positivists, which will be as valuable for art as for the human sciences; but, on the other hand, *Erlebnis* and the cult of lived experience incorporate a vaguely "pantheistic"[34] aspect, in the sense that *Erlebnis* is supposed to make us part of a universal experience of life that escapes from the cognitive categories of rationalism. It is the great age of the philosophers of life, and Bergson was undoubtedly the greatest catalyser. To understand *Erlebnis* is to commune with the whole of the senses, with an experience of life which transcends knowledge. It is a case of contradictory tendencies (positivist and pantheistic) which go hand in hand: in the age of science, art and the human sciences must also be concerned with ultimate givens if they wish to be respectable enterprises, but these givens will emerge on an irrationalist horizon, as the whole domain of reason is finally administered by the sciences. Gadamer here sees a false alternative which proceeds from a fatal abstraction.

The abstraction of aesthetic consciousness

We still today succumb to interpreting works of art and of the mind in terms of creation and of expression. Gadamer usefully reminds us that they are only a matter of recent developments found in the nineteenth century. Specifically aesthetic categories tacitly presuppose that art is not, or no longer, allowed to be described in terms of knowledge. Every work of art is essentially the *expression* of a lived experience and every aesthetic experience is consumed in the recreation of the original lived experience.

Against this scientific reductionism, Gadamer recalls that art has always had, and continues to have, other tasks. He finds a first witness in allegory, which was originally a form of rhetoric, then a way of interpreting texts, before it became an artform in allegorical painting in particular. Allegorical painting is thus a cryptic writing which goes beyond what is immediately expressed. Gadamer remarks that it is not chance that allegory was so systematically discredited in aesthetics and creativity in the nineteenth century. The aesthetic consciousness could not admit that art could refer to anything except itself. Allegory was once more an experience of reality, rather than an experience of itself.[35] But the fact that allegory was an experience of reality and truth led Gadamer to reinstate the participation of truth in allegory. It is one of the forms of art, and of discourse, that underlines the fact that the pernicious separation of art from truth can never be total. Gadamer questioned this radical, fatal cut when he spoke of the abstraction of aesthetic consciousness. If it is true that aesthetic experience rescues us from the routine of everyday life, which we have always known, it does not, for all that, disrupt the hermeneutic continuity of our existence in the networks of meaning, which are always more than just aesthetic. If the work of art allows us to escape from ordinary life, it is only to drag us back all the more, so that we rediscover our reality, unveiled by art, with new eyes and ears. Far from erasing it, art always presupposes our continuous existence.

Thus, from the nineteenth century, it is an abstraction to separate art from nature or even from reality. It is the price of autonomy in aesthetics. Gadamer divulges the clearest testimony in Schiller's *Letters on Man's Aesthetic Education*. From then on, it was an education in art and no longer through art.[36] If Schiller wanted to reabsorb the Kantian dualism between nature and freedom, between theory and practice, he created an even deeper abyss, that between art and reality. Art, cut off from reality, became a matter of appearance and illusion. Gadamer saw here the consequence of modern science's nominalism: if the whole of reality is reduced to the order of spatio-temporal matter, which is studied by science, art consists of nothing but fiction. Besides, it is revealing that the word in English (the language of modern science) for the whole of literature is "fiction".[37] And everything which is not fiction bears the illuminating name of "non-fiction". Such is the empire of modern science that its nominalism extends to characterizing a whole branch of literature, or even the whole of literature.

Gadamer determinedly combats this non-reality attributed to art, not only because it trivializes the truth of art, but because it makes us lose the most precious feature of art: the remarkable experience of reality in its meaningful whole. This is what, in the constructive part of his aesthetics, leads him to insist on the ontological contribution of the work of art. All his thoughts on art can be put under the title "The ontology of the work of art", because art for him is first and foremost an experience of reality, of being, of truth. Gadamer insists so much on it that his preferred term to nail this truth in art is *Seinszuwachs*, "surfeit of being".[38] Art is not in the least degree a part of being; on the contrary, through art a being becomes more than itself (*dass das Sein mehr wird*[39]). These terms appear to give an almost quantitative turn to the "excess" of being in which art makes us share, but they are only the reverse of the ontological encumbrance to which modern science has constrained art, in confining it to a cult of appearance. The difference, or the "aesthetic distinction", is thus a pure abstraction induced by the secret empire of science over hard, pure reality. Art acquires sovereignty, but it is finally concerned only with the imaginary, with non-reality. Certainly this has led to the creation of specific "sites" for art: permanent concert halls and museums have been built, where aesthetic enjoyment can be exercised in an autonomous way. All large towns nowadays have their "arts centre", carefully separated from the rest of civic reality, which is dominated by the hard realities of science and economics. All newspapers have an arts section, and to subscribe to an arts charity is to act generously, to promote art as appearance *sui generis*. But to turn art into an autonomous world of production and creation is to cut it off from the rest of reality. The artist thus loses his place in the world. Since the age of Puccini, the artist has led a Bohemian life, at the centre of a universal cult. For we must talk of cult. In a world secularized by science, the Bohemian artist has become a saviour.

In fact, we are talking about a new mythology. Its tragedy is that it maintains just as it is the division between (scientific) knowledge and (illusory) myth. But the worst is that the abstraction of the aesthetic distinction also makes an abstraction of art itself.[40] Artists have always had a more prosaic conception of their own work. Where the aesthetic consciousness likes to talk of creation, of genius, of inspiration and of profound meanings, the artist most often stays with matter-of-fact considerations that are concerned with the work and its production. And far from being a purely aesthetic matter, art has always responded to a certain function and most often to commissions. Assuming that art always originates from free, creative inspiration, aesthetic consciousness has naturally discredited commissioned art. Thus architecture is for us an exceptional case, even a less pure art because it responds to commissions and to practical imperatives.[41] This is to forget that art has almost always been a matter of commission, and a matter of craftsmanship. Velazquez's *Las Meninas* is after all a portrait of the royal family and almost the whole of Bach's works consists of cantatas which he had to compose for each Sunday's mass!

CHAPTER TWO

Truth after Art

The critique of subjectivism in modern aesthetics: the game of art is elsewhere

If we wish to recognize that art has a claim to truth, or better still, to learn what truth is from art, we must above all overcome the Kantian "subjectivization" of aesthetics. For Gadamer, it is a case of the great impasse of aesthetics, if not of the whole of modernism. The vice of modern science is the notion of objectivity that constrains the aesthetic experience to being understood in subjective terms, as if there were no question of its being understood in anything other than spiritual states and the "lived experiences" of the subject. To reduce everything to the level of subjectivity concerned only with itself is to subscribe to the nominalism of modern science. Gadamer's positive and polemical thesis is that the experience of art, on the contrary, remains an experience of being, and even a surfeit of being, to such an extent that subjectivity plays only a secondary role. The vital thing in an adequate ontology of a work of art consists from then on in recognizing that subjectivity is not the master of what happens to people in an aesthetic experience. Think here of *Geschehen*, of the character of the non-instrumental event, of understanding according to Gadamer, where the advent of art is the first revelation.

How do we describe the aesthetic experience in itself? This question holds a trap, because aesthetic experience is not one that we truly control. We can only properly speak of control in cases where we concentrate on technological development of external nature (where subjectivity can do anything). But, in aesthetic experience, it is we who are captured, rather as if we were taken up by a *game*. Gadamer uses the metaphor of a game in his investigation into the ontological density of the aesthetic experience. What "captures" us here? It was perhaps Rilke who expressed it best in saying that the capacity for capture which is given to us here is not truly our own, but that of the world. We are capable of capture (*Fangenkönnen*) because we are first captured and challenged. Rilke's example is that of a ball which is thrown to us and which brings us into the game, without our taking the initiative.

The concept of a game thus serves as the conducting wire in the rediscovery of aesthetic truth. But it is evidently a case of a notion already "occupied" by aesthetic consciousness. Schiller recognized its cardinal function in the foundation of aesthetic education when he radicalized Kant's opening. Whereas Kant spoke of the interplay of the faculties of *knowledge*, Schiller retained only the pure concept of a game, which would indicate the true liberation produced by art when it distinguishes between the spheres of art and of ethics. In opening a game's space of aesthetic liberty, art delivers us in some way from moral imperatives and from the "seriousness" of knowledge. In this spirit, we continue today to associate art with a certain form of "entertainment", as if art were nothing but a diversion. It is implied that in aesthetic experience, subjectivity always and only plays with experience. We know that Gadamer intended to destroy this banality, but he would do so by using the means of aesthetic consciousness, as if he took a wicked pleasure in taking his inspiration from his seminal categories to draw from them a new sense and an understanding of the truth: just as he counteracts the *unreality* of aesthetic consciousness by stressing the *surfeit of being* which it brings, and just as he opposes to the simple game of subjectivity the seriousness of a game where subjectivity undergoes metamorphosis.

There is something serious, even sacred, about the game. We say of those who do not play seriously, and who prefer to take the lead, that they *violate* the rules of the game. Effectively, the game has its own autonomy in which the player lets himself be carried away. As he often does, Gadamer follows the wisdom of language, which speaks here of a game of light, of waves, of colours and of language, following the expression that existed long before Wittgenstein; or a game in sporting competition, such as the Olympic games, or tennis (we note that the German here speaks freely of a game, or *Spiel*; English distinguishes even more clearly between *game* and *play*). Gadamer thinks that in all these examples, what is imposed is never the autonomous activity or arbitrariness of subjectivity, but the autonomy of the game itself. In subjectivity, to play is to allow oneself to be caught up in a game which imposes its rules, its movement and its supremacy. Ball games are an example here. What is demanded from the player is that he responds to a game situation where he is not in command and where he must respect the essential given. The ball is thrown to him and he must react. He can do so with more or less dexterity, but it will always be the game situation (or that of the opponent) which dictates the range of possibilities. Gadamer observes that it is impossible to play on your own. Even when there is no other player, there is always an opposition "with which the player plays and which automatically responds to his move with a counter-move":[1] a game of patience, a crossword puzzle, a book, etc. The true subject of the game is the game itself: "We have seen that play does not have its being in the player's consciousness or attitude, but on the contrary play draws him into its dominion and fills him with its spirit. The player experiences the game as a reality that surpasses him."[2]

The analysis of the game that Gadamer proposes is anthropologically impressive. To play is not a free act of subjectivity, but a being played, which possesses its own seriousness and reality. But we can wonder what his analysis has to do with the ontology of the work of art. There is first of all the polemical motivation which consists in recalling that the fundamental category of Schiller's aesthetics, that of the game, is less game-like and less subjective than it seems. The game does not mean subjectivity's folding back on itself; to play is, on the contrary, to conform to an order, to a logic, to seriousness, which brings in subjectivity. But besides this polemical aim, Gadamer seems to have been fascinated by this idea of the hold of a subjectivity which is transported elsewhere, into the realm of art, where it persists all the same in being called upon in its full continuity. The experience of art implies, if you like, two aspects which could seem contradictory, but which hermeneutics judges to be constitutive of aesthetic experience and which it is tempting to think of together with the help of the notion of a game: the experience of an autonomous reality "which goes beyond us" but with which we are, paradoxically, at the same time directly concerned. Art is thus, if we can use worn-out categories, both powerfully objective (it is "there", in the work which imposes its diktat from the heights of its majesty) and at the same time very subjective: because we are always mysteriously apostrophized, or "put into play". The later Gadamer seems to have heavily stressed the absolute[3] or this quasi-sacred separation of art: the poem always imposes its diktat,[4] the great literary texts are "eminent" texts,[5] and paintings as well as poems always speak from a certain "height" or majesty (Hoheit[6]). The Gadamer who speaks in this way is the great admirer of art; he has a fine knowledge of aesthetic "separation", of the extent to which art allows us to take part. We could be worried here that he is coming dangerously close to the "aesthetic distinction" which he contests so vigorously elsewhere. This is not the case. For terminological reasons, we will differentiate in what follows between the aesthetic *distinction*, which Gadamer judges excessive, and the *separation* which makes art art. The work of art that is in an enigmatic way "separate" from the rest of the world is never wholly distinct. There is an entire separation between the world and art, because the game of art can be encapsulated in a form or a work, but

41

aesthetics proposes a reading of it that is much too short, by celebrating a radical split from reality, which is ruled by scientific nominalism. In Gadamer's eyes, the true aesthetic distinction is something more and something other than what is made of it by aesthetic knowledge. Far from being pure entertainment, the game of art challenges us directly as if it was imparting to us a surfeit of reality (*Zuwachs an Sein*). The work of art addresses itself to us, as *Aussage*, as enunciation or message before which we cannot remain indifferent. Besides, *Kunst als Aussage* is the title of the important volume 8 of Gadamer's *Werke*, entirely devoted to the theoretical basis of aesthetics: art as enunciation, message, "proposal", "suggestion". We can translate Gadamer's title by the words, "Art as proposal". And the proposal of art is always addressed to us from a certain height, which raises us up to it. This art which "looks" at us provokes a response from us. The poem that is the *Gedicht* unfolds not only as the diktat which we must follow, but also as *Gespräch*, as dialogue. Gadamer's collection of interpretations of poetry bears the title, *Gedicht und Gespräch* (*Poetry and Dialogue* (Frankfurt: Insel, 1990)). The speech (*Wort*) of art inevitably calls for a response (*Antwort*), which implies the wholeness of our being. It is unnecessary for all art to be "poetic", in the linguistic sense of the term. Music equally evokes a response, an echo. It is impossible to listen to a melody without silently humming it, without wanting to tap your foot and probably to dance to it.[7] Everything happens in the recognition of existence, and in a more instinctive than conceptual way, in what is rhythmed. Is there a confusion here in making us believe that the hermeneutic continuity of our existence is broken?

Metamorphosis and recognition

The idea of a "game" of art allows us to think of the dialectic of address and response as the "unity" of a whole process: the remarkable "separation" of art, and also its dialogical magic, the fact that we are in it. The response, or the reading, that art calls forth is also its vindication. For Gadamer, this means that the form of art is found in its presentation (*Darstellung*), in which we always participate. Gadamer said later that the work of art only has its being in its implementation or accomplishment (*Vollzug*). So we cannot ontologically distinguish the work of art from its presentation (or, following Fruchon's translation, from its representation), for example an original play of Shakespeare from its contemporary adaptation, or a poem by C. F. Meyer from its recitation. The musical work, which exists only in its execution on the platform, is for Gadamer the clearest example of this, but he extends this requirement of execution to all forms of art. Later, Gadamer liked to speak of a "reading": "To read is always to allow something to speak."[8] The final version of his aesthetics, that of *Kunst als Aussage* (1993), in effect conferred an unparalleled extension to this idea of a "reading", even going so far as to speak of a "reading" of architecture and of paintings.[9] To appreciate an architectural monument, a piece of music, a poem or a painting, is to let it act on me, to let it transform me. Every aesthetic experience is one where the *proposal* of art resounds in my interior ear, as in the act of reading.[10] In *Truth and Method*, this role of the interior ear, of the sound which responds to the appeal of art, is again rendered by the rather Plotinian notion of "presentation", which evokes the idea of the work as a procession or an emanation.[11] It is linked with Gadamer's other great Platonic metaphor, that of participation, which is composed of activity, passivity and wonder. We are there, but without ever seizing everything. To speak of the interior ear is to recognize a larger area for the game, with the capacity for hearing and response.

This is the true form of art for Gadamer. If the separation or the idealism of art never totally break their links with reality, it is because reality itself is found there, but in so dazzling a way that it appears to be transfigured. Gadamer speaks, in a term difficult to translate, of a "transformation into structure", of *Verwandlung ins Gebilde*.[12] Gadamer means that the game of art is set out in a form which has its own "ideality". This ideality corresponds to what we can call, with Paul Ricoeur, the opening of a space, of a world.[13] In assuming the form (*Gebilde*) of a work of art, this world is certainly "separated" from our daily lives, but it is its configuration, indeed its elevation, that allows us to rediscover our world. In the work's artistic separation, reality becomes "transfigured". "The transformation into structure means that what existed previously exists no longer. But also that what now exists, what represents itself in the play of art, is the lasting and the true."[14]

Art thus induces a transfiguration of the real, in the revelatory sense of the word, so much and so well that we can ask what exactly is transfigured: reality, or us? Obviously, both at the same time, because what art reveals is always also the whole of our being, the totality of our being-in-the-world consigned to a form (*Gebilde*). It is not by chance that here, more than anywhere else, Gadamer's text teems with Heideggerian metaphors. Art appears as an unfolding of truth, an ontological process, a surfeit of being, the opening of a world. In the world of everyday life, we are so wrapped up in the business of the world of beings that we lose the sense of being to which art recalls us.

From this point of view the transfiguration in Gadamer's work reminds us to mistrust the "use of truth" in "The Origin of the Work of Art" (1935–6), where Heidegger had so suggestively brought out the remarkable revelatory capacity for art as a theatre of being.[15] But in his analysis of the ontology of the work of art, Gadamer did not refer even once to Heidegger's famous text. Perhaps this was because he was too close to it. It is not unhelpful to recall that in 1959, the year when he finished his major work, Gadamer wrote an important introduction to the Reclam edition of Heidegger's essay on the work of art, at the request of Heidegger himself. It was then entitled "The truth of the work of art",[16] and shows what Gadamer owed to Heidegger, even if his passion for poetry evidently preceded his meeting with Heidegger.

The notions of *being*, of *truth*, and of *work* (*Gebilde*), had the right emphases. With Gadamer, *being* designates what goes beyond the simple thought of subjectivity: what is produced over and above our actions and our knowledge. Rather, it is concerned with a being or with an opening in the game, where subjectivity is borne away. And this process of *truth* is one of knowledge for Gadamer. We have seen that the term "knowledge" can be misconstrued, but Gadamer did not make that mistake. Art allows us to go beyond the meaning. Knowledge of art is that of recognition, in the sense of anamnesis: it allows us to rediscover our world for what it is, in revealing to us its "essence", to talk in Heidegger's terms. What stands out in a work of art is the truth of the world such as is intercepted or surprised by its metamorphosis into a work, which is for us an experience of recognition in both its meanings: that of knowledge and that of thanks. Art opens our eyes. The most natural reaction to the revelation which it lavishes on us comes from the "it is so"[17] ("*es kommt heraus*"), as Gadamer said in his last articles on aesthetics, in which he took up Goethe's fine verse, "so much truth, so much being" ("*so wahr, so seiend*"[18]). Art allows us to rediscover the world that we already inhabit, but as if it were for the first time. We discover what we have always known ("it is so"), but as part of a revolution which drags us from our ontic sleep, because being is in some way remembered there in all its dazzling evidence. From there, Gadamer thus continually has this idea of a "surfeit of being": Van Gogh's shoes have more being than those of the peasant. If they are more than a copy, it is because they are revelatory of their essence. This cognitive or "recognitive" aspect of art led Gadamer to revive the obsolete notion of art as *imitatio* or *mimesis,* which goes back to Plato. The imitation of reality is never its double, an imperfect copy, but rather that which allows us to recognize being itself, what it is. *Mimesis* therefore represents more of a cognitive than an imitative, and thus servile, process. We must always take account of the *anamnesis* in the *mimesis*, as etymology requires us to do. The world is most often lived in the mode of forgetfulness, forgetfulness of oneself and of the world, and to allow us to (re)discover reality for its own sake is the anamnetic function of art. The lost aspect of the notion of *mimesis* is that of its cognitive function, universally acknowledged up to the appearance of aesthetic knowledge. Such knowledge is now burdened by this concept, which is unusable because art is considered to be devoid of reality.

> [T]he concept of imitation sufficed for the theory of art as long as the cognitive significance of art went unquestioned. But that was the case only as long as knowledge of the true was considered to be knowledge of the essence, for art supports this kind of knowledge in a convincing way. By contrast, for nominalistic modern science and its idea of reality, from which Kant drew agnostic consequences for aesthetics, the concept of *mimesis* has lost its aesthetic force.[19]

If there is no place for *mimesis* in aesthetic knowledge, the latter can have no place in reality. Artistic creation is less a clear mirror of reality than the effusion of subjectivity, and aesthetic experience seeks to recreate a memory or an expression rather than to make sense of existence.

But Gadamer also went further than Heidegger in speaking of *Verwandlung*, of the process of *metamorphosis*. Not only is reality transformed because it is rediscovered, but we ourselves are the subjects of metamorphosis. The term might appear too strong, perhaps too religious, but Gadamer was determined to return to something of the solemnity, of the sacred experience of art, when art was at least a carrier of truth. To speak of metamorphosis is to implicate the spectator in artistic presentation.

Gadamer expresses this implication of the spectator in the presentation of a work with the help of the Hegelian notion of mediation (*Vermittlung*). The ambiguity of the German term *Vermittlung* serves Gadamer's intentions well, as it conveys the *transmission* of the work, its execution, its interpretation, as well as the *appropriation* or the "mediation" of the work by the spectator. Gadamer speaks of "total mediation" because the work of art has being – *Vollzug*, a mode of execution – only in its interpretation, which Gadamer tends to assimilate – perhaps rather quickly – to the interpretation of the spectator himself, who is taken up in the game of art. We can see, in this assimilation of the spectator's sense of the *presentation* of the work, a distant echo of Bultmann's conception of *kerygma*: what is proclaimed, what constitutes the basis of the Christian message of salvation, is not so much the historical life of Jesus, but the predication (the *kerygma*) of the Apostles themselves. The content or the object of this proclamation was in any case a historically inaccessible given, as the given and the primordial reality of the Christian faith go back to this first predication of the Apostles. The life and indeed the resurrection of Jesus are less important than the meaning which they had for those who proclaimed them, and for those who today recognize themselves in the self-understanding which constitutes the act of faith (to the point where Bultmann seems to identify Christ's resurrection with the "resurrection" of the Christian faith): an understanding equivalent more to a lack of capacity for self-understanding or self-justification without the help of grace.[20] We note the consequences for Gadamer's hermeneutics: the meaning of the work is not to be sought anywhere except in its *Vermittlung*, in its transmission or its "mediation": it has being only in its presentation. Even if the theological aspect of this notion is foreign to Gadamer, we will find an echo of it in his concept of the work of art.

The temporality of the work of art and the exemplary status of tragedy

For Gadamer, art is only in the presentation, which is simultaneously dialogue and address. In this way, we can say of art that it is always contemporary. Gadamer insists at length on this contemporaneity or temporality of the work of art so as to play down the aesthetic and historicizing distance of works of art which classifies all works of art according to their historical era: baroque, classicism, impressionism, etc. Do we really look at one of Renoir's paintings in order to confirm that he was an impressionist, as is repeated *ad nauseam* by all the guides? Is Baudelaire nothing but a manifestation of Romanticism? This historicization of works of art remains inevitable, but the issue is to know whether the temporality proper to works of art is well embedded.

Historicism presupposes that there is a distance between the work and the viewer, and also a distance between the historical work of art and its contemporary execution. This distance is reabsorbed in the Gadamerian concept of the work, which is realized only in its actualization. The viewer "is included whatever the remoteness of his opposite".[21] Gadamer was here inspired by the Kierkegaardian notion of *contemporaneity* in order to unlock the double distance of historicism and aesthetic knowledge. Kierkegaard had underlined the contemporary urgency of the message of salvation in the framework of theological meditation. He recalled that sacred texts do not relate historical events that happened in distant centuries, but they are concerned with a call to salvation which concerns me directly, here and now. I am always directly challenged in the "now" of my existence. Like Heidegger, Gadamer was fascinated by the rediscovery of Kierkegaard in dialectical theology, first by Barth, then by Bultmann.

These two thinkers appealed to the Kierkegaardian idea of contemporaneity to combat the historicism of liberal theology that had a tendency to acquiesce in a sovereign distance which led to the understanding of biblical texts within their historical context, where they at best underlined a vaguely Kantian "moral" message, rather as if the Bible had to be read through *Religion within the Limits of Reason*. Barth replied that it was God who directly addressed him in the biblical texts. Less theocentric than Barth, which explains their last schism, Bultmann said that it was the disquiet of our existence which is evoked in the biblical texts. In his famous essay of 1925, "What Meaning does talk of God have?", reprinted in *Glauben und Verstehen*,[22] Bultmann said that to talk of God is to talk of my existence, which is its task, its decision and its concern. The peaceful assurance of historical distance and superiority claimed by liberal theology are found to be relativized in the name of an address which is always contemporary because it cannot leave me indifferent.

Gadamer was less directly involved in theological considerations, but he retained the idea of a demand or an address (*Anspruch*[23]), which he applied to the experience of art. He thus opposed the Kierkegaardian notion of *contemporaneity* to historical *simultaneity* of works of art for aesthetic knowledge. Simultaneity means here that works from different periods can be the object of one and the same aesthetic experience as it is only a case of reliving the lived and the expressive. Thus in a museum the paintings are most often arranged historically, but in a "simultaneous" way for aesthetic knowledge, which thus moves from the "lived experience" of the Baroque to that of impressionism, of expressionism, etc. This aesthetic simultaneity, Gadamer maintains, is once again equivalent to a levelling of original contemporaneity, of the address of truth that emanates from all works of art worthy of the name and which says to me, following Rilke's verse which Gadamer loves to quote, and which echoes the exhortation of Mozart's commander, "You must change your life!"[24]

We might believe that this is perhaps too emotional a conception of art. But if Gadamer insists so much on the existentialist force of the aesthetic address, it is because he intends to combat the loss of substance and of *pathos* proper to aesthetic simultaneity. It was not by chance that Gadamer found the primary example of testimony to this contemporaneity in the example of tragedy. Certain thinkers have believed that they should exclude tragedy from the restricted framework of their aesthetics because it is more an issue of an ethico-metaphysical phenomenon than a properly artistic one.[25] But it is precisely this non-distinction that inspired Gadamer, because it is clear that the tragic work directly reflects the tragedy of life. Contemporaneity is integral to it. But Gadamer is fascinated by another aspect of tragedy. The famous definition of tragedy that Aristotle gives in his *Poetics* gives rise to a purification of the passions, as if to indicate the essential participation of the spectator in the game, which is also that of life. Aristotle writes that tragedy produces a purification (*catharsis*) of the passions of distress (*eleos*) and anguish (*phobos*), which Gadamer understands above all in the sense of the subjective genitive (we are not purified of them, but the passions themselves are purified, relieved). But the question of the genitive, heavily debated and perhaps insoluble, as there are reasons for both readings, is not crucial here. What is essential for Gadamer is that the spectator is implicated and that he experiences a purification of his essential passions. Tragedy, emblematic of all art, always implies a confrontation with yourself. The spectator finds himself led back to his own reality, to the tragedy of destiny and of existence. Can there be here a true aesthetic distance, asks Gadamer?

> The spectator does not hold himself aloof at the distance characteristic of an aesthetic consciousness enjoying the art with which something is represented, but rather participates in the communion of being present. The real emphasis of the tragic phenomenon lies ultimately on what is presented and recognised, and to participate in it is not a matter of choice.[26]

It is clear that being present at a tragedy is exceptional and it makes us rise above everyday experience. That is obvious, but the continuity of existence itself is not interrupted. Is this discovery not aesthetic? Is it not rather an experience emblematic of truth and which art alone allows us to glimpse?

The presentation of truth in the non-performing arts

For Gadamer, tragedy is exemplary in more than its title. Three consequences clearly follow: first, that tragedy has being only when it is performed; secondly, that it implicates the spectator in its game, in its festivity, even in its definition; thirdly, that it is never entirely cut off from the tragedy of life to which it leads us inexorably back, a tragedy which for Gadamer remains the model of all hermeneutic experience. In all three cases, aesthetic autonomy is badly placed.

Of course, all philosophical aesthetics has its privileged models (natural beauty for Kant, poetry for Hegel and Heidegger, music for Adorno) and their consideration often detracts from the other arts, which risk losing their specificity. So we can ask if Gadamer's paradigm, that of tragedy, is not a little too well chosen. The distance from tragedy on stage to tragedy in life could appear a little too close, and to speak of presentation in the case of the interpretative arts, which we will here call the performing arts (theatre, music and dance), is a little too obvious. What is it about the less tragic, or non-performing arts: painting, sculpture, architecture, literature, etc.?

It is not certain that *Truth and Method* has answers to all these questions. Gadamer developed his poetics of literature after 1960, and they are to be found in volumes 8 and 9 of his *Werke* (where it can be determined that it was finally poetry, his grand passion, which remained the primary model of aesthetics for Gadamer). But the purpose of Gadamer's work was not to offer an integrated theory of art, an aesthetics, but to begin with art in reconquering an experience of truth which goes beyond the sphere of art, so much and so well that this truth can serve as the foundation of a general theory of hermeneutics. Gadamer's thesis is that art is a game, that is, that it has no being apart from its presentation, which means a surfeit of being for what is represented since what appears is there rediscovered in its truth. In the end, this rediscovered truth is always a confrontation with ourselves.

From this perspective, there is no doubt that we must recognize a methodological pre-eminence[27] in the performing arts, and more particularly in tragedy, where the confrontation with ourselves takes, so to speak, a temporal dimension. But Gadamer finds this presentation of being in the plastic arts as well. The painting (*Bild*) represents in Gadamer's eyes the great fiefdom of aesthetic knowledge. Its frame already contains a certain closure, which seems to confer its own autonomy and allows it to be shown in a gallery, a museum, where it is exposed to purely aesthetic consideration. The presentation that is constitutive of the performing arts seems to be dismissed from the game by this autonomy of the painting which always reflects back on itself.

Perhaps Gadamer, in his analysis of paintings, strongly underlines what he understands by presentation. It is at once a presentation of someone or something (it is not by chance that Gadamer prioritized the portrait) and a presentation to the viewer who contemplates the painting. Presentation is at work at the beginning and end of a painting. Far from having an autonomous reality, the painting always reflects a reality or a model, but in such a way that this reality does not have access to its own being except through the painting (we think again of Van Gogh's shoes or of Frans Hals's painting which makes us see and understand who Descartes was). Here, the translation of *Darstellung* by "representation" is deliberate. It completely corresponds to Gadamer's thesis on *Darstellung*: what has access to presentation is always a being that exercises the function of representation:

This characteristic is easy to establish in the particular case of the representative image. The way in which the sovereign, the statesman, the hero shows and presents himself is in the image which is embodied in the representation. What do we mean by that? Certainly not that the person who is represented gets from the image a new and more authentic way of manifesting himself. On the contrary, it is the other way round: *because* the sovereign, the statesman, the hero has to show himself and to present himself to his own, because he has to comport himself as his representation, the painting has access to his true reality.[28]

In other words, according to Gadamer's rather curious thesis, the painting only exploits this propensity to presentation which the person or thing represented already has: the king, the hero, such-and-such an aspect of sacred history, such-and-such a historical event, some great battle or other which is to be commemorated. But we wonder what veils hide the most banal realities, peasant shoes or still lifes. We could say here, even though Gadamer does not, that the function of representation is to act as compensation: because such realities are forgotten in the business of daily life, the painting returns their reality to them, assigning to them in some way a new onto-logical dignity. The painting alone allows us to rediscover for them, by conferring a surfeit of being, a "presentation" of those realities which are "under-represented" in the world and in life. We could say the same about the forms and colours which seem to be cast higgledy-piggledy into non-figurative art. It is art that allows us to appreciate them for themselves.

Presentation is actually therefore constitutive of the plastic arts. And presentation is always linked to the world, which is in some way itself dedicated to representation. Even if we do not always know the model for a portrait, it is clear that the painting reflects it, in concentrating (by the difference of the sign or the symbol) all our attention on it, because it is only in the painting that the being of what is represented emerges in its truth, in its presentation. The reference to the world which is presented is always essential to art. Gadamer calls this reference "occasionality": art always remains linked to the world from which it has arisen, as is exemplified in commissioned works, dedications or historical inscriptions. But according to Gadamer, occasionality, which aesthetic knowledge seems to belittle, is still more profound: it is integral to the work itself,[29] which always retains something of the situation from which it is born, even if it is metamorphosed in form. Every work is inscribed in this way in a horizon of life.

All the same, we must see that Gadamer moves on slippery ground and perhaps he wishes to avoid it. In criticizing aesthetic knowledge in the name of the occasionality intrinsic to a work of art, he risks making us believe that he rather favours the historicizing consideration in works of art, which would explain them from their historical context. But for Gadamer, it would be to go from Charybdis to Scylla. He is seeking a way between these two rocks (which are in mythology two "monsters"): if aesthetic knowledge forgets that works are rooted in the continuity of life, historical knowledge forgets that we are considering works of art! This is why Gadamer prefers to speak of a "general occasionality".[30] To avoid historicism, he even underlines that it is unneccessary to know all the historical references for their own sake. Here Gadamer fought against taking aim at a restorative or reconstitutive understanding in the original mearing which he associates with Schleiermacher and his hermeneutics. "This is not occasionality in the sense intended here",[31] Gadamer insisted. More basically, occasionality means a work's demand for meaning, its *general* attachment to the world, *which is also our own*, and which can be realized without all the historical references being mastered (which anyway is never the case).

So occasionality, from the angle of what can be called a fusion of horizons, also implies *our* world in the work of presentation. The meaning of occasionality in the work is always also the meaning which the work takes for us, according to historical considerations. The young Bonaparte's portrait takes on a particular connotation when he became Napoleon, and the traces of a completed past for us acquires a meaning and a value that it did not have in its own age. The occasionality of works is also that which befalls them in our world. We could name the presentation the "downstream" of the work, what confers on it a presence and a stature in our world. If the painting is the primary model of the "upstream" presentation, what acquires a surfeit of being in representation, sculpture and architecture carries the greatest confirmation of the work's contemporary occasionality. If the sculpture or, still more obviously, the monument goes back to a past creation, it still inscribes itself into our world, where it fulfils a certain "function". It is obvious that aesthetic knowledge tends to belittle this functional or useful aspect of architectural works. But Gadamer heavily underlines architecture's practical destiny because it allows him to make a show of both aesthetic knowledge and historical knowledge: considerations of pure aesthetics never take account of the practical vocation of architecture, which is sometimes excluded from the domain of aesthetics. But historicism does not succeed either, because the work of architecture is raised in the present where it displays a particular valency, as it inevitably has to absorb new constructions, from traffic and the architectural and natural work of centuries. The occasionality of the work is not uniquely what gave it birth; the work still has to be integrated into our present. All contemporary "completeness" in the meaning of the work must take account of these factors. In this way, architecture also has an exemplary status with Gadamer, as his last writings confirm.[32]

Gadamer therefore succeeded in showing that presentation is equally essential to the non-performing arts such as painting, sculpture and architecture. Presentation always comes back to a being which presents itself, which has access to its truth, but the spectator always participates in this presentation himself, from his own present. The last form of art that Gadamer deals with, but only very briefly, in *Truth and Method* is literature. On this point, the later additions on poetry are particularly valuable. But we must recognize that Gadamer's theory of presentation is here at its most evident, as is shown by the evolution of his literary studies since 1960. In 1960, Gadamer was still battling against the conception that the literary work is an aesthetic entity closed in upon itself, and exists only in the ideality of the text, as if "there does not appear to be any presentation that could claim an ontological valence of its own".[33] From today's perspective, to which Gadamer has made an important contribution, we have the feeling that the work of 1960 is knocking on an already opened door. His thesis there is that the "the reading of a book would still remain an event in which the content comes to presentation", even if the reading shows "the maximum degree of freedom and mobility".[34]

The indelible contribution of reading to the understanding of the text is today one of the greatest contributions to literary studies. It has largely been developed in Germany by the Constance school, notably in Hans-Robert Jauss's aesthetics of reception and Wolfgang Iser's theory of reading.[35] The aesthetics of reception was directly inspired by hermeneutics when it sought to deepen the two dimensions of "literary presentation", as it has its roots in a deterministic historical context (to which the work has always been the reply), leading it to historicize literary works, and it becomes actual in the act of reading. Perhaps Gadamer was influenced by these developments, because (as we have seen) he greatly extended the idea of reading in his later aesthetics, recognizing that the way to finish (*Vollzug*, execute) the work of art was to undertake a reading which participated in a productive way to the event in the sense of the work, whether it be literary, musical, pictorial or architectural. In making us confront ourselves, the inherent presentation of every work of art invites us to an exercise of reading and attention. In this way, all the arts are, like us, transitory.

Hermeneutic consequences of truth rediscovered in art

We must speak of hermeneutic consequences because Gadamer's enquiry was part of an interrogation of the epistemology of the human sciences:

how should we understand their claim to truth? It is obvious enough that the concept of method is badly appropriated, as it is so closely modelled on the exact sciences. The temptation of the human sciences is therefore to be understood according to the model of aesthetics. As is maintained by the Gadamerian reconquest of truth from art, the human sciences have everything to gain, but the problem is that the human sciences are most often understood from a narrow aesthetic knowledge, which is still tacitly imposed on them by the scientific model. This model consigns the understanding of art to the periphery, in all the senses of the term: to the periphery of science, of truth, of reality and of society where, under the cover of the avant-garde, art developed an autotelic cult of marginality.

Gadamer ultimately spoke little enough of "truth" as such in regaining truth for art, insisting above all on the function of *presentation* in the game of art, which at its roots is an ontological process. But the ontological process[36] is one of truth for Gadamer. From *Truth and Method*, we should listen to the words of Goethe, which became Gadamer's leitmotiv in 1992: "so wahr, so seiend"; "so much being, so much truth". But what is the opposite of truth? Is it error, or falsehood? Yes, if we think of kitsch, for example. But the true opposite of truth is emptiness.[37] If the true work of art is the revelation of a being, its opposite is an empty or hollow presentation, which raises up nothing. In his 1992 essay on Goethe, Gadamer rediscovered the later Heidegger's passion for the impersonal words of the event, in commenting very simply on the ontological discovery accomplished by art: "it emerges", "it is so".

Art is therefore less aesthetic than aesthetics believes. It is the experience of truth, but of a truth in which the viewer knows that he is always implicated. We learn the lessons first, that truth does not depend entirely on the distance of the viewer, and secondly, that truth (always understood as justice) enhances the event. To speak of event is to recall that we are not masters of everything which happens to us in the game of art; in art as well, there is being more than knowledge. As Adorno said, no one understands art, but we can say at most that we understand something of it.[38] The truth of art is not one of mastery, but of participation. Even if we do not understand fully, we do not understand less.

The human sciences can therefore be inspired from this test of art. But the hermeneutics of the human sciences has preferred to follow another model, that of the aesthetic knowledge which is a reject of modern methodological knowledge that claims a monopoly on knowledge and truth. For such hermeneutics, interpretation essentially aims to recreate the lived experience that has come from an original creation. This is no longer truth, but a phenomenon of expression which we seek to understand either from its author (on the psychological model) or from its historical context (as historicism would wish). In these two derivatives, psychologizing and historicist, hermeneutics is excluded, without its always being realized, from the world of knowledge. The aestheticization and the historicization of hermeneutics from now on describe the two faces of one and the same fundamental loss, that of truth. After reconquering the truth in art, Gadamer's great task was now to find the meaning of hermeneutic truth.

CHAPTER THREE

The Destruction of Prejudices in Nineteenth-Century Aesthetics and Epistemology

The critique of Romantic hermeneutics

For Gadamer, the experience of the work of art is not primarily a specifically aesthetic experience, but one of understanding. This is why aesthetics should be conveyed by hermeneutics. All the rest of Gadamer's work is therefore taken up with hermeneutics. But the shadow of aesthetic consciousness continues to hover over hermeneutic development. To be concerned with understanding, or with the human sciences, is not enough to pretend to have grasped the complete radicality of hermeneutics. The whole of Gadamer's thought can be seen as an attempt to reconquer this universality of the hermeneutic problem. In his work, the cascade of sectional titles, such as that of disengagement (*Freilegung*), of overstepping (*Überwindung*), of enlarging (*Ausweitung*), of the rediscovery and reconquest (*Wiedergewinnung*) of the hermeneutic problem finally emerges in the universal aspect of hermeneutics. Throughout, Gadamer seeks to disturb the ease with which we seek to avoid the finitude of human understanding and to make it an issue of method or technique. In the second part of *Truth and Method* his "destructive" task is directed against the hermeneutics of the nineteenth century, which are essentially those of Schleiermacher and Dilthey.

In his great debate with the preceding hermeneutic tradition, of which he is the inheritor, Gadamer concentrated on showing how Schleiermacher and Dilthey, despite their best Romantic intentions, succumbed to the modern concept of method, which caused them to miss the radical nature of the hermeneutic problem. Numerous specialists in the works of Schleiermacher and Dilthey have incidentally reminded us that Gadamer's "presentation" is rather unilateral as it is silent about the respects in which certain elements of their hermeneutics anticipated his own.[1] In the vast literature that has appeared since Gadamer's "errors" have been pointed out, it has perhaps been forgotten that Gadamer denounced Schleier-macher's and Dilthey's aphorisms essentially from a basis of solidarity. It is precisely because they were *also* aware of the specificity of the hermeneu-tic problem that Gadamer sought to destroy the methodological form in which they finally presented their thought. It is equally forgotten that without Gadamer's destruction, which hoped to radicalize the hermeneu-tic thought of the Romantics, we would today perhaps have forgotten Schleiermacher's and Dilthey's hermeneutics. Schleiermacher would have remained what he was before Gadamer, that is to say the author of the *Discourse on Religion* (1799) and of the *Glaubenslehre* (1821–2), and therefore a great Protestant theologian, who would also have been remembered for his translation of the whole of Plato's works, but who was not interested in hermeneutics, as he did not write any work on it, but treated it as a peripheral topic. As for Dilthey, he would have remained a great historian of philosophy – we owe to him the rediscovery of the young Hegel and the Academy edition of Kant's works – and a methodolo-gist of the human sciences, that is to say, the author of an *Introduction to the Human Sciences* (1883), where curiously the word "hermeneutics" does not appear even once.

Still, there is no doubt that Gadamer's destructive work in the debate with the two great "hermeneuts" of the Romantic movement aimed at giving a higher profile to his own conception of hermeneutics. He recognized it himself in his self-critique of 1985,[2] but from the time of *Truth and Method* he specified that he would be content "to pursue the development of the hermeneutical method in the modern period, which culminates in the rise of historical consciousness".[3] But his explanation of 1960 does not prevent the emergence of crucial problems in their hermeneutics. Even if it is legitimate to complete Gadamer's partial interpretation, we would be blind if we ignored those aporiae that Gadamer's destruction brought to our notice for the first time.

Essentially, Gadamer's critique is that the hermeneutics of Romanticism has diluted understanding's aim of truth (or of content), to the advantage of the aim of meaning which from then on became oriented more to expression. The meaning understood would be less a truth than the expres-sion of an individuality or of an era. Gadamer saw the first indication of this in Schleiermacher's new interest in understanding. Gadamer could certainly have recognized himself in the acknowledged priority of understanding, so much so that for Schleiermacher it was the foundation of the universality of hermeneutics: when traditional and special hermeneutics were defined by the specificity of their contents (sacred texts, profane texts, legal texts, etc.), general hermeneutics concentrated exclusively on the *process* of under-standing which constituted their common basis. But for Gadamer, that also meant that hermeneutics was not really determined by "the unity of the content of tradition to which understanding is applied", but by "the unity of a procedure".[4] Here Gadamer's argument appears a little quick. It is not *because* the understanding is now the object of privileged attention, as is still the case with Heidegger and Gadamer, that the aim of content is necessarily sacrificed. We could also discern, in this acknowledged priority given to the understanding, an anticipation of hermeneutic universality which Gadamer sought.

If we can speak of a loss of content, it is because we are witness to a certain inflexibility in the meaning of understanding from Schleiermacher onwards. More and more the understanding seems to aim at the *opinions* of others. As that became still more apparent in Dilthey, who built his theory of the human sciences on the triad, "understanding–expression–lived experience", understanding was concerned with individual opinion, which was displaced or alienated in such-and-such an expression. Gadamer's first argument was that understanding aims less at expression than at truth. But we already know this argument since it directed the whole of the critique of aesthetic knowledge. Gadamer's most subtle argument lay in the elaboration of another insight into understanding, perhaps difficult to follow because it relies on the wisdom of the German language. In German, to understand means first of all "to agree mutually on common ground". In a certain way, that is also true of the French word *entente* (often the translation for *Verstehen*). But Gadamer draws from this the controversial thesis that "understanding is first of all agreement (*Einverständnis*)".[5] If Gadamer is worth attacking on this point, it is because a superficial reading makes him say that understanding necessarily means to be in agreement with what is understood. As if understanding *Mein Kampf* is to agree with its arguments!

The meaning of Gadamer's remark lies elsewhere. It arises, like almost everything else with him, from the experience of dialogue, which is the natural place of accord and understanding. Gadamer says that, in conversation, which is – like art – a game where the true *subjectum* is the dialogue itself, the accord which prevails between the interlocutors does not essentially bear on the opinions that come to be expressed in the course of the exchange, but on the "common ground", the very thing that the exchange is about. The underlying agreement is, besides, always greater, breaking out of the precise objects of discussion. Habermas's ethics of discussion reified these presuppositions in speaking of the "transcendental conditions" of dialogue, which have the characteristics of the rationality and veracity of the interlocutors. But it is not necessary to speak of transcendental conditions to follow Gadamer's argument. The fact of sharing a language and common preoccupations is enough to understand that in understanding or mutual accord, the interlocutors do not only share "in this or that . . . but in all the essential things that unite human beings".[6]

We understand the bearing of this insight on understanding as "accord on common ground", which determines the rest of his hermeneutics, only in opposition to Schleiermacher. With regard to this initial accord, others' opinions – or mine – do not at first enjoy a particular profile. It is only when the accord is disturbed that the opinions of others come to be fixed as such. It is only when my understanding hears something shocking, unrealistic or unintelligible that it comes to consider the *opinions* of others as such and to wonder *how* they came about. If we can stay with the example of *Mein Kampf*, we read the book as the document of Hitler's defective opinions because we cannot agree with what he says, and we can wonder how he came to his affirmations. But no one judges this question to be primordial in the reading of Euclid's *Elements*, or of Sophocles' plays, or of a good poem by Rilke. Of course we can *also* ask questions about Euclid's opinions, or those of Sophocles or Rilke, and there is a whole critical literature from the nineteenth century onwards, but its orientation is secondary to understanding. Gadamer sees it as a detour from the natural aim of understanding, even if it recognizes that it can be *essential* in certain cases. What is determining for Gadamer is that what tends to become the rule for Schleiermacher is really always an exception.

Gadamer is quite right in seeing here a reversal[7] of order in hermeneutic priorities. It also presupposes a universalization of *foreignness* in what must be understood. If a common sense can no longer be presupposed, all understanding from now on will try to reconstruct the process of meaning for itself, so as to understand how everyone else came to their opinions. The clearest witness is found in the famous adage, often evoked by Schleiermacher, according to which the task of understanding is *to understand an author better than he understood himself.* Gadamer recognizes in this the real problem of hermeneutics,[8] since according to him it allows a line of separation between the two insights of the hermeneutic task. What has to be better understood is whether it is the author or the thought which has to be expressed. Gadamer thinks that, originally, it was probably only a maxim which had bearing on the common ground, on the truth of what was trying to express itself. Thus Kant could write with regard to his transcendental dialectic that he understood Plato better than Plato understood himself because he interpreted his ideas as concepts of pure reason. Kant's intention was not to better understand Plato himself, but to better understand the truth which Plato could only imperfectly express. But Schleiermacher gives a different meaning to the formula. What is better understood is not truth itself, but the unconscious process of the creation of meaning. In this sense, Schleiermacher could write that "the hermeneutic task consisted in reconstituting in the most perfect way the whole internal development of the writer's activity of composition".[9]

According to Gadamer, hermeneutics here takes a psychological turn. It is no longer an issue of presenting a fundamental rational defence of the well-foundedness of meaning, but of reconstituting unconscious production. To this ideal of the *reconstruction* of meaning, Gadamer opposes the Hegelian idea of an integration of meaning with contemporary consciousness. Here his hermeneutics relies on the teachings of his aesthetics. Just as the truth of the work of art is achieved only in its contemporary presentation or reading, so the hermeneutic completion of meaning is effected in the application conferred on it by contemporary understanding. The meaning that is transmitted to me from the past is one which challenges me, and which I always interpret in the light of my own possibilities, of my categories, or, better, of my language. The reconstruction of which Schleiermacher speaks, where the legitimacy cannot be questioned, is always effected on the basis of an addition to the meaning communicated. But the ideal of reconstruction presupposes distance in relation to meaning, which is the daughter of scientific method, but which despises the relation of addition in the sense understood. For Gadamer, to understand is always to understand yourself as well.

Gadamer therefore prefers to speak, with Hegel, of an integration of meaning transmitted by the work of history. In integration, distance is not always eradicated: meaning inevitably comes from the past, and is understood as such, but the horizon of the past is always fused with the present and represents its welcoming ground. This is the meaning of the eminently Gadamerian idea of a *fusion of horizons* in the process of understanding. I always understand the past from the perspective of my own horizon, but the latter has itself been formed by the past as much as by the possibilities of the language of actual understanding. What in understanding really comes from "me", and what is taken up from the "past"? Can we really know, with complete assurance? Can understanding be completely transparent to itself? This is why it appears more prudent in Gadamer's eyes to speak of a melting of horizons, of an encounter which mysteriously succeeds. The understanding is more event and effects meaning more than historical or methodological consciousness is prepared to admit.

If Gadamer is right to be opposed to the project of a strictly methodological hermeneutics in favour of event which intervenes in all successful understanding, it could all the same be that his opposition to the aim of truth combined with the psychological aim (*mens auctoris*) is a little too rigid. The latter, if it is well understood, is in the service of the former. The "transposition" into the mind of the other only has meaning in understanding its pretension to *truth,* precisely in its concern for objectivity. To take the *perspective* of the other into account completely corresponds to the idea of understanding in today's language. "To test understanding" is to try to put ourselves in the place of the other. To speak here of psychologism is perhaps to yield to a facile positivist reductionism, as if the whole concept of empathy implied a "psychic transfer". To transpose oneself into the soul of the other, as Schleiermacher says, is not necessarily to reconstruct a psychology, but rather to acknowledge that we should recognize the well-foundedness of, the reasons for, another's position. In this sense, we can defend Schleiermacher against Gadamer, even if the Gadamerian opposition between truth and psychology was doubtless necessary in its time to allow hermeneutics to emerge from the impasses of historicism and aesthetic consciousness.

Everything depends on the meaning that is suitable for the crucial concept of *expression* in this debate. Gadamer devoted an important *excursus* in an appendix to his work, where he made it clear that his whole enterprise can be read as an account of the psychologizing insight into the concept of expression.[10] We know that the term played a key role in the hermeneutic thought of Dilthey and Georg Misch.[11] To understand, for them, is to understand how an expression relates to an *Erlebnis,* a lived experience. Gadamer relentlessly criticizes this conception because he suspects an aestheticization of understanding, dangerous as it is accompanied by a loss of truth, which is the business of scientific methodology. But, for all that, we must not conclude that Gadamer is trying to get rid altogether of the notion of expression which he attacks so ferociously. As the important *excursus* on the concept of *expressio* shows, he wants by contrast to restore to it its original *rhetorical* meaning. In good rhetoric, *expressio* first refers to the formula or the expression which is impressed, which marks us.[12] What makes an impression is always the thing present in an expression ("*im Ausdruck ist das Ausgedrückte da*"[13]). What is expressed rhetorically is always the thing itself, and not the subjectivity which is its vehicle: "To find a good expression is to find an expression which aims at a certain impression; it is not at all expression in the sense of the expression of what has been lived."[14] In this spirit, Gadamer tries to free the word "expression" from its modern subjectivist colouration. He suspects that language has been forgotten – as expression of things rather than of subjects – that is to say, forgetting rhetoric as a source of truth. Once again, we have established that Gadamer "destroys" the history of ideas, here the carrier of the psychologizing concept of expression, only to rediscover a meaning that modern subjectivity tends to make unrecognizable by interpreting each mental phenomenon as an almost mechanical production of subjectivity. It is to miss the rhetorical intentionality of the expression, which is always the expression *of something*.

Self-effacement in the historical school

Gadamer's intuition is that the mechanism of subjectivity or of expression finally emerges in a structure of aesthetic thought in the unverifiable sense of the term.[15] This aesthetic thought in expression, after Schleiermacher, finds its most symptomatic expression in the school represented by Ranke and Droysen. Leopold von Ranke (1795–1886) and Johann Gustav Droysen (1808–84) were great historians: we owe to the former a monumental *History of the World* and to the latter great works on the history of Prussia, on Alexander the Great and on Hellenism (a word invented by Droysen). But they were also historians who, in the spirit of the century, reflected on the foundations of their discipline. They did so in their role as historians, because they were mistrustful of philosophical constructions. But from a philosophical point of view, the methodological reflections of both Ranke and Droysen were first and foremost replies to Hegel. All historians of the nineteenth century sought to defend the scientific nature of their discipline in distancing themselves from an idealist philosophy of history. Although Hegel was one of the first to recognize the historical character of all thought, a merit which the historical school recognized, it is clear that his historicist philosophy reacted to the historicization of the concept, of reason and of philosophy, by an *idealization of history,* reconstructed as a function of the demands of the rationality of the philosophical concept.[16] What the historical school denounces in Hegel is the wish to impose an *a priori* teleology on the course of history, since it does not do justice to facticity, to the individual, even to liberty, which properly characterizes historical facts.

This critique of the idealist conception of history in the name of facticity is well known. What the historical school itself proposes, in order to escape from the dangers of a philosophy of history, remains to be seen. Its reply is sometimes marked by positivism and sometimes by an aestheti-cizing hermeneutics. Following the spirit of positivism, it goes without saying that history should become a science; it should deal with phenom-ena and avoid imposing a metaphysical superstructure on them. Historical facts must no longer be deduced as a function of *the* a priori requisites of a metaphysical system, but must be interpreted in themselves. To interpret phenomena in themselves is to understand them in their "historical context". What is presupposed, and where hermeneutics takes over what is handed on by positivism, is that the whole of history constitutes a great text which must be deciphered.

We can wonder here if the historical school leaves behind all forms of idealism. Historical phenomena remain dumb if they are not set in a wider historical context, that of an era, and in the last analysis, that of universal history. Even for the historical school, there is no such thing except for historical facts which can speak for themselves. The particular has sense only in its function in a more general context. But where does this dialectic of the part and of the whole come from, if not from hermeneutics and its model of interpreting texts? Gadamer says that in this way philology has served as a basis for historical science. But can the textual model really be transposed to history (it will soon be to existence, when the issue of "the meaning of life" is raised), and does it offer a sufficient basis to allow us to grasp facticity in its entirety in historical understanding? In contrast to history, the texts interpreted by philology form a relatively finished totality, where we can identify the beginning and the end. But where, in history, is there some such thing as a beginning or an end susceptible of being understood? It is in this way that the historical school is led back to the problem, Hegelian as it is, of universal history which it still tries to avoid like the plague.

What distinguishes the historical school from Hegel is in the end its rejection of teleology, the idea of progress in history in the sense of a more and more complete actualization of reason. The historical school considers itself to be constrained to replace this concept of progress by that of an equivalence, or a principle of equity between centuries, which is a feature of relativism.[17] If eras should not be interpreted in the light of a superior philosophical *telos*, but for their own sake, they all enjoy an equal value "before God", as Ranke noted. The Lutheran idea of a direct and immediate relationship of the believer to God is thus also applied to the succession of eras.[18] For an infinite intelligence, all eras are found in the indifference of a relative simultaneity (which Gadamer shrewdly likens to the simultaneity of aesthetic consciousness), if it is true that each era possesses its own legitimacy. The role of the historian in all this is to "efface himself" so as to let the phenomena speak for themselves, according to their own legitimacy for an infinite intellect. The famous metaphor of the *self-effacement* of the interpreter seems to assimilate the historian's concern for objectivity with that of the scientific concern. Just as the results of science should be independent of the observer, so should the historian efface himself before phenomena which can be explained in their proper context. But does this objectivity do justice to meaning in the historical context?

The concept of self-effacement, apparently a carrier of objectivity, passes over in silence the historicity of the historian himself, that is to say the extent to which he also belongs to the history that he relates, if only because the questions that he asks must always carry the mark of his own time (the powerful apologetic character of Droysen's own history of Prussia is an outstanding example). In a formula which anticipates that of the historical work (*Wirkungsgeschichte*), Gadamer speaks of an "anteriority" (*Vorgängigkeit*[19]) of the historical link in relation to the historian's consciousness. There is no such thing as a historical consciousness that is itself placed above history. Even according to Ranke's principles, God alone, or an infinite intellect, is capable of writing such a history. The proof of this is that history must be rewritten by every new generation. Histories written in the past are still of interest and scientific value, but they confirm that history is understood differently in each age. The historian's historicity does not sufficiently take the historical school into account. In the name of historicity and of facticity, the historical school promises to escape from Hegelian idealist presuppositions. Again, it could be that the Hegelian idea of an *integration* of history *understood* in the present has taken better account of the essential anteriority of history.

The historical school appeals to aesthetic categories by silently transposing the philological model to that of history. If every event is only the expression of an age, the attitude of the historian in the face of history is amenable to the order of aestheticizing contemplation or to self-effacement. But does this self-effacement by which the historian is allied to an infinite intelligence stand up to our radical addition to history and to the truths which we encounter there? Can we take on the indifferent attitude of detached spectators in the face of history? We always continue to be concerned by the history which we practise, whether or not we are conscious of it. To make history is not only to reconstruct the great text of universal history from an objective and aestheticizing perspective; it is always to be placed in opposition to a history which surrounds us and which is always reflected in the questions of the present. This historicity of the historian and the fact that history is always of concern to us are not really taken into account by the historical school. A radically historical thought must begin from our essential addition to history.

Droysen certainly developed a deeper conception than that of Ranke when he took account of the meditations of understanding in all historical knowledge. But according to Gadamer the concept of *understanding*, which in Droysen acquires a methodological value, considers historical phenomena to be manifestations or exteriorizations of an interiority. For Gadamer, it reveals that Droysen is "entirely Cartesian".[20] It could be that Gadamer's judgement here is a little severe, even if it goes without saying that Droysen's intentions are methodological. In explaining that historical knowledge, according to the famous formula, enhances "understanding in enquiry" (*forschend verstehen*), Droysen takes good care, as Gadamer recognizes, to distinguish this knowledge from that which is current in the natural sciences. The infinity of research which is offered to historical understanding is not that of the infinity of the object, but that which can never directly be seen or understood. The understanding never has access to an ultimate and Cartesian datum; it always relies on previous testimony and understanding. To understand, in Boeckh's great formula, is to recognize what is already known (*Erkenntnis des Erkannten*), to understand again what has already been understood, and which is always and only offered in favour of those meditations of understanding. For historical knowledge, "'hearsay' is here not bad evidence, but the only evidence possible".[21]

It is not certain that this concept of understanding, which, all to the good, seems to take account of meditations of finitude, is altogether Cartesian. Gadamer even recognizes that it has religious and pietistic overtones, which we can understand according to the idea of a search or an examination of conscience (*Gewissensforschung*). Doubtless Gadamer is seeking to attach religious connotations to the very basis of a "pantheist metaphysics of individuality" which he had already noted in Schleiermacher, but we must not forget what his own concept of understanding owes to theology, notably to that of Bultmann. For theology at Marburg, self-understanding has nothing to do with a Cartesian mastery of one's own interiority. Rather, it consists in recognizing that understanding will always only be partial, that it will never completely succeed, as if failure is most essential to understanding. If, to put it in Hegelian terms, the *Dasein* is a being of understanding, fundamentally it does not understand very much. This condition of finitude allows us to understand ourselves, between human beings, knowing that all understanding carries a large component of hearsay and tentativeness. Does this congeniality, better, this complicity in human understanding, go back to a "ultimate immediacy"[22] of Cartesian inspiration, as Gadamer believes, or is it not a reminder of its absence? In distinguishing his concept of seeking from the knowledge of the exact sciences, Droysen was perhaps closer to Gadamer than the latter realized.

But when he does not denounce a *Cartesian* base (most certainly present in Droysen's *methodological* project) Gadamer is ready to assimilate the concept of expression to a structure of *aesthetic* thought. In thinking more radically of the anteriority of history to consciousness, Hegel would have seen further than the historical school. If this is beyond doubt, it remains that Droysen understood historical phenomena as the expressions of "moral powers" which formed the "actual reality of history".[23] Certainly this concept of ethical forces appears rather gross, in that it recalls the vitalism of natural forces. But it would be unfair to see in it nothing but an aesthetico-hermeneutic category, as Gadamer does.[24] The idea of ethical powers reminds us of Hegel, who himself thought of history as progess in historical consciousness. Here again we should modify Gadamer's verdict according to which Droysen interpreted history only with the help of aestheticizing categories which retained from Hegel the concept of the exteriorization of the mind.

The three aporiae of Dilthey and historicism

The historical school was essentially the reaction of historians to Hegel's idealist philosophy. As Gadamer well saw, their rejection of the idealist philosophy pushed them towards philology.[25] From this perspective, hermeneutics became the unacknowledged presupposition of the historical school. But this philologization of history itself proceeded from idealist presuppositions (historical facts always having to be understood in a wider context), positivist presuppositions (the self-effacement of the interpreter), and finally aesthetic presuppositions (each phenomenon being only the expression of something lived, or of an era). Dilthey alone delivered a full philosophy of historical knowledge, and he saw himself as the great methodologist of the historical school when he undertook the task of developing a "critique of historical reason". This critique sought to give a philosophical foundation to the human sciences, analogous to that which Kant undertook in the pure sciences with his *Critique of Pure Reason*. It was an ambitious project, but above all Gadamer regarded it as symptomatic. We know that none of Dilthey's publications ever carried the title "critique of historical reason", which was always for him a great undertaking. But Gadamer thought that his project could not be carried through because he was haunted by very fundamental aporiae.

Several contradictory tendencies seemed to clash with Dilthey, who was an extraordinary historian of philosophy, a penetrative interpreter of history, a methodologist of the human sciences and a master of methodology in the exact sciences. Essentially, Dilthey never came to acknowledge his Cartesian foundations, which alone allowed the human sciences to withdraw from arbitrariness and from subjectivity, with its thought of a more Romantic historicity that still remained aestheticizing. Dilthey was therefore split between Romanticism and positivism, as Gadamer pointed out in an important article of 1984.[26] According to Gadamer, the two aspects were intertwined: aestheticizing Romanticism is always and only the reverse and the consequence of Cartesian positivism. If Gadamer speaks freely of Dilthey's aporiae, we must also see that Dilthey was *coher-*

ent in trying to reconcile his Cartesian foundationalism and his aestheticizing thoughts on historicity. For Gadamer, they are products of one and the same mind. Gadamer sought to combat this approach on behalf of a more radical idea of historicism, which is liberated from the spectre of Cartesianism and consequently of relativism.

We cannot overstress the strategic importance of Gadamer's debate with Dilthey. In many ways, the latter represents his interlocutor and principal adversary in *Truth and Method*. The whole of the historical preparation therein devoted to the history of hermeneutics in the nineteenth century was aimed at recalling the idealist, Romantic and aestheticizing presuppositions which were those of Dilthey. And the hermeneutics of understanding that Gadamer defended can be understood only in opposition to the project of a methodological hermeneutics whose most eloquent mouthpiece was Dilthey. Dilthey's thought represented the latest advance in philosophical hermeneutics. Heidegger, who was obviously Gadamer's greatest inspiration, had also spoken of hermeneutics, but it appeared only in the framework of an existential ontology which seemed to have burnt its bridges with the methodological approach of a hermeneutics of the human sciences. Despite Heidegger, who is more easily associated with phenomenology or a "philosophy of existence", hermeneutics is still identified with the thought of Dilthey and his school, represented by authors such as Georg Misch, Hermann Nohl, Josef König, Bernhard Groethuysen, Erich Rothaker, Otto Friedrich Bollnow and Frithjof Rodi. In France, as Raymond Aron and Georges Gusdorf would have it, the descendants of the Diltheyan school are perhaps less direct.[27]

Dilthey could also ask fundamental, and therefore philosophical, questions on behalf of hermeneutics. The most crucial problem, more prominent than those of relativism and nihilism, was that of historical consciousness. As he came out of the historical school, his questions were still in epistemological terms: if every historical manifestation must be understood within its era, is an objective and universally valid knowledge possible? The problem is thus one of knowledge, of truth, and it is asked above all in the historical, and thus human, sciences. These "sciences" have suffered from an inferiority complex in comparison with the objective natural sciences (of which Kant, it seems, had defined the conditions of possibility and the methodology), which has threatened their scientific credibility. Dilthey therefore looks for the salvation of the human sciences in a "methodology".

Hermeneutics is doubtless implicated in this debate by reason of the following "syllogism": all of the human sciences are sciences of understanding, but hermeneutics is understood, from Schleiermacher (whose biographer Dilthey was) as a science of understanding; it could therefore be that hermeneutics is called to serve as the foundation of all the human sciences. As he said in his article of 1900, "The Emergence of Hermeneutics", the essential role of hermeneutics is "to establish in theory, against the constant intrusion of Romantic arbitrariness and sceptical subjectivism in the domain of history, the universal validity of interpretation, the solid basis of all historical certainty".[28] In seeking to "resolve the question of the scientific knowledge of individuals and even the great forms of particular existence in general", hermeneutics should allow us to determine "if knowledge of the singular can acquire a universal validity".[29]

Rather oddly, Gadamer does not refer to these compromising texts in his confrontation with Dilthey in *Truth and Method*. They would easily have confirmed his thesis on Dilthey's latent Cartesianism. Gadamer prefers to attack head-on the problem of historical consciousness as Dilthey asks it, and as it is asked in Gadamer himself, in spite of, but also since, the hermeneutics of existence promoted by Heidegger. When we study the works published by Gadamer throughout the 1950s, we realize that they are dominated by this Diltheyan problem of historical conscious-ness and truth in history. We think of the pamphlets on truth in the human sciences,[30] the conferences held in Louvain in November 1957,[31] and also the first version of the manuscript of *Truth and Method*, which opens with a debate with Dilthey.[32] We can also say that the whole of Gadamer's work begins with Dilthey, to which his hermeneutics is the reply.

If the work published in 1960 carries a section devoted to art, it is because Gadamer was trying to develop an original, non-methodological concept of truth which he could then set up in opposition to Dilthey's. In his 1975 preface to the English edition of *Truth and Method*, Gadamer recognized that the two points of anchorage of his hermeneutics were found in his attack on historical consciousness and the experience of art.[33] But from the viewpoint of the hermeneutic tradition, the debate with Dilthey is crucial.

But Dilthey was already so in evidence in all the arguments of the work that the chapters devoted to him come as no real surprise. The first two sections have prepared the ground so well that the only thing remaining is the citation of Dilthey's aporiae where Dilthey buries himself in his reply to historicism. The basic aporia (Gadamer speaks of the aporiae of historicism in the plural) is certainly that of positivism as the final foundation and in historicity. Dilthey is not only a Cartesian methodologist, but the inheritor of the Romantic tradition and of the philosophy of life. Because he has a keen appreciation of the relativity of all life, Dilthey poses the problem of historical consciousness in methodological terms: historicity is so invasive, so universal, that only a rigorous methodology would be able to contain its effects. But, Gadamer wonders, if we are thoroughly historical beings, is knowledge that totally transcends this condition not excluded?

Dilthey hopes to find a solution to this dilemma in the very fact of historical consciousness. *Because* we are aware of this historicity, we are capable, to a certain extent, of getting away from its influence and studying history objectively. Everything happens as if historical consciousness had become the remedy for its own ills. But here Gadamer puts his finger on a still more savage aporia than historicism, that which assimilates historical consciousness to a form of self-knowledge.[34] It is indubitable that historical consciousness can adopt a reflexive attitude in opposition to history and its own historicity. But does this awareness of history succeed for this reason in objectifying the full extent of its historical determination? It is not certain. Dilthey is once more the victim of a Cartesian paralogism, in identifying historical reflexion with the hold of the objective consciousness of history which determines us. Can we know which tradition or traditions really determine us? Do we not find in the idea of a historical consciousness that would like to dissolve the attachment to history an *instrumentalism* of knowledge and of subjectivity which gives us an illusion about its own possibilities of knowledge? On the boldness of historical consciousness, in the *geschichtliches Bewusstsein*, Gadamer comes to graft a "consciousness of the work of history", a *wirkungsgeschichtliches Bewusstsein*, which recognizes that historical consciousness is being more than knowledge. In this sense, the whole of Gadamer's hermeneutics can be understood as a reply to Dilthey. The thesis of his hermeneutics is effectively that for a historical being, historicity itself is never resolved in self-knowledge.[35]

The mistake is to believe that Gadamer nevertheless tries to undermine the foundations of the possibilities of reflexion, and more particularly those of historical consciousness. Gadamer does not disqualify the acquisitions of historical consciousness in the manner of an ostrich who puts its head in the sand of historicity to avoid the obvious attack of historical reflexion. Rather, he appeals to a more reflective awareness of historicity that is also aware of its own historicity, which Dilthey tends to ignore in abandoning himself to the superiority of a historical consciousness that understands itself, rather in the manner of Aristotle's *noesis noeseos* or the absolute mind in Hegel. Gadamer always speaks of a "consciousness" (*Bewusstsein*) of the work of history. And that consciousness is accompanied not by a loss, but if all well and good by a reflexive gain. It not only allows us to understand ourselves better, but more modestly it also allows us to understand better how historical consciousness is itself the daughter of its time, by applying historical consciousness to itself. The self-effacement that promotes historical consciousness is itself the product of its age, and its ideal of scientificity. It comes from a model of knowledge that is incompatible with the historicity of understanding. Such an unrealizable ideal has as its consequence the paralysis of effective possibilities of historical understanding, which never conform to the model of the exact sciences, as there are different objectives and experiences of knowledge. So the consciousness of the work of history puts us in a position to better understand the human sciences and historicity, which is not nothing, but is historical consciousness itself.

And Gadamer is so little the enemy of historical consciousness and reflexion that he follows Dilthey when he proposes that historicity is always accompanied by a knowledge of itself that is rooted in the depths of life itself. According to Dilthey, in effect, the human sciences only prolong a virtuality of reflexion that proceeds from the most elementary objectivations of life and which allow life to grasp itself. From this aspect of reflexions, Dilthey himself goes beyond the methodological framework of his own enquiry and he anticipates the more ambitious hermeneutics of historical existence that would be developed by Heidegger and Gadamer, but whose trace we also find in authors such as Misch, Yorck and Husserl, who in their way radicalize Dilthey's intuitions. Philosophical hermeneutics is very sympathetic to this possibility of deriving scientific knowledge from practices and procedures which plunge their roots in the lived world (*Lebenswelt*). But according to Gadamer, Dilthey's consideration of the lived world and its immanent reflexion in life remains vitiated by Cartesian presuppositions. Thus Dilthey likes to raise the doubt of the scientific method – a Cartesian theme if ever there was one! – on doubt or on scepticism which can afflict the mind at certain times of human existence. Also it is true that human life instinctively seeks forms of solidity so as to acquire a certain stability in existence. According to Gadamer, doubt and solidity here do not have the same meaning. Cartesian doubt, which doubts in order to come to an indubitable certainty, cannot be confused with existential doubt, because the latter doubts the very possibility of such certainty. Far from being its extension, Cartesian doubt in Gadamer's view starts from a movement directed against life and its essential doubt.[36] And the solidity that life encounters in the stability of customs, of the family and of social life has nothing of Descartes's *fundamentum inconcussum* which is the object of an integrated foundation or even deduction. This solidity is dependent more on a solidarity, on a community of belonging, than on a foundation. This stability or this trustworthiness of human experience cannot be confused with that of scientific method. Dilthey too hastily identified the two in his attempt to found knowledge in the human sciences in a methodological way. Dilthey therefore remained the son of his times and the prisoner of historical aporiae. They came from a common source, but we can, in the interests of clarity, distinguish three orders of aporiae or of difficulties. The most fundamental aporia is that of Cartesian foundationalism, which cannot be reconciled with the Romantic thought of historicity: Dilthey seeks to impose on the human sciences, even on life and on historical consciousness, a model of methodological consciousness that he knows to be incompatible with the radical experience of historicity. The second aporia, which is probably the most pertinent if we wish to understand Gadamer's final hermeneutics, is that of the *intellectualism* of historical consciousness and of the historical *being*. Dilthey assimilated too rapidly historical consciousness to a mode of *knowledge*. For Gadamer, instucted here by Heidegger, historicity is perhaps more a mode of being than of knowledge. We must be able to integrate this intuition, which is also a matter of consciousness, to a more consequential historical consciousness. In the end, if Dilthey saw that the hermeneutic problematic was in a wider framework than a general philosophy of historicity, and life, he was often the victim of the paralogism which consists in interpreting the hermeneutic manifestations of life from the categories of modern science. Thus he came to assimilate the experiences of doubt and the search for stability and even the meaning of experience to Descartes's methodic enterprise that transformed them into instruments of certainty. An instrumentalist and too epistemologizing a conception of historical consciousness screens the insight of the hermeneutic experience that life has of itself.

The phenomenological opening

If Gadamer focused on Dilthey's aporiae, the last great advance in the problematic of the hermeneutic sciences is to enquire into his own contribution. Gadamer's more positive hermeneutics can now be put to work. It can be inspired by Dilthey's more Romantic, more historical, intentions, but it is clear that its fundamental impulse is from Heidegger's phenomenology. But which Heidegger? We know today, in the light of the young Heidegger's manuscripts and published courses, that Gadamer was inspired much less by *Being and Time* than by his early hermeneutics of facticity where, very soon, he also recognized the impulses that led to the later Heidegger's reflections. Gadamer never paid much attention to the distinction between the early and the later Heidegger, because that risks, in his eyes, the unified direction of his thought. Gadamer always saw this essential direction in "the overcoming of the subjectivity of modern thought",[37] where instrumentalism comes from forgetting finitude and time. From *Truth and Method,* he saw in the direction of Heidegger's thought only the culmination of his youthful intentions, momentarily suspended by the transcendental interlude of *Being and Time.*[38]

In his conferences in Louvain,[39] as in *Truth and Method*, Gadamer claimed to be appealing to Heidegger's hermeneutics of facticity, which announced the intuitions of the later Heidegger on the dispossession of human subjectivity. The critique of technical or instrumentalist thought and the rediscovery of the power of truth in the work of art and in language became its most visible fruits. In persisting in talking about hermeneutics, we can say that Gadamer attached the term to Heideggerian thought at its hermeneutic point of departure.[40] There was audacity, but also clairvoyance, in Gadamer's interpretation. He had, in effect, recognized an unsuspected coherence in Heidegger's development, which had escaped many thinkers, even Heidegger himself. And the discovery of the young Heidegger's courses which Gadamer had heard helps us today to measure that coherence.

But in 1960 the situation appeared completely otherwise. Since his *Letter on Humanism*, Heidegger seemed to have rejected his early philosophy (the dominant interpretation of those close to him, such as Karl Löwith, Max Muller, Walter Schulz and soon William Richardson and Otto Poggeler confirmed it), even renouncing the term "hermeneutics" to the advantage of a more poetic concept of being, which did not avoid being followed by laboured imitations. As for the hermeneutics of facticity, it was not at all well known. Gadamer could not authorize it, when the youthful courses or manuscripts of which there was then no trace had not been published. Since their publication, Gadamer has written many articles on the young and the later Heidegger, where he gives a luminously clear account of himself and his relation with his mentor. If Gadamer were to write *Truth and Method* today, it is clear that the chapter devoted to Heidegger would partly take the form of the book *Heideggers Wege*,[41] which he published in 1983, and which with new additions became part of volume 4 of his *Werke* in 1987. We must note, too, that there are also more recent additions in volume 10, which appeared in 1995. *Heideggers Wege* is the book that Gadamer never stopped writing, that is to say the dialogue that he never stopped having and that serves as the entry-point to his whole hermeneutics, mirroring how in *Truth and Method* his hermeneutics follows immediately after a chapter on Heidegger. To philosophize, we know from the time of Plato and Aristotle, is always to hold a dialogue with your masters.

In 1960, Gadamer had to show how his project was inspired by Heidegger, but without using the sources or the historical distance which today are his and ours. As he spoke of hermeneutics, Gadamer had to refer to *Being and Time*, even if he had never appreciated its surface transcendentalism. But in 1960, it was quite difficult to say that *Being and Time* was for Heidegger only a circumstantial adaptation to the transcendental framework of thought, as if, in his great masterpiece, Heidegger was momentarily unfaithful to his most private intuitions on the finitude and historicity of understanding. Since we know the young Heidegger, this interpretation has acquired a certain amount of evidence.[42]

This situation gives a rather elliptical character to the chapter devoted to phenomenology in *Truth and Method,* all the more regrettable as it is concerned with an obviously crucial moment. But Gadamer had neither the sources nor the distance nor the authority to explain, as he should have done – and as he perhaps wished to do – his whole debt to Heidegger. Another study should take up the debate from the augmented versions in *Heideggers Wege.* In 1960, for lack of anything better (which sounds rather presumptuous, but which does not mean to be), Gadamer had to lean on *Being and Time* to show that Heidegger's thought, by its radicalization of historicity, represented an unexpected unblocking, which allowed him to free hermeneutics from the epistemological framework which was also Dilthey's. But the apparent transcendentalism, the project of foundation and the recovery of the question of being in Heidegger did not help Gadamer's cause (there are after all aspects which lead an author like Georg Misch to see in Dilthey the most radical perspective on the map of historicity). To strengthen his thesis, which went beyond Dilthey's epistemological aporiae, Gadamer also referred to Yorck and Husserl, as did Heidegger in *Being and Time.* Thus Yorck, Husserl and Heidegger would become the great godfathers of overstepping the "epistemological" interrogation, or the instumentalism of understanding, in hermeneutics.

Yorck was Dilthey's correspondent, and Heidegger refers to him with such wholehearted enthusiasm that he was content to cite large extracts from his letters in section 77 of *Being and Time.* Yorck had put his finger on Dilthey's essential aporia, which was to wish to grasp life with the help of the Cartesian categories of modern science. By insisting so much on the objectivations of life and on an epistemological platform, Dilthey had cut off life from its essential mobility, missing also its essential historicity that is the true condition of possibility in the human sciences. Yorck had been the first to question the aestheticization underlying Dilthey's theoretical perspective. Besides, it is not unreasonable to think that perhaps Yorck, whom Heidegger read, was the great inspiration of the Gadamerian critique of the aestheticization of the historical school. Yorck particularly took notice of the importance that Dilthey attached to the comparative method.[43] Yorck pointed out that we can only compare the forms towards which we adopt an aesthetic distance and those in which the observer is not himself directly concerned. Is it not this implication of knowledge in life and in history which should be at the centre of a philosophy of historicity and of the human sciences? Dilthey would have missed historicity in attempting to conclude with the help of categories that were too contemplative or too visual, borrowed from the physical world of the natural sciences. As Rodi well saw, Dilthey's work never really came out of the shadow of Yorck's critique, taken up so powerfully by Heidegger.[44] We can obviously wonder if, over and above this critique, the Yorck account itself had a more satisfactory conception of the relationship between historical knowledge and historical life. It is an issue only in Yorck's posthumous works, published in 1956 under the promising title, *Attitude to Knowledge and to History*, when Gadamer edited his works. But the developments which Gadamer devotes to them, and which he never takes up anywhere else, are not particularly illuminating, because Yorck's reflections remain so speculative.

Husserl, thanks to his demand for a phenomenological vision that tries to free thought from pre-established methodological concepts, was a greater liberator. First, he contributed to the deliverance of philosophy from the epistemological primacy of the neo-Kantians, which condemned philosophy to being only a second-degree reflection of the primary fact, that of science.[45] To return to things themselves means that philosophy could be something other than a scientific methodology. Husserl was also a liberator in his critique of objectivism in science, which maintains that it is involved in the independent data of consciousness. In his concept of intentionality, Husserl recalls that every object has the mode of being of consciousness. There is therefore no object in itself, no objectivity possible without the implication of the intentionality of consciousness. Lastly, Husserl was a liberator in recognizing that this intentionality cannot always accompany the effort of establishing a sovereign subjectivity. The whole aim of meaning is elaborated in a horizon that breaks out of the framework of subjectivity alone. Gadamer is very keen on this term horizon, because it recalls that all intentionality is inscribed in a framework that is never entirely thematic, but without marking a rigid boundary, as it is always with us and invites us to go further. Husserl also saw very well that the horizon implicates understanding. He sometimes speaks of passive syntheses, resorting to the order of an underground temporality of the life of consciousness. Husserl spoke in this way in the *Krisis,* in the unexpected formula of an "absolute historicity" of the absolute mind which incorporates everything.[46] A happier notion is that of a "world of life" (*Lebenswelt*), which serves as a foundation, or, better, a background to every position or intentionality of consciousness. This Husserl raises above the consciousness of intentionality, to the pre-donated soil of the world of life, to which hermeneutics progresses after Dilthey. But, according to Gadamer, Husserl did not go to the end of his intentions in continuing to speak, paradoxically, of "establishing the world of life",[47] which always revealed a transcendental "original me" (*Ur-Ich*). Here Husserl did not succeed in freeing himself from epistemological and idealist thought, which tried to derive every datum from a foundationalist and autonomous subjectivity, in favour of a philosophy devoted to the ideal of an apodictic knowledge. Rather like Dilthey, Husserl did not succeed in freeing himself from the grip of Cartesian categories in his attempt to close in on life and the history of consciousness.

Heidegger exploded these schemes when he radicalized the experience of historicity with which Dilthey and Husserl were concerned. This is the meaning of his hermeneutics of facticity. But facticity does not, as the Young Hegelians and the representatives of the historical school would have it, represent the ultimate foundation, a new positivism which can be opposed to the aspirations of a metaphysics of absolute mind. It wishes rather to expose the metaphysical presuppositions of the very notions of foundations and of subjectivity:

> Thus it was clear that Heidegger's project of a fundamental ontology had to place the problem of history in the foreground. But it soon emerged that what constituted the significance of Heidegger's *fundamental ontology* was not that it was the solution to the problem of historicism, and certainly not a more original grounding of science, nor even, as with Husserl, philosophy's ultimate grounding of itself; rather, *the whole idea of grounding itself underwent a total reversal.*[48]

Heidegger questioned the notion of foundation because he made the ontological implications explicit. To escape from its finite temporality, subjectivity seeks an absolute foundation, regarded as permanent presence. The demands of a solid and ultimate foundation come from an erasure of temporality which haunts human experience. But the notion of subjectivity springs from the very ontology of permanence. The *subjectum*, the *hypokeimenon*, is what is found at the foundation of everything else. And for Aristotle, the "underlying element", the subject *par excellence*, is not the human being, but matter (*hyle*), from which all beings are made. For modern thought, humankind, by a singular self-promotion, becomes the point of reference of the being in its totality. Heidegger notes the enormity of this presumption when he recalls the *Dasein* to its essential temporality. Is the human subject really the foundation of everything else? Is he not rather projected in his being, for a time and like a bolt of lightning of which he is never the master? This dispossession of "subjectivity", which is everything except a permanent present and a foundation, preoccupies the hermeneutics of *facticity*. If we keep to the notion of the subject, it is perhaps the "throw", the "projection", indispensable to the *Dasein*, which we should stress. We must speak of a hermeneutics of "projection", because facticity does not indicate a fact, an ultimate datum which we can oppose to an idealist metaphysics, but its opposite, the indispensability of the deal "where" we are, in so much as *Dasein*. Heidegger's powerful concept of projected being (*Geworfenheit*) thus runs counter to that of subjectivity. The safe promotion of the human being to the rank of subject is only the reverse of his essential projection. To speak of hermeneutics leads us to mean that everything should from now on be understood from this experience of temporality,[49] beginning with the experience of understanding itself. From the perspective of a hermeneutics of facticity, the understanding no longer means a cognitive or methodological process appended to the human sciences, but a possibility of being. Heidegger brilliantly adopts the German expression, *sich auf etwas verstehen* (to understand oneself, to know oneself in something), to mean that the understanding relates to practical knowledge, to a practical skill, a power, a capacity to do something. The person who "can" read a poem, for example, is not the person who has knowledge or who has mastered a particular technique, but the person who is capable of doing so, who can set about it.[50] Understanding also means knowing how to set about something, where we remain implicated because each time it is a matter of a possibility of my being. For Gadamer, the decisive unblocking is there: understanding is no longer an "operation" (which would go the opposite way from that of the integrated life), but an originating mode of being of life itself.[51] Gadamer says that the understanding no longer indicates a method, but the way of being of the *Dasein*, its essential fluidity. To be a *Dasein*, to be "there", is always to live in a certain understanding, intended in the sense of "being able to set about it", "being good at it". It is clear that it is less a case of an intellectual or mental process than a way of behaving, of an ability to be, in our existence. And understanding always arises from a basis of lack of understanding. I can get out of something by immersing myself in projects of understanding which are so many possibilities of my being in time, because I never completely exist in the present. In forcing the similarity, but only a little, we can say that the *Dasein* is fundamentally an understanding being, but only because, at root, it understands nothing at all. All understanding is always only a project, only provisional. It is a "being able to set about it", in a situation that will never be mastered once and for all. Here we must understand the part of hermeneutics in the term hermeneutics: what is to be understood is the emblem which rebels against understanding. Hermeneutics is not the title of a philosophical project that aspires to complete understanding, but the name of vigilance in thought which rests on its absence.

Perhaps Heidegger seems to reinforce thoughts of subjectivity in talking here of "projects" of understanding. However, it is clear that it is not a case of plans or designs of which subjectivity is conscious. This is why Heidegger speaks, from *Sein und Zeit* onwards, of a "projected project". There is no project without being projected, no *Entwurf* without *Geworfenheit*. It could be that the early Heidegger put more stress on the *Entwurf* and the later Heidegger on the *Geworfenheit*. The whole issue probably revolves around this.

What interests Gadamer, again, is probably the unified aim of Heidegger's thought and its hermeneutic consequences. Understanding is a project in which I am always co-implicated, where the the "object" of understanding has, like me, historicity as its mode of being. But this project never uniquely arises from me, from my projection or from a process which is only instrumental. It is also the fact of a work of history, of an addition to a tradition, which is less a matter of method than of event and participation. Gadamer's intention is not to make of the addition to a tradition a source of legitimacy for knowledge. It would be absurd. He always recognizes that there are "immanent criteria" of scientific knowledge,[52] which emerge from method, and remind us with all desirable clarity that we cannot confuse an "ontological" addition to history with emotive dependence:

> "Belonging" is a condition of the original meaning of historical interest not because the choice of theme and inquiry is subject to extrascientific, subjective motivations (then belonging would be no more than a case of emotional dependence, of the same type as sympathy), but because belonging to traditions belongs just as originally and essentially to the historical finitude of *Dasein* as does its projectedness toward future possibilities of itself.[53]

The addition to history means something other than dependence with regard to such-and-such a prejudice, which can be controlled in many cases. It means an ontological condition of finitude, the impossibility of assuring a final foundation to all the projects of meaning. To speak of assurance and of foundation is already symptomatic. These terms already betray a forgetfulness of temporality. Gadamer's hermeneutics tries to value this productivity of temporality and of history in order to unsettle the assurance that leads us to conceive of the understanding in terms of method, instrument and procedure. This instrumentalism also affects the understanding of tradition, often understood as if it were only an object of research. There is tradition and event in all understanding, Gadamer notes, and to forget it is to be exposed still more blindly to the hold of unmastered prejudices.

Thus the "ontological radicalization" led by Heidegger can contribute to the development of historical hermeneutics.[54] The whole of Gadamer's hermeneutics is thus devoted to "this new aspect of the hermeneutical problem" which is profiled "against the background of this existential analysis of *Dasein*".[55] In *Truth and Method,* Gadamer speaks of an appeal to the *transcendental* meaning of the Heideggerian project.[56] The expression is ambiguous and aims above all to recall the *philosophical* and universal aspect of hermeneutic questions. Knowing the addition of an interpreter to his object and to a tradition is an issue of a very particular transcendence. It is transcendental only to the extent to which it is, for Gadamer, an issue of a condition essential to all understanding. But it is obvious that above all it marks the limit of every strictly transcendental perspective which aspires to explain understanding from a principle. Modern transcendental thought is still instrumental. Do we always know where understanding comes from? To speak of tradition and event is not to put one's finger on a new principle, but to remember finitude. When all is said and done, it is finitude which becomes the new "transcendence". The whole of Gadamer's questioning lies in the ambiguity of this transcendence.

CHAPTER FOUR

Vigilance and Horizon in Hermeneutics

The constellation of understanding

The main point of the hermeneutics of facticity and its contrast with the transcendental constitution research of Husserl's phenomenology was that no freely chosen relation toward one's own being can get behind the facticity of this being. Everything that makes possible and limits *Dasein*'s projection ineluctably precedes it. This existential structure of *Dasein* must also leave its trace in the understanding of historical tradition, which is why we initially follow Heidegger.[1]

As he starts with Heidegger and *Being and Time*, Gadamer also starts with the circle of understanding. To the circle of understanding Heidegger gave an ontological, non-epistemological direction, because *Dasein* is an object of care and its future forms the priority of care, which he understands as the function of more or less implicit anticipations. Through these anticipations of meaning, he tries in a way to ward off attacks, knowing that existence itself will still reserve some for him, up to the unanswerable blow, death, which all the dispositions of metaphysics seek to escape.

The reason is that there is no understanding without anticipation, no interpretation without prior understanding, which the circle raises from *Dasein's* mode of being. But already Heidegger does not like to speak of "circle", as the imagery is spatial, or more precisely geometric. In Heidegger's terminology, it is of an image modelled on subsisting being, and therefore misplaced in the unquiet flexibility of *Dasein*. This is why Heidegger stipulates, twice in *Being and Time*,[2] that we "must avoid" (*vermeiden müssen*) describing *Dasein* in terms of the imagery of a circle. He resigns himself to it in reaction to the suspicion of a "logical vice", or *petitio principii*, which could arise from his concept, according to which every interpretation (even those aspiring to be scientific and objective) is governed by the anticipations of understanding. "According to the elementary laws of logic", the circle intended here can only be *vicious*. Whence Heidegger's irony: if we insist at any price on talking about the circle, so be it! What is essential is perhaps not so much to avoid it as to enter it resolutely, even if we scandalize logic! From this perspective, Heidegger comes to talk about the circle.

To see it more clearly, it is useful to distinguish between an epistemological concept and a more phenomenological understanding of the circle. From a logical perspective, the circle effectively represents a vice because it consists in presupposing what has to be proved. To speak here of a vicious circle is a tautology. But what interests Heidegger and Gadamer is the phenomenological tenor of the concept of a circle: it describes the fact that all understanding necessarily ("ontologically") proceeds from an anticipation of meaning. Here the dogma that presuppositions are absent is revealed at its most naïve, since the understanding that complies with it succumbs all the more blindly to the hold of presuppositions which it does not wish to recognize (the idea of a lack of presuppositions already being one).[3] Gadamer insists on the phenomenological dimension of a circle because it allows us to consider the double components of the interpreter with his object, and with a tradition, in a positive way, or a way which does not incorporate the idea of a scientific understanding. The methodologism of the human sciences is incapable of doing justice to this indelible moment of our historical component because it is inspired by the model of objectivity in the human sciences. Thanks to the Heideggerian awareness of the circle of understanding, "the interpreter's belonging to his object, which the historical school was unable to offer any convincing account of, now acquires a concretely demonstrable significance, and it is the task of hermeneutics to demonstrate it".[4]

But there are important differences of emphasis in the Heideggerian and Gadamerian applications of the hermeneutic circle. First of all, it is striking that Heidegger *never* speaks of the whole circle and its parts, but rather of the circle of precomprehension and of its exposure in the process of interpretation. Heidegger evokes the idea of a circle because it exposes the fact that every interpretation arises from a prior project or prior understanding. Besides, this line of argument very naturally gives rise to the suspicion of a logical vice (is interpretation only the confirmation of a meaning decreed in advance?), to which Heidegger seeks to reply by his ontological radicalization. As for Gadamer, from the beginning he associates the circle as a whole and in its parts with the classical, descriptive and less epistemologically exacerbated problematic. He helpfully recalls that the rule(!) of the circle comes from ancient rhetoric,[5] where it has a purely phenomenological meaning because it indicates the necessary coming-and-going of all understanding. Far from indicating a logical vice, on the contrary the circle comes to describe the constant process of revision in the anticipations of understanding, in the light of a greater knowledge of the parts and in the name of a greater coherence of interpretation. Besides, Gadamer sees in the coherence of the whole and its parts an interpretative "criterion of accuracy".[6]

Gadamer explains that every interpretation is elaborated on the basis of an "anticipation of perfection" recognized by the thing to be understood. The lessons from Louvain luminously specify that this anticipation completes the deal of the hermeneutic circle.[7] This coherence, initially lent to the *interpretandum*, leads one to revise one's first projections of meaning when they are revealed to be untenable. The compatibility of interpretation with this coherence in the meaning to be understood continues to represent the *teleological norm* of every interpretation. Only when this anticipation of a coherent meaning is disappointed is there recourse to more historicizing or psychologizing interpretations of meaning. What is confirmed here is that to understand first means to listen to something. Historicism celebrated historical and psychological methods in hermeneutics so much only because it did not recognize this evidence and this positive dimension.

Gadamer's circle is therefore, in a sense that must be well understood, initially *less* epistemological than that of Heidegger, since it does not come from the suspicion of a logical vice which is raised by the concept of a precomprehension forever governing the interpretation which it brings to light. On the contrary, the circle describes a constant process, or a rule of coherence open to all interpretations: previous projections must be revised to make them conform to the thing. But in another way, the circle appears *more* epistemological than with Heidegger, because the emphasis is placed on the revision of provisional "hypotheses" of interpretation. The field of the application of the circle does not initially appear to be the same with the two authors: whilst Heidegger tries to detach the anticipation of existence that is at work in all projects of understanding, in order to elaborate his hermeneutic analysis of *Dasein*, Gadamer concentrates on the typical, and certainly more limited, case of textual interpretation in the human sciences. We could say that Gadamer "philologizes", or more accurately "re-philologizes", what was for Heidegger an existential circle. This displacement makes Odo Marquard say that Gadamer has replaced the being-for-death of the *Dasein* by the being-for-the-text.[8] But this is a very superficial reading. It is true that Gadamer's acknowledged project is to apply the Heideggerian concept of the circle to a hermeneutic of the human sciences (a concretization for which Heidegger himself had opened up the possibility), but he did not forget for all that his master's more radical hermeneutic gains. In effect, can we interpret texts in abstracting from the issue that is always existence for itself? To think that Gadamer's thoughts are elaborated by the abstraction of the whole foundation of the problematic of being-for-death would be to mutilate them fatally. The text which I interpret is always addressed to the finitude of the text which I still am for myself.

Gadamer sees the point of the Heideggerian analysis less in remembering that there is a circle in the comings-and-goings of understanding, because rhetoric and Romanticism have already detected this circularity, than in the idea that this circle has a "positive ontological meaning".[9] In Gadamer's view, that means that the circle "is not a 'methodological' circle, but describes an element of the ontological structure of understanding".[10] We can see in the circle a methodological or epistemological problem only from a Cartesian, and thus resolutely *linear*, perspective, where every proposition must flow from a previous proposition, until we reach an ultimate principle (that of the *cogito*). But Gadamer wonders whether we really understand in this way. Does understanding not always emerge in the light of the anticipation of meaning and on the basis of adherence to a tradition? Even if this is not explicitly developed in Heidegger and Gadamer, we can object to the metaphor of a circle from a strictly linear conception of meaning and of understanding. The circle here means that all understanding emerges in favour of a universal context of which we are always and already a part. Against the idea of a mastery of meaning, the fruits of a linear deduction, hermeneutics opposes a conception according to which the understanding is more a matter of participation, of sharing, as the meaning understood is always one which we share with others (the first syllable of com-prehend incorporates mutuality). If we wish to avoid the idea of the circle, we could perhaps here speak of a constellation of understanding, which brings about its luminosity. All understanding is held under a constellation specified each time: at such a moment, it appears in time and space, in response to such a dialogical context, in such a "stellar" horizon. Walter Benjamin and Theodor Adorno have spoken in this sense of the constellation of all historical understanding. The subject of understanding always inscribes himself in a universe, in a horizon, of vision and sharing, where he allows himself to be challenged by a constellation of questions. Here the crucial idea is to amputate this constellation of meaning from its prejudgeable character, which methodology alone can control, and to recognize the legitimacy of this constellation in the hermeneutic field of the human sciences.

There is a final difference between the two conceptions of the circle: whilst Heidegger insists on the primacy of the future for the anticipations of understanding (which seeks to forestall criticism), Gadamer thinks that he is more faithful to the purpose of a hermeneutics of projection in speaking of a primacy of the past over the future. The future is just what is not in our grasp,[11] and can be "anticipated" only in the light of acquired experience, of the work of history which has formed us.

Perhaps it is useful to tabulate these differences between Gadamer and Heidegger, which emerge from an essential solidarity on the subject of the ontological nature of the circle of understanding:

	Heidegger	Gadamer
Terms of the circle	Circle of interpretation (*Auslegung*) and of the understanding that governs it	Circle of the whole and of the parts
Logical pertinence	Circle born of the appearance of a logical vice (*circulus vitiosus*) or a *petitio principii* – "epistemological circle" (from the point of view of logical criticism)	Circle which indicates a rule of interpretation (rhetorical issue) – phenomenological circle (which describes a process)
The limit of the metaphor	Spatial, geometric diagram, not suited to the flexibility of existence (because modelled on the subsisting being, *Vorhandenheit*)	There is no true circle, since there is a demand for coherence which invites constant revision of the hypotheses of meaning (in the name of the anticipation of perfection) – here Gadamer is more epistemologizing than Heidegger
Area of privileged application	Hermeneutics of existence	Textual hermeneutics
To understand is above all	To understand oneself in, on to find oneself in	To listen to each other about the thing
Source of anticipations	Primacy of the future	Precedence of the past (work of history)

The essential agreement begins with the ontological nature of the circle, and also with the reflexive gain which it means for hermeneutics. The metaphor of the circle allows us to take note of the constellation which is always that of the understanding. All understanding emerges with the aim and in a context of meaning, of which the circle invites us to take note. The dominant scientific model induces a mistake in allowing us to believe that the ontologization of the circle is accompanied by a loss of rigour in the order of scientific knowledge. Really, it is the deductive, linear model which offers only the appearance of rigour. If we recognize the part of components and of events at work in each constellation of understanding, we could also be aware of prejudices susceptible of distorting the understanding. But how do we distinguish between legitimate and illegitimate prejudices?

Prejudices and things themselves: which aporia?

An understanding that acknowledges its essential contribution to a constellation of meaning which makes the understanding possible will try to develop an explicit knowledge of its own constellation, of its own prejudices. Gadamer is so reluctant to renounce the ideal of a critical elucidation of prejudices that he himself criticizes a Cartesian prejudice: the prejudice against prejudices! The expression, ingenious, presupposes that there are prejudices prejudicial to the understanding and that the prejudice against prejudices is a part of it. This prejudice assumes that what constitutes the object of an ultimate and certain foundation is the only thing that can be held as true. If we leave aside the sphere of mathematical truths, which are the constructs of pure reason, where do we find such ultimate certainties in the order of our knowledge and our practices? For Gadamer, the concept of an absolute foundation is not a possibility of our finite existence. The discredit thrown on all prejudices by the Luminaries rests on this demand. Should we not re-examine this ideal if we wish to be fair to the reality of historical understanding? Then we will stop seeing in the neutrality or the auto-effacement of the interpreter a realizable or even pertinent model for a radically historical hermeneutics.

Gadamer conducts his own critique of prejudice against prejudices in the spirit of the Luminaries. He puts into question a prejudice that *distorts* the reality of historical understanding. There are therefore prejudices which open up access to the thing, which makes understanding possible. After Heidegger, Gadamer says that the first task is not to allow anticipations to be imposed by "intuitions and popular notions", but to elaborate them from things themselves. Gadamer even says that the

> central question, the fundamental question from the point of view of the theory of knowledge can be formulated in this way: on what

is to be founded the legitimacy of prejudices? What distinguishes legitimate prejudices from all those innumerable ones which critical reason must incontestably overcome?[12]

An important question, but one that hides an even more important paradox: if we see in prejudices the conditions of understanding, do we not, by the very fact of the same confirmation, cut ourselves off from the things themselves? Gadamer is always asked this question. The greatest aporism of his philosophy has always been detected here: how do we reconcile the essential ("ontological") anteriority of prejudices with the incessant call – shocking for some – to things themselves?

Let us make a frontal attack on this great epistemological paradox, in order to see if it holds up or if it hides, as we are tempted to reveal, an even more stubborn aporism. To begin, let us remember two considerations: first, for Gadamer, all understanding emerges entirely in the light of anticipations (which we can call "prejudices") so much and so well that the correction of a prejudice, shown to be illegitimate, is always only made in the light of a new anticipation which replaces the previous one; and secondly, to speak of things themselves is not to speak of "things-in-themselves" such that they could be understood independently of an effort of understanding (which would be a manifest contradiction). From then on, how do we take the idea, constantly reiterated by Gadamer and Heidegger, according to which the understanding should try to render itself conformable to things themselves? To have access to the "thing" itself is rather like the equivalent of the French expression *"en venir au fait"* ("to come to the point") in the sense of *"cesser de tourner autour du pot"* ("to stop going round the houses"), that is to say, to go for the essential. The German *Sache* ("point") is always the *Streitsache*,[13] the Latin *causa*, that is to say the thing debated, the thing that matters. To develop anticipations that are conformable to the thing, is therefore to elaborate pertinent conceptions, which are at the nub of the thing to be understood. It equally presupposes that the thing also matters to us, that it concerns us. We cannot develop suitable or fertile anticipations without entering into the debate with the thing itself. It is precisely this dialogical model of understanding that Gadamer seeks to value against the epistemological paradigm of a subject which is initially separated from its object. But is the understanding subject not at the same time judge and judged? That is to say, in understanding certain presuppositions care must be taken at the same time that these anticipations are conformable to the thing. But according to Gadamer, it is effectively this constant concern of adaptation, always undertaken anew, which is the catalyst of all understanding that is ready to allow itself to say something in what it seeks to understand.[14] We note that he never here gives up talking about adequacy or fairness. Of course, it is not a matter of a pure algebraic equivalence between the subject and the object, but of a movement towards the object which is already a part of the *ad-equatio*. Adequacy is literally carrying across, the *ad*, which seeks to adjust itself, to raise itself to the heights of the thing to be understood. To understand fully the idea of adequacy is not to forget this carrying across of the person who understands, because he constitutes the whole definition of truth, understood as *adequatio*. The ideas of accord, of consonance, of concordance, of adjustment recall it with the same insistence: the truth is a matter of accord in the almost musical meaning of the term, in the sense in which the *interpretans* is at the pitch of the *interpretandum*. The essential in the knowledge of truth is not the objectification, the reification of an object, so much as the consonance, the accord between the understanding and what is to be understood. In this sense, all truth is hermeneutic and a matter of adequacy. When a truth emerges, German expresses it well: *es stimmt!* that is to say, there is accord. Agreement is here that of the reply which seeks to raise itself to the level of what wants to be understood.

We must also hear a Bultmannian resonance behind this emphatic conception of the *Sache*. We know that for Bultmann, the *Sache* of the Christian message exists only in the message itself, that is to say in its *kerygma* or its proclamation by the Apostles. It constitutes the first component of the whole Christian proclamation. We must measure every proclamation by the yardstick of this *Sache*, but also in a certain way the original proclamation itself, which was not perhaps itself at the height of the thing that it seeks to explain, because it formulates the thing in mythological terms when it speaks, for example, of an "above", of a cosmic ascension, etc. This is the reason for Bultmann's "demythologiz-ation" of the Christian *kerygma* so that it speaks – and it is anew "proclaimable" – in our age. Every mythological or inadequate proclama-tion can itself be criticized only by *another* proclamation which hopes to be adequate, that is to say, which seeks to conform to the thing itself. This thing will never be given without proclamation, or in the terms of the first part of *Truth and Method*, without presentation. Nonetheless, it is crucial to speak here of a thing which can be resistant to each inadequate or too partial a presentation to be offered. But this inadequacy can only be brought to light by a new proclamation.

Thus understood, *all* understanding is nothing other than an adjustment to the thing, which *seeks* to become "equal" to the thing, but the movement in the *ad* recalls that equality, for us human beings, is never total. We also say of a response (or of a performance) that it is "adequate" when we wish to say that it is barely sufficient, that it could be better, more complete. All of our truths are only adequate, approximate. Only the truth of the gods is entirely "equal" to the thing. Gadamer's aporia is not to speak of an agreement of prejudice with the thing itself. Far from being a misconstruction, this conception allows us to rediscover the original meaning in terms of "accord", an adequacy between intelligent anticipations and the thing under investigation. This rediscovery of the truth also allows us to unmask in the encompassing relativism – which seeks to deny, with Nietzsche or Rorty, all objective truth – the vestige of a conception of truth still implicitly governed by an epistemology with an absolute foundation where the subject does not have a vote in the chapter. It is not because such a truth is an impossibility of our historical existence that there is no truth.

In our sense, Gadamer's aporia, if indeed we have to talk about aporia, so valuable is its hermeneutic insight, is perhaps to be found elsewhere. It does not consist in speaking of an agreement between the anticipation of meaning and of the thing, because the truth always emerges from such an adjustment, always redistributed to suit the possibilities of the language, but in speaking here of a "prejudice". The term perhaps still gives too epistemological an emphasis on the debate which is essential to the truth. The term "prejudice" in fact suggests that the anticipation or the waiting which constitutes the sphere of welcome to the truth can one day be transformed into a declaration. The accord that is at the root of the encounter with truth perhaps does not lend itself to such an instrumental conception of knowledge. Do we always know what are the prejudices that determine us and which make accord possible? Is a prejudice not defined by the fact that it does not form a part of knowledge? Gadamer well realized this from *Truth and Method* onwards, when he wrote

> The prejudices and fore-meanings that occupy the interpreter's consciousness are not at his free disposal. He cannot separate in advance the productive prejudices that enable understanding from the prejudices that hinder it and lead to misunderstandings.[15]

But if it is so, can we still hope to find a criterion to distinguish good from bad prejudices, as if they were at our disposal? The text of *Truth and Method*, which reminds us of the ultimate unavailability of prejudices that can influence us, also sets the limits of epistemological interrogation, in that area where Gadamer seems to be searching for an epistemological criterion. To express the aporism in another way: in *Truth and Method* at least, has Gadamer clearly succeeded in "going beyond epistemological interrogation" in hermeneutics when he still gives such an epistemological emphasis to the problem of the truth of prejudices? Does the concept of truth that he tries to elaborate from the experience of art not try to frustrate too epistemological, too instrumental an understanding of truth?

We should perhaps speak of a tension rather than of an aporism, because Gadamer knew from 1960 onwards that a willing mastery of one's own prejudices does not give one the right to contribute a full understanding to history. From *Truth and Method* onwards, he displayed a fine knowledge of the limits of an epistemological and objectivist approach in hermeneutics. This is in evidence above all on the issue of prejudices, to which he devoted some of his most dramatic lines:

> In fact, history does not belong to us; we belong to it . . . the focus of subjectivity is a distorting mirror. The self-awareness of the individual is only a flickering in the closed circuits of historical life. *That is why the prejudices of the individual, far more than his judgements, constitute the historical reality of his being.*[16]

Help from temporal distance?

Let us resume the aporia: Gadamer promised to go beyond the epistemological framework in which historicism attempted to enclose the hermeneutic problem. He puts into question the epistemological ideal with a photographic objectivity because he abstracts the addition of the interpreter from the constellation of understanding. This dimension of addition has to receive its legitimation in an adequate hermeneutics of the human sciences, and of our historical experience. Gadamer is thus led to restore prejudices as a source of truth. The truth is therefore rediscovered, re-heard as accord between understanding and the thing. But accord is effectuated on the basis of prejudices. How, then, do we separate fertile prejudices from those which are not fertile? If this is a legitimate question, we can ask ourselves whether it does not perpetuate, in certain respects, the epistemologism which Gadamer denounces as an instrumental distortion of understanding. Is not Gadamer himself in search of an epistemological criterion in the investigation of the transcendental foundations of legitimate prejudices? What increases the difficulty is that prejudices often remain subconscious. Can we fend off all prejudices that invade us? Are those we believe we have found those that really rule us? In *Truth and Method*, Gadamer perhaps still does not ask these questions with the desired rigour.

It could be that the overly epistemological project of a hermeneutics of the human sciences limits the expected application of Gadamer's investigation. In *Truth and Method*, he is still seeking a solution to the "fundamental question from the point of view of the theory of knowledge . . . on what do we found the legitimacy of prejudices? What distinguishes legitimate prejudices from all those innumerable ones which it is the task of critical reason to overcome?"[17] This is of course the central question, but "from the viewpoint of the theory of knowledge". Does not the most consistent reply from the hermeneutic viewpoint consist in remembering that we are looking for a foundation which always already supports us? If we belong to history more than it belongs to us, can we hope to find a metaphysical solution to the general problem of the legitimacy of prejudices?

In *Truth and Method*, Gadamer wanted to find the outline of a solution to this problem in the productivity of temporal distance. With good reason. Often it is the receding of time which allows for fertile interpretations to emerge as such. Gadamer's outstanding example is still that of art. How do we distinguish true art from that which engages only the tastes of the time? It is clear, as Gadamer rightly underlines, that the judgement applied to contemporary art is "desperately uncertain". The receding of time is of great help to us here. It operates a filtering function that allows ill-founded judgements to disappear, and allows durable prejudices to emerge as such. But in 1960, Gadamer went as far as to see in it the *only* solution to the epistemological problem of the foundation of prejudices: "Temporal distance alone places us in a position to reply to the properly critical question of hermeneutics, to know what is asked by the distinction in operating between *true* prejudices, or those which guarantee *understanding*, and *false* prejudices which bring in *misunderstanding*."[18]

Gadamer's text affirms something profound about temporal distance by reminding us that distance in time is not so much what separates us as what ties us to meaning, but he goes much too far in making the solution of the greatest epistemological question rely on the virtues of the filtration of temporal recession. Not only does it not touch the issue of prejudicial legitimacy in contemporary works, but it passes over in silence the effect of obstruction that can be provoked by a tradition which consolidates mistaken interpretations. History offers many examples of this. It is, for example, entirely conceivable that passages judged unfit in a certain age, without which they will perhaps remain forever unintelligible, have been expurgated from classical texts. And who has ever compiled the history of the conquered or of peoples decimated so that they have been lost without trace? If it can be of great help, temporal distance can also be obscuring.

What is most problematic in Gadamer's chief work is the little word "alone", as if the truth of understanding depends on temporal distance alone. But Gadamer modified this passage in the fifth edition of 1986, replacing the problematic term "alone" by the more modest "often", so that it now reads "*Often* temporal distance can solve the question of critique in hermeneutics." A fine and precious modification, as it bears witness to a true accomplishment in the circle of understanding, which consists in remaining open to any modification if the initial project is found to be untenable. It could be that in this opening, that is to say in the dialogue, the issue of legitimate prejudices has to be decided each time.

The modification of the text also reveals that the later Gadamer better realized the limits of a strictly epistemological approach to the issue of understanding. For him, the essential is in fact less to find a solution to the problem of the legitimacy of "prejudices" (a term which has remained stuck to his work, but which he seldom used after *Truth and Method*) than to free the hermeneutic problem from an even more instrumental approach. The criticisms which Gadamer made of the thought of the nineteenth century, in knowing that it was still dominated too much by the the fetishes of procedure and method,[19] was perhaps more worthwhile for the issue of prejudices in *Truth and Method*. By showing clearly the problem of the criterion of the distinction between fertile and useless prejudices, perhaps he gave himself over to methodological thought. The proposed solution of temporal distance is not really a solution at all, and Gadamer's correction to his own text shows that he saw that it was not. It does not mean that the issue remains insoluble or meaningless. On the contrary, freed it from its its narrow epistemological framework, the issue becomes once more one of hermeneutics, that is to say a matter of vigilance which must be exercised at every moment.

The silent work of history

It is still a notion unsurpassable in importance in *Truth and Method* which allows the effective frustration of the instrumentalism of historical method: that of the work of history (*Wirkungsgeschichte*). It represents the true speculative summit of the work. Gadamer even turns it into a "principle" (*Prinzip*) and the whole of the rest of the work is only its development. Gadamer's translators have had trouble in finding an equivalent term. In the most recent French translation of *Truth and Method*, the expression "work of history" has even been variously translated by two rather indifferent terms: history of action (*histoire de l'action*, which is a better translation of the German *Handlungsgeschichte*) and history of influence. This latter term above all translates the *pre-Gadamerian* meaning of the term, which has relevance to the reception of a work throughout history, to its posterity, to its efficacy, etc. (for this reason the term was translated in the former version by "history of efficiency" (*histoire de l'efficience*)). The guises according to which classical works and events have been read and received over the centuries bear witness to an authentic historical productivity. Along the thread of reception, every work and every event (the French revolution, the discovery of America, etc.) is enriched with new meanings and new relevances that are determined by the attempts of their historical context of reception, and also by the previous interpretations to which they react. For example, in 1992, in the quincentennial celebrations of the discovery of America, we no longer always saw, as had been the case in previous commemorations, the glories of European civilization being spread to barbarians, but instead, in reaction to this history of conquest, the discovery of America was interpreted as the beginning of the annihilation of non-European civilizations. Every event and every work is thus submitted to the context of reception, which goes beyond and enriches the original meaning, and bears witness to an ineradicable fertility of temporal distance and of the addition of understanding to a given constellation.

The discipline of *Wirkungsgeschichte* was thus developed by historicism in the nineteenth century as a particular discipline which was interested in the effectiveness of works in history. Evidently, if historicism was based on the aftermath of facts and works, it was in the hope of extracting itself from its influence: someone who wants to get back to the "original meaning" of Aristotle's works or the "real course" of events in the French Revolution will do well to study, as a secondary topic, their aftermath through history so as to resist distorting prejudices. The idea is thus that if someone wants to study original works and the work of history objectively for himself, he must distinguish between the two. As with Dilthey, the distance of historical knowledge must allow an escape from the consequences of this historical conditioning which would be neutralized by its objectification.

Historical knowledge thus understands itself as the last and proudest achievement of the Luminaries.[20] Here we rediscover what can be called a "dialectic of the historical Enlightenment". This historical Enlightenment is so illuminating or lucid that it has rejected the dream of the Luminaries, which was to recognize a rational teleology in the course of history. The idea of historical progress would thus only be a metaphysical presupposition of the Luminaries, which ceased to be constraining for a clearly historical Enlightenment. The critique of the Enlightenment led by historicism was therefore accomplished in the name of an even more radical Enlightenment: from then on, the wish to understand the course of history from rational norms was criticized in the name of historicism. The latter even started from the opposite presupposition, by knowing that every historical process in principle rebels against reason. That is why everything can only be understood historically. Historicism is thus understood as a universal and radical Enlightenment.

Gadamer attacked this pride of historicism by taking note of the notion of the work of history.[21] For historical knowledge, the *Wirkungsgeschichte* is always only the history of reception which allows itself to be objectified and placed at a distance. But does history, in which we are and which passes through us, lend itself to an integrated objectivity? The *geschichtliches Bewusstsein*, "historical knowledge", forgets that it remains a *wirkungsgeschichtliches Bewusstsein*, a "knowledge borne by history". The term *Wirkung* translates this idea that history continues to work even where it is not in the least suspected of doing so. Even the scholar who makes a separate study of the aftermath of the French Revolution is determined by its aftermath over succeeding generations. If I talk in a generally well-received translation of the "work" of history[22] (less, in any case, to translate an untranslatable term than to promote philosophical understanding[23]), it is to underline this working of history that is at the same time an allowing, a permitting, and also a process of being childlike, which happens to us and which produces unforeseen fruits. To speak of the "action" of history is still not enough. The term remains too instrumental. The notion of work gives us a better idea that history is active in us, works in us or penetrates us, to a greater extent than knowledge can penetrate and suspect. Further, in French, "work" (*le travail*) means at the same time "working" (*oeuvrer*) (of history) and its product, its work.

With this concept, Gadamer perhaps best realized his project of going beyond the epistemological and instrumental approach in hermeneutics. The work of history revealed a working of history that is active over and above the historical knowledge we can have. Here, the understanding is properly a traditional event that brings subjectivity into its game. Besides, it is not by chance that the category of "game" makes an appearance again in this context: it describes a process which takes us up, which encompasses us, but of which we are not the masters.[24] In one of his most incisive texts, Gadamer writes that *"understanding is to be thought of less as a subjective act than as participating in an event of tradition,* a process of transmission in which past and present are constantly mediated".[25]

But at the moment when we could expect that he will explain that this work of history is a great Moloch which swallows up every form of knowledge, as if it were a new version of Heidegger's destiny of being, Gadamer tells us that what matters above all for hermeneutics is to develop an explicit knowledge of the work of history. What knowledge is at issue?

The vigilance of a historically effective consciousness

My hermeneutics seeks to maintain the later Heidegger's orientation of thought, and to make it accessible in a new way. It is to this end that I am resigned [*in Kauf nahm*] to keep the concept of knowledge, to which Heidegger's ontological critique has raised his function of ultimate foundation. But my enterprise was precisely to establish the limits of this concept of knowledge ... Without doubt it is necessary, in *Truth and Method*, to read as is necessary my chapter on the knowledge of the work of history. We cannot see in it a modification of self-knowledge, let us say a knowledge of subsequent history, or even a hermeneutic method which has succeeded in being founded on knowledge. We must, rather, recognise that the work of history in which we are all held limits knowledge. It is something which we can never wholly penetrate. Knowledge of the work of history is, as I have said before, "more being than knowledge".[26]

Knowledge that knows itself to be worked, but also borne by history, will be knowledge that incorporates its historicity, but which will not seek to avoid it entirely because knowledge of historicity will make it take note of the limits of objectivation. It thus represents the achievement of historical knowledge which will eventually be the consequence, as it will also be radically aware of its own historicity. Rather than being knowledge totally transparent to itself, what it cannot and does not want to be, it is fitting to speak of an exercise in lucidity, better, of vigilance.

We can distinguish three layers in this knowledge of the work of history: first, in the sense of the objective genitive, it initially takes the form of *historiographic* knowledge, that is to say, of knowledge which is forced to clear up its own hermeneutic situation; in the case of scientific knowledge in the human sciences, it is a matter of the vigilance that consists in undertaking the history of interpretations of its subject, of the state of research, knowing that this work of history is also part of the whole constellation of research. A subject, a problematic, an interrogation will always be inscribed in a tradition, in a debate, of which we must take note. The clearest of the time, this presentation of the "state of research" in the human sciences is practised to show the originality of a new approach. This novelty has meaning and can be sensed as such only if it is in the context of current discussion and of a process of transmission. What is important is not so much to be at a distance in relationship to this discussion and this tradition as to be aware of engaging in the debate with it and its presuppositions, so as to better avoid one's own. An entire avoidance is of course never possible, but the vigilance which it is crucial to cultivate will be all the more alive.[27]

Secondly, the vigilance of the work of history then above all takes the form of *philosophical* knowledge of the work of history in all interpretations. This time, it is less a matter of timely knowledge of the "when" and "how" of historical workings than of a recognition of the activity of history in *all* understanding. We can if it comes to it speak here of a "transcendental" principle of reflexion of which the whole of the rest of *Truth and Method* is the philosophical explanation. Thirdly, we can also understand the knowledge of the work of history in the sense of the subjective genitive. The knowledge which we have of our own historical determinism also arises from the work of history, a work which is never completely transparent to us. To talk of a subjective genitive is to recognize that knowledge proceeds from a source of which it is not the origin, but from which it always nourishes itself.[28] Gadamer magnificently says of this knowledge of the ultimate work of history that it is "more being than knowledge". But we must take note of that as well, if we wish to avoid the sirens of an even more instrumental conception of knowledge as history. As Schelling has said, knowledge of the work of history is a small memorial to the immemorial work of history.[29] In the name of this knowledge, Gadamer later criticizes the pretentions of this reflexive philosophy which is the victim of an even more idealist preference for knowledge.

Under the name of reflexive philosophy, Gadamer above all attacks Hegel's philosophy, which seeks to arrive at a knowledge capable of appropriating to itself in an absolute knowledge the whole of historical determinism (of which the historical knowledge of the nineteenth century is for Gadamer only an incarnation). For Hegel, the essential in philosophy was in effect to recognize in each substance, in each being placed before knowledge, a manifestation of subjectivity or of reason.[30] This wish is to integrate the totality of being, or even the totality of what determines knowledge, with subjectivity, to which hermeneutic thought is opposed, in the way that it must "go against the grain of the direction of Hegel's *Phenomenology of Spirit*, to the extent that the substantiality which determines it is brought out in all its subjectivity".[31] By the idea of substantiality, we understand here the opaqueness of the work of determining history, which also supports knowledge. Modernity perhaps makes us forget too often that there is more shade than light in knowledge and that the border between the two is thinner than we think.[32] In fact, every idea of light presupposes the anteriority of such a basis, of such a dialectic between obscurity and the candle which flickers in the night. We are reminded here of Heraclitus' fragment 26: "we light a candle in the night". Rather than of knowledge, perhaps we should speak of a vigilance in the work of history if we want to avoid idealist connotations in the notion of knowledge.

This idea of vigilance is not a commentator's fancy. It is perhaps essential to what could be knowledge instructed by hermeneutics. It already plays a role of the first order in the young Heidegger's hermeneutics of facticity. In there, *Dasein* is itself expressly defined as "the indication of a path towards a possible awakening" (*Anzeige des Weges des möglichens Wachseins*).[33] To be "there" is to be able to wake up to one's own possibilities of being. And the role of hermeneutics is to bring forth the *Dasein* to this possibility of awakening which slumbers within itself. Thus hermeneutics "opens to *Dasein* the possibility of understanding itself, and of being". But this understanding does not aspire to a total translucidity of *Dasein*; we know that it is impossible. As Heidegger explains, "What is aimed at in this understanding [*Verstehen*] can be terminologically fixed as a *Wachsein*, an awakening, a vigilance." The hermeneutic task is thus "each time to make *Dasein* individual and accessible to itself, to remind it of itself and to keep track of the self-alienation of which it is the victim".[34] Vigilance is the mode of knowledge of the person who is forced to keep his eyes open in the middle of the night, who at every moment takes the risk of swallowing everything including himself. Not by chance has the metaphor known such an aftermath since Heraclitus. It is found in Plato (where philosophers are first of all guardians, watchers,[35] *phulaka*, *Wachter* in German), and also in the New Testament (Matthew 24, 42: "Watch therefore: for ye know not what hour your Lord doth come"; see also Luke 21, 36, and Mark 13, 33), and even in the very idea of the Enlightenment, defined by Kant as the effort of awakening after a long sleep. But the idea is also found in Gadamer, at the very end of a strategic chapter on the work of history. Here it is the case of a term which Gadamer has once again added to the last edition of *Truth and Method* in 1986. It is made clear that the controlled exercise in a fusion of horizons signifies what is called "the task of . . . historically effected consciousness".[36] He also allows us to clarify the central concept of a fusion of horizons: to know the past is to penetrate it by transporting yourself into its horizon, by leaving the framework of the present. But, Gadamer wonders, is there some such thing as a horizon of the past which is radically cut off from the horizon of the present? Does not the construction of the horizon of the past always operate on our terms, even if it aims precisely to trap in the past that which is not of the past? And does not the horizon of the present, its constellation of questions and research, remain carved by the past? The separation of the distinct horizons of the past and present therefore perhaps represents a new instrumental illusion of the understanding. This is why it is perhaps more important to recognize that *"understanding is always the fusion of these horizons supposedly existing by themselves"*.[37] When understanding takes place, when it bursts into flame, the horizons of meaning, of the past and of the present, are fused together.

But if the horizons do not allow themselves to come apart with a surgical precision, why do we talk of a fusion of horizons, as the idea of fusion seems to presuppose their prior separation? Gadamer wants to preserve the heuristic legitimacy of separating the horizons of the past and present for the special case of scientific understanding in the human sciences. It is beyond question that this separation is here wholly legitimate and that the explicit elaboration of horizons of interpretation is part of the vigilance of historical knowledge which no longer intends to let itself be governed by anachronistic prejudices. On this point, Gadamer concedes a certain legitimacy in the objectivation of historical knowledge. This is why, in 1960, he characterized the "controlled achievement of such a fusion as the *task* of the knowledge of the work of history". But in 1986, Gadamer replaced the more scientific term "task" (*Aufgabe*) by that of "vigilance" or "watching" (*Wachheit*). The "controlled" achievement of the fusion of horizons also arises from the work of tradition. It is perhaps less important to control this fusion than to be warned of it, by the vigilance of a knowledge which knows itself to be worked by history. It is the dialectic between this determinism and this knowledge which must now be developed.

The immemorial canonicity of tradition and of the classical

The work of history does not paralyse knowledge, but reminds it of itself, of its possibilities of awakening. The knowledge which it limits is the knowledge which the Western philosophical tradition tries to assimilate to an absolute transparency. But as Aristotle knew, this knowledge is reserved for the gods, for the sovereignty of the *noesis noeseos*. In a sense, the whole of Gadamer's hermeneutics wishes to remind us that we are not gods. The knowledge of the gods is a transparent matter, but ours is of awakening. As our language also says, to be aware is first of all to be awake, to be present, to have our eyes open, to be "there", as Heidegger insists. Is that not first of all knowledge? Is knowledge not to be awake, to be exposed to a "there" in a daylight of which we are not the source? To have knowledge, in this sense, is less to have knowledge of this or that, with the goal of mastery which remains objectivizing, but to to be there, "in" the meaning which challenges us. In this "being-there", the achievement of meaning is not a case of mastery, but of participation. For hermeneutics is less the intellect being transparent to itself than a presence to something, a being awakened to something.

This knowledge which is a matter of awakening and constellation is necessarily worked by "history". By that, Gadamer recalls that our capacities of awakening or opening are not wholly at our free disposal. The idea of a subterranean work of history, in *Truth and Method*, comes under the often misunderstood term of tradition. Tradition means the whole of the capacities of awakening that are freely taken up, but in no way created or founded in their validity by a free discernment.[38] Tradition is thus what is imposed on knowledge without its having previously been founded on reason. There is always tradition, that is to say event, in reason. We would be wrong to identify this "imposition" of tradition with something irrational, arbitrary, even authoritarian. Gadamer contests this identification, but in the name of a still human rationality. We forget too often that what is imposed is first of all what inspires knowledge, what carries it away, but also what supports it. When Gadamer speaks of a tradition "freely taken up", he is thinking less of a tradition, which would have made the object of a reflexive appropriation (which is rare), than of the rationality in tradition which is conserved or perpetuated because its setting constitutes the basis of every reasoned project and every foundation. Gadamer sees in this tacit perpetuation of tradition an act of freedom and of reason:

> Even the most genuine and pure tradition does not persist because of the inertia of what once existed. It needs to be affirmed, embraced, cultivated. It is, essentially, preservation, and it is active in all historical change. But preservation is an act of reason, though an inconspicuous one. For this reason, only innovation and planning appear to be the result of reason. But this is only illusion.[39]

It is an appearance induced by an understanding of reason which is still too instrumental, which associates rationality too hastily with an integral mastery of the order of causes, that is to say, with the ideal of a foundation independent of tradition. But there is also a rationality, a legitimacy, in what is perpetuated, in what is conserved over and above transformations. Gadamer judges this "basis" to be more fundamental than the foundation, which is proclaimed to be strictly linear. This basis can in principle be recognized by reason. Besides, in *Truth and Method*, Gadamer reproaches Karl Jaspers and Gerhard Krüger for not having recognized this "principle". He insists that the recognition of the principle is an act of freedom and of reason.[40] The term "act" is perhaps rather strong, because it is not always a case of a conscious action or process, but it is right to talk of freedom and reason. What arises from tradition that is "authority become anonymous"[41] can in principle be understood and it is always so to the extent that the process of transmission is perpetuated. A tradition whose rationality has become problematic always ends in atrophy, and to maintain it is no longer anything but a question of restoration or folklore. But what characterizes such a tradition is that it no longer supports the present. Gadamer is not preoccupied with those traditions.

The tradition that interests him is that which makes our present possible, which is at work in him, above the knowledge he has of it, but which circumscribes the very horizon of our knowledge, of our being-there, of our capacity of awakening. Gadamer considers the primary example of the efficacy of tradition that ties contemporary knowledge to the authority that we recognize in the *classical*. Numerous commentators are ready to denounce here a classical prejudice in Gadamer. It is also a misunderstanding. Gadamer only drew an example of the efficacy of the work of history from his own discipline, his area of expertise, classical studies. Gadamer's only fault was thus to have done philosophy from his own facticity (only the gods philosophize otherwise, but that is so true, says Plato in the *Symposium*, that no god does philosophy in the way that we exhaust ourselves with it). But sometimes a limited example emerges in a universal truth. This is the meaning of "classical" for Gadamer. Previously, the term had a purely normative meaning, rather naïve, rather oppressing for us: the classics represented the insurpassable summits of the mind and *models* to imitate. This ideal gave life and legitimacy to the discipline of "classical studies", what is called in German, since F. A. Wolf, the *Klassischen Altertumswissenschaften*. In reaction to this judgement of normative value, historicism wanted to make of "classic" a simple concept of the age that characterized a temporal phase, without the implication of a value judgement made by the historian, because such a judgement would compromise the objectivity of his proposal. The classical thus found itself reclassified in a historical distance, which imitated scientific objectivity. So the specialists in classical antiquity put back into positions of honour other periods of history, the archaic period, Hellenism, etc. But Gadamer asks whether things are so simple. Can there be such a thing as a stricly historical concept of the past? We must see that Gadamer's intention is not to rehabilitate a normative concept of the classical – he is too much the inheritor of historical knowledge for that – but to recall that a normative element never disappears altogether from historical knowledge. Already the fact that other eras find themselves evaluated by reference to the classical shows, *a contrario*, that the classical keeps some of its authority even when it is challenged. The classical means for Gadamer the "canonical basis" that is presupposed by the historical knowledge which claims that it is detached from its objects of research. Who decides what are the important moments of history, or the great works which we should know, if not the "classical" character that history or a certain history has given them? Is the historian's scientific knowledge ever free from this efficacy of the work of history? To the extent to which it is awakened to ..., knowledge is always tied by a certain canonicity, of what merits attention, of what can be pertinent, and of what can constitute a credible argument. Where does this canon of what is authoritative for knowledge come from if not from the work of history? The example of the classical in Gadamer thus recalls that "historical consciousness always includes more than it admits of itself".[42] Historical knowledge makes an abstraction of the fact that a historical work or event challenges us, belongs to us as well, before even the will of objectivation of historical distance intervenes. It goes without saying that the contents of what is classical or canonical are infinitely variable, since it is a function of the capacity for awakening of each era. The classical never therefore represents for Gadamer a "supra-historical value",[43] but a modality *par excellence* of the historical-being which makes of it a past charged with meaning and for which the force of challenge precedes historical knowledge: "The classical is fundamentally something quite different from a descriptive concept used by an objectivising historical consciousness. It is a historical reality to which historical consciousness belongs and is subordinate."[44]

It is therefore not the classical as such – or such a classical – which matters to Gadamer as much as what he teaches us on the subject of our essential addition to history, and on a certain canonicity. This addition can be read in two ways: we belong to history, to its work, but it is also history which belongs to us, to the extent to which it is always appropriated, read, received, understood by the present and in virtue of its own possibilities of awakening. This mediation of the past and the present appears constitutive of historical knowledge, which it is a case of reconquering. We thus stop seeing in the reciprocal addition of the interpreter to his object, to his history, a hindrance to objectivity:

> This discussion of the concept of the classical claims no independent significance, but serves only to evoke a general question, namely: Does the kind of historical mediation between the past and the present that characterises the classical ultimately underlie all historical activity as its effective substratum?[45]

This mediation allows us to rediscover the essential problem of hermeneutics, the application that all understanding realizes.

The ethical vigilance of application

When Gadamer introduced his important metaphor of a fusion of horizons, he did not avoid attracting attention to a particular connotation of the term "horizon" in German:

> The concept of "horizon" suggests itself because it expresses the superior breadth of vision that the person who is trying to understand must have. To acquire a horizon means that one learns to look beyond what is close at hand – not in order to look away from it but to see it better, within a larger whole and in truer proportion.[46]

French usage is a little different, but it is also said that a book, a journey or a meeting has broadened our horizon, or in the plural, they have opened up new horizons to us.[47] The term "horizon" here denotes a certain generosity of spirit, and also wisdom. This wisdom is essential to Gadamer's concept of horizon. The vigilance of the work of history also has something to do with the elaboration of such a breadth of horizon: as I know that I have been worked by history, I am aware that I am in its debt, but I am also aware of the limits of my knowledge. This knowledge allows me to open myself to the perspective of others. As Gadamer often says after *Truth and Method*, "The soul of hermeneutics consists in recognising that perhaps the other is right."[48]

Knowledge of the work of history thus emerges in an ethics of understanding. It is not by chance that, in the economy of *Truth and Method*, the three chapters which are used to "reconquer the fundamental problem of understanding" from the "principle of the work of history" are devoted to the problem of application, to the actuality of Aristotle's ethics, and to the exemplary meaning of legal hermeneutics (if it had been written at another time, this chapter in *Truth and Method* would doubtless have included a section on rhetoric). The thought of Hans-Georg Gadamer, who began his career as a lecturer in ethics and aesthetics in Marburg in 1929 and whose doctoral and teaching theses were on Greek ethics, thus rejoins its ethical sources.

Gadamer's thought returned also to some of its *hermeneutic* sources. In the "profiling" history of hermeneutics that he presented in order to introduce his own, Gadamer had begun his study of hermeneutics with Schleiermacher. But it is clear that he did so to denounce a loss of substance, of content and of truth in the hermeneutic task, which Schleiermacher had twisted in the direction of a psychologizing and historicizing reconstruction of the process of the author's creation. Strong in the principle of the work of history, Gadamer could return to what had been lost, and find again what he estimated to be the essential problem of hermeneutics, that of application. Gadamer's line of argument can appear to be rather forced, in the sense that the theme of *applicatio* occupies a secondary role in eighteenth-century hermeneutics, without the common ground with the meaning that Gadamer gives to it. But it is right to remember that pietist hermeneutics had recognized an important function in the idea of application, a function that had scrupulously been put aside in the more epistemologizing hermeneutics that have appeared since. If this problem became "completely invisible to the historical self-consciousness of post-romantic scientific epistemology",[49] it is because it was thought that the application of a meaning to the present situation was prejudicial to the objectivity of interpretation. But Gadamer saw in this ideal of objectivity and its concept of interpretation an even more damaging distortion of what is at the root of every interpretation. With this attitude, Gadamer went over to the model of pietist hermeneutics which had added to the subtlety of intellection and exposition a *subtilitas applicandi*, of which the resolution was to apply the meaning understood to the present situation. The typical case is that of the preacher who must "apply" the meaning of a biblical text to the present situation of the faithful. We might think that this is a limited case. But Gadamer finds it equally in the situation of the judge who must apply a general law to a particular case, and he also discovers it in every form of understanding, in the historical and philological interpretation where the interpreter belongs to the events and the texts which he enables to communicate with the present. Gadamer here moves to a completely new reversal, of those who have the genius to produce revolutions in their disciplines, as they lead us to consider their foundations – here those of hermeneutics – in another way: instead of using the cognitive model of philological and historical interpretation – which aims at objective understanding – Gadamer reclaims the practical model of legal and theological hermeneutics, to rethink from top to bottom what philological and theological interpretation is itself.

Gadamer's ambition is to reconquer lost evidence, to know the idea that meaning is always understood in the present, in the terms of and for the present: "Formerly it was considered obvious that the task of hermeneutics was to adapt the text's meaning to the concrete situation to which the text is speaking."[50] This truth, which Gadamer usefully remembers had its foundation in our addition to language, announced the consequences of the third section of *Truth and Method*, which subsequent hermeneutics denounced when they preferred to follow the safer model of the objective sciences, where the involvement of the interpreter was found to be tainted with anathema. But how do we understand meaning without making it speak, without conferring on it a resonance in a language that we can understand? The first lesson of the notion of *subtilitas applicandi* is for us to remember that an understanding without application is no understanding at all. In reclaiming the hermeneutics of the eighteenth century, which did justice to the task of application, Gadamer aimed in a way to "marginalize" nineteenth-century epistemology in the name of a conception, better, in a practice of interpretation that was not ashamed to admit that texts had something to say to him.

The second great lesson of the hermeneutics of *applicatio* in the eighteenth century concerns the very term *subtilitas*. He had the good fortune to remember that understanding – or application – is less a mechanical process than a capacity (*Können*, or in French,[51] *aptitude*[52]), less a matter of rules than an ability-to-be, less a procedure than a mental subtlety. It places in relief once again the marginal character of the intellectualism of methodological hermeneutics which tries to subject the understanding to rules sufficient to guarantee objectivity. It could be, as Gadamer had already suggested with Helmholtz, that feeling, instinct, flair and the sense of tradition are more important factors than method alone.

But the epistemological method is tenacious. We could in effect believe that the meaning which should be applied to a current situation must *at first* be understood in a more cognitive and objective way. Here Gadamer *radicalizes* the classical concept of application in maintaining that application is not added to a cognitive (philological or historical) understanding, but that it constitutes the core of it. The idea is thus not to return to the distinction between the three subtleties (*intellectio, explicatio, applicatio*), but to recognize that understanding is always application. And Gadamer here is not thinking of a conscious application, let us say of an updating of meaning (which is always noted as such), but of an event of understanding itself. We can illustrate this with the help of the example of translation, which aims to capture the meaning of a text. It is always the meaning to be captured that guides the translator, but the meaning wants to be captured, to become intelligible in another language. The best translation will be that which captures the living meaning in a different era and a different language. And the less apparent the effort of translation, the more it will succeed, a success which is always the fact of mediation between the past and the present. Understanding, translation, always emerge from such an application, where the interpreter succeeds in making a text speak. The French term "*application*" has another meaning which would perhaps have served Gadamer's purpose: we say of a work that it has been done with application, to mean that it has been accomplished with diligence, devotion and assiduity, in the service of the thing. Thus the person who understands, in applying the meaning of the past to the present, makes a vow to the meaning which he seeks to understand. It is *that* which must be given. This translation of meaning emerges from a successful mediation of the past and the present. Gadamer gives the name of application to this insertion of the interpreter into what he understands.

This revolutionary conception of application represents an open provocation for methodological knowledge. It is why Gadamer is inspired not only by the models of legal and theological hermeneutics. We can still assert that in these two cases application represents a factor that perhaps is important, but secondary in relation to the primary task, which remains that of intellection in the objective sense. Gadamer's analysis tries to be more fundamental. He proposes, no more no less, to reconquer a model of knowing where application, and application to itself, is constitutive of the understanding of meaning, and also of the rightness of understanding, of its claim to the truth. Before he reactualizes the models of legal and theological hermeneutics, it is necessary to give to the knowledge of application in question the appropriate philosophical basis. Gadamer discovers this model in Aristotle's practical philosophy.

Gadamer appeals to this model at highly strategic times in his work. In the lectures on *The Problem of Historical Knowledge*, a chapter on Aristotle (which was largely reproduced in *Truth and Method*) bridged the chapter on the young Heidegger's hermeneutics of facticity and the last lecture which sketched out the "foundations of hermeneutics". In the work of 1960, the chapter on Aristotle offered the first concrete manifestation of the fundamental problem of application and became the chief work in reconquering the unity of the hermeneutic problem. But Gadamer often came back to it in other texts and at the most unexpected moments. Thus he devoted a whole section to the theme of "practical philosophy" in his autobiographical text of autopresentation in *Philosophical Hermeneutics.*[53]

What can we learn from Aristotle (and perhaps better from Plato, as Gadamer later insisted)?[54] There is a very extensive way of interpreting the links between hermeneutics and Aristotle, which in fact touches upon a very minor aspect of the debate. It concerns, in a word, the "relativism" that we like to give to "knowledge of the situation" which is that of Aristotelian ethics, just as of hermeneutics. This reading is only possible if we judge to be constraining the empire of relativism and its invariable corollary, the monopoly of truth held by the Cartesian knowledge of certainty and ultimate foundations. In this situation, in effect, if there are no absolute norms and certain proofs, everything becomes a matter of *ethos* and of situation in the relativist and dangerous sense of the term. "Situational knowledge" becomes the utilitarian knowledge of the person who acts conformably to his interests or those of his clan, because they are his own and he was formed in this *ethos* from which it is impossible to extract himself. In fact, this situational knowledge is more apparent in the calculation of the person who "knows how to profit by his situation". It is true that this neo-Aristotelianism of values has played an important role in recent discussions of ethics, where it has been most often contrasted with the universal norms of Kantianism.

But Gadamer is not preoccupied at all by the debate between universalism and relativism, even if the opposition between Kant and Aristotle plays an appreciable role in his work.[55] The crucial debate is rather how to deal with the intellectualism of moral knowledge. If Aristotle's ethics represents a model for Gadamer, it is not because he maintains that all values are relative (and does Aristotle say so anyway?) but because he sees clearly that moral knowledge is not a purely intellectual knowledge: ethical wisdom does not consist in mentally knowing an ideal norm (an idea, an abstract good, a mathematical universality), but in being able to apply the good in a concrete situation. In other words, moral knowledge is not one of objectivation, but in contrast is one of application.

If we must be opposed to Kant, it is not because Kant has maintained in an anti-realist way that there are universal norms of acting. Gadamer never opposes Kant's categorical imperative in the name, let us say, of a Nietzschean relativism of values. Gadamer here is much nearer to Kant's universalism.[56] We have seen besides that his conception of *Bildung*, of "formation", is linked to an elevation to universality, to a transcendence of simple particularity. That is not a little Kantian. What gives him a problem is certainly not universalism, but intellectualism – and, consequently, unacknowledged intellectualism – which intends to make the rectitude of moral action depend on the cognition of an abstract norm. This knowledge of moral action proceeds from an objectivist conception, a tributary of the objectivation of modern science, which makes it overlook the specificity of human action and moral knowledge. But moral knowledge is not one of objectivation, but of action and practical application. Aristotle proposed the clearest model of it in his ethics. His intention was to set out the limits of a purely instrumental knowledge – whether epistemological or technical – of the norms of action, as if human action was always in the situation of objectivizing the norms that determine it. Thus its importance for Gadamer's hermeneutics: just as to be a historical being means never being able to resolve yourself in self-knowledge, so to be an ethical being means never being able to objectivize all the reasons for your actions. This is not to deny that moral action is always brought about from a certain normative foundation. Far from it, because in all our moral actions and judgements we remain, even if we do not know it, determined by the ethical heritage of the categorical imperative, and also by the Ten Commandments, the Sermon on the Mount, the Golden Rule, the Greek ethic of honour in war, etc. In this sense, moral action is indebted to a tradition, to a foundation that carries it. Are we in a position to untangle all the threads that weave our moral constitution? But the most pertinent question is the following: does the rightness of moral action depend on such intellection? Of course it does not. It is the hegemonic model of scientific knowledge, which is a knowledge of universal scientific laws, that makes us believe that moral action is also defined by its conformity to universal and objectivable norms. Is this model really appropriate to moral action? Is not to act morally always to accomplish the good in a situation of action? Is not to demand absolute norms for such action, for the Good itself, to overlook the situation of all ethical action in intellectualizing it? This is the meaning of the Aristotelian critique of Plato. Gadamer takes lessons for hermeneutics from it.

The reference to *ethos* therefore has nothing to do with a plea in favour of the relativism of action or, in applying it to hermeneutics, of understanding. It has the unique function of recalling that rightness here does not depend on *detachment* in relation to the situation of action, as can be true of authoritative knowledge in the spheres of science and technology. Besides, it is the delimitation of ethical knowledge in relation to *epistēmē* and *technē* which matters more than anything else to Gadamer. Understood from the critique of intellectualism, its meaning and its bearing become very clear. It is manifest that ethical wisdom does not arise from the order of the *epistēmē*, of which the model provided for the Greeks is mathematics: it is not a matter of mathematical good, but of human good. It is more difficult and thus more crucial to distinguish this knowledge from technique. Technique is also knowledge of doing, but it aims at the production of an object that is exterior to myself. Practical wisdom is not knowledge of an object, and does not allow this distancing:

> The objectifying methods of modern science, characteristic of the hermeneutics and historiography of the nineteenth century, appeared as the consequence of a false objectification. My purpose in returning to the example of Aristotelian ethics is to help us realise and avoid this. For moral knowledge, as Aristotle describes it, is clearly not objective knowledge – i.e. the knower is not standing over against a situation that he merely observes; he is directly confronted with what he sees.[57]

The acting being does not therefore have in relationship to himself the distance which is that of the artisan to his object. If I am implicated by my action, it is because I am always in the situation of the one who must act.[58] But we should not understand too quickly this concept of situation in the sense of a "situational ethics" that is still thought of in too utilitarian a way (which perhaps still hides a technical knowledge: how to extract advantage from the situation). A little earlier, Gadamer appealed to the concept of situation developed by Jaspers, a concept which truly meant that we find ourselves in a situation in such a way that we have no objective knowledge of it.[59] In one sense, the situation (whether an ethical or a hermeneutic one) has something of the invisible, because we are plunged into it, but this invisibility does not exclude discernment, the sense of what is right: "For although it is necessary to see what a situation is asking of us, this seeing does not mean that we perceive in the situation what is visible as such, but that we learn to see it as the situation of action and hence in the light of what is right."[60] This capacity of discernment is not a matter of objectivation, but of vigilance, of awakening to the situation. In his 1963 article on the ethical foundations of hermeneutics, Gadamer spoke of a "vigilance [Wachsamkeit] of ethical knowledge".[61] Vigilance is always borne by normative foundations, by a sense of good, but its awakening to the challenges of particular situations remains the only area in which it is exercised.

What characterizes this ethical wisdom for Aristotle is therefore that it escapes from objectivation. To measure this knowledge by the yardstick of unchanging knowledge or of what is technically feasible is not a "deficiency", but we are leaving the area of practical philosophy. In rejecting objectivation, practical wisdom can neither be learnt (unlike mathematical knowledge) or be taught (unlike technical ability). But it is still legitimate here to talk of knowledge – or of wisdom – and of its rightness. But its rightness is a matter of vigilance and application. It is a case of knowledge in which it is not possible, or desirable, that we put ourselves in brackets if we wish to understand what is right, and in which orientation in too abstract a norm, inspired by a scientific model, runs the risk of obscuring the task that we all undertake. Gadamer is fascinated by this model of knowledge that is not detached from the subject and from its concrete application and he applies it in turn to questions in hermeneutics. It replaces the model of auto-effacement in hermeneutics.

Fortified by this philosophical basis, Gadamer can return to the problem of application such as he sets himself in "practical" hermeneutics, in law and in theology, but better to close in on the practical foundation of all understanding. Legal hermeneutics here plays an exemplary role. As seems to be the case for the model of predication, the example of a judge who applies a law to a precise situation can appear limited, but as a continuation of the model of practical wisdom, the limited case allows us better to apprehend the universal. The Italian jurist Emilio Betti had already spoken of the normative function of application that is exercised in the magistrate's verdict but he saw in it a supplementary effort which was added to the original hermeneutic task of understanding: the magistrate who has to apply a concrete law must for Betti have already understood the sense or the intention of it in its original meaning.[62] The philological model of the penetration of meaning remains determining for Betti. Here again, Gadamer inverts the perspective in maintaining that, on the contrary, it is application that represents the true and primary understanding worthy of the name. To show this, Gadamer turns to the legal historian who seeks only to understand the original meaning of a law (repealed or otherwise), an example which Betti had also used to distinguish the supplementary work of application accomplished by the magistrate who himself represents the law. According to Gadamer, the legal historian must carry out "exactly the same thing as the judge"[63] if he wishes to understand the meaning of the law; that is to say he must himself make an effort of application. This exercise of application works at two levels: first, if he wishes to understand the meaning of a law, he must also understand its possible applications, because a law has meaning only in the function of its adaptation to a particular context: in "reconstructing" this context, he must himself try to understand how the law can be applied. The law has *no meaning* without the context of possible application. Secondly, and still more fundamentally, the legal historian cannot "understand" this "original" context of application in abstracting from his own legal expectations and his sense of the law. This does not mean, of course, that the historian must submit the law which he studies to his own legal norms, but that his understanding of the law is dictated by such expectations, even and above all if it is a case of incommensurable legal contexts. In distinguishing former legal contexts from his own, the norm of his own governs the distinction. Thus Gadamer draws the conclusion:

> The hermeneutical situation of both the historian and the jurist seems to me to be the same in that, when faced with any text, we have an immediate expectation of meaning. There can be no such thing as a direct access to the historical object that would objectively reveal its historical value. The historian has to undertake the same reflection as the jurist.[64]

Gadamer is well aware of the differences that there may be between the two types of application (the first has immediate consequences and represents the law, the second is more contemplative), but the community matters more to him, and in the end we are concerned less with the application of law by a magistrate than by the legal historian. Here we can speak of one and the same effort to understand, devoted to a concrete application. The legal model is not only about the effective application of a law by the magistrate. What the legal (and theological, because Gadamer always speaks of the two at the same time) model exemplifies for all understanding is that it is animated by an essential tension between the fidelity of the text (to the law, to the biblical text) and the necessity of its application to the present context. In effect, it would be a serious mistake to see in the concrete application which completes the law a form of arbitrariness or of freedom in relation to the original meaning of the law. To be faithful to the spirit of justice intended by the law itself is to adapt its application to the particular circumstances of a precise case.[65] The person who has not understood this has not understood the law itself, that is to say the spirit which animates it and which knows that it has to be applied differently to do justice to precise situations and to their inevitable particularities. Not to realize this would be to misrepresent the law. Legal and theological understanding is thus divided into two headings: that of the law (of the past), and that of the present, and always special, case. Gadamer thinks that this essential bipolarity covers every case, and in this sense, legal hermeneutics always enjoys an exemplary status. Thus Gadamer's conclusion:

> We can, then, distinguish what is truly common to all forms of hermeneutics: the meaning to be understood is concretised and fully realised only in interpretation, but the interpretive activity considers itself wholly bound by the meaning of the text. Neither jurist nor theologian regards the work of application as making free with the text.[66]

The present application can be understood as arbitrary only if we first of all decree that the intervention of the actual situation puts into question the objectivity of the interpretation. Legal hermeneutics recalls that, on the contrary, it is ignorance of the present situation that represents a lack of objectivity and justice. The addition to the present, but also and therefore to tradition, is not a restrictive condition, but a condition of possibility for accurate understanding.[67] In the light of legal hermeneutics, there is therefore room to revise false models of objectivity that prevail in the field of philological and historical hermeneutics. We have seen above that the nineteenth century served as the model for philology to realize the historian's concern for objectivity: to understand is to understand a meaning from a given totality, from the context. The particular is understood only as the result or the expression of a wider totality, but this, in history, is never given. If we have spoken of a philologization of history, the strength is to recognize that there is room to speak of a growing historicization of philology. In effect, according to the model of historical hermeneutics, which ended by imposing itself on philology, texts are no longer understood according to their own intention to express themselves, but as witnesses or vestiges of a grand narrative, that of history. To the extent of its being seen in texts as nothing other than historical expression, without exemplary bearing, philology has ended by becoming a simple branch of history.

This solidarity between history and philology is attested by the qualification *philologisch-historisch* which often serves to characterize all the *Geisteswissenschaften* in Germany. The Academies of Science thus have their *philologisch-historische Klasse* for cataloguing publications in the human sciences. Gadamer's debate with history and philology therefore aims not only at bringing out the hermeneutic basis of the human sciences, but also at freeing them from the model of scientific objectivation that imposed the universal model of history. Gadamer wishes to put into question this pretension to the universality of historical hermeneutics. In effect, he thinks that it is worthwhile neither for philology nor even for history such as it is effectively practised. Even under the aegis of historical knowledge, the texts that the philologist or the philosopher studies continue to be texts which speak, which we study because they have something to say to us. It is also true of so-called historical phenomena since they are studied only by reason of their *historical meaning*. From where does this meaning come? From the phenomena themselves or from their historical efficacy, such as has been recognized and transmitted by a history which determines us? The "facts" which the historian studies are always witnesses, vestiges, remains, as Droysen brilliantly saw. We never have dealings with the past as such, but always with the past as it is conserved in witness. There is already a work of history and application in the material that is offered to the historian. Certainly the historian can and must give himself up to the critique of this witness, but where do his questions, his doubts, his revival of questions, come from, if not from other witnessing and from his own intervention in the past that he seeks to understand and to make speak today? It could thus be that the "truly decisive factors" of knowledge pre-exist all application of historical method.[68] Gadamer thus finds the common denominator of all hermeneutic disciplines, those of history, philology, theology and law, in the event of *application* where the past and the present interpenetrate. The unity of hermeneutics therefore resides neither in the universality of the method of understanding, nor in the universality of historical knowledge, nor in the contemplative ideal of philology, but in the task of application of which legal and theological hermeneutics are only the most eloquent reminders. The whole of Gadamer's conclusion is worth quoting, as it is so important:

> Thus we too acknowledge that there is an inner unity between philology . . . and historical studies . . . but we do not see it in the universality of the historical method, nor in the objectifying replacement of the interpreter by the original reader, nor in historical critique of tradition as such but, on the contrary, in the fact that both perform an act of application that is different only in degree. If the philologist or critic understands the given text – i.e. understands himself in the text in the way we have said – the historian too understands the great text of world history he has himself discovered, in which every text handed down to us is but a fragment of meaning, one letter, as it were, and he understands himself in this great text. Both the critic and the historian thus emerge from the self-forgetfulness to which they had been banished by a thinking for which the only criterion was the methodology of modern science. Both find their true ground in *historically effected consciousness*.[69]

Such is the great conclusion of hermeneutics in the human sciences, developed by Gadamer in the second part of his work. Once delivered from the distorting model of auto-effacement and the reduction of all meaning to the expression of an objectivizing process of history, understanding perceives in its addition to the work of history its condition of possibility and its most intimate task in the vigilance of application. But Gadamer's project is not, or no longer, limited to that of an accurate understanding of the human sciences. His purpose takes a more philo-sophical and more universal turn which overflows the still-limited framework of a hermeneutics of the human sciences. The principle of the work of history, which has allowed the reconquest of the unity of the hermeneutic disciplines and their relationship with the truth, is a universal principle of all understanding, and of everything in relationship to the world: that is to say, of all language. All the rest of Gadamer's hermeneutics relates to the directing idea of this universalization of hermeneutics under the conduct of language. Before taking this last turn, a final "analysis of knowledge of the work of history" must specify the relationship between hermeneutics and the philosophy of reflexion.

The mirages of reflexion and the bugbear of relativism

The oracle at Delphi – know yourself – reminds us that we are not gods, but men. Should we accuse her of relativism?[70]

Hans-Georg Gadamer

In the whole of *Truth and Method*, Gadamer always appealed to Hegel in order to overcome historicism. Better than Schleiermacher, Hegel saw that the understanding was less the reconstruction of a past meaning than its integration into a present constellation, with contemporary application incarnating the true effectiveness of meaning. Better than historicism, Hegel understood that it represented less an object of enquiry for knowledge than its most intimate constitution. Knowledge is never anything except the tip of the iceberg of its own historicity. In its capacity of awakening, this knowledge embedded in history is required to become self-knowledge. Gadamer's hermeneutics itself culminates in the elaboration of a knowledge of the work of history. But does not this knowledge incarnate an avatar of Hegelianism? Gadamer is constrained to engage with the idealist philosophy of history to mark the important but evident differences, but without all the same "renouncing Hegel", as Paul Ricoeur did in his own hermeneutics of historical knowledge outlined in *Temps et Récit*.[71] It is a case of upholding the "truth of Hegelian thought"[72] against the reflexive ambition of his system.

Gadamer is particularly anxious to dissociate himself from the attraction exercised by the philosophy of reflexion. In 1960, he had not expressly specified what he meant by that, but it is clear that he was essentially aiming at Hegelian philosophy and its pretensions to integrate history into the sphere of knowledge. If the term "philosophy of reflexion" is more or less a happy one, it is because Hegel himself severely criticized the *Reflexionsphilosophien* which he identified with the thought of Jacobi and Fichte (which explains the irritation of the Hegelians faced with the term retained by Gadamer). The defect of these philosophies was for Hegel that they never really emerged from subjectivity and they were thus deprived of a real effectiveness. But by using the expression "philosophy of reflexion" against Hegel, Gadamer reproaches himself for lacking in effectiveness, that is to say for finally preventing the full effectiveness, the work, of history on knowledge. In trying to dissolve the reality of history in the mind's awareness of itself, Hegel did not succeed in extracting himself from the admittedly impressive sphere of the philosophy of reflexion. The hermeneutics of the awareness of the work of history forces itself to resist this temptation in attaching this awareness not to its transparency, but to the awakening of awareness which is that of the experience of language, an awakening which is never the mind's pure seizing of itself, but its presence to the world, to being. The "foundation" of language is no longer an instrument in the service of sovereign thought, but its medium, its way of being achieved, its condition. The linguistic texture of our awakening-to-the-world in this way becomes the new *a priori* of hermeneutics.

The vigilance of the work of history rather wishes to become the memorial of the immemorial historicity that is at work in all knowledge. It is necessary to maintain this "truth" of Hegelian thought against the claims of his system to absolute knowledge that, on the faith of reflexion, would end by abolishing the history of this self-awareness, which becomes entirely transparent to itself. For Gadamer, the historicity of knowledge is such that it never lets itself be dissolved entirely by the work of reflexion. In this context, the accusation of relativism or of self-contradiction surges inexorably, and Gadamer also associates it with the perspective of the philosophy of reflexion. For him, relativism represents a pure figure of reflexion without an effective hold on things. The problem did not appear until the nineteenth century, when neo-Kantianism sought to immunize the *a priori* nature of reason against the suspicion of "relativism", which historical knowledge allowed to spread out over everything that the mind produced.

Gadamer's attitude in the face of relativism is not the easiest to encompass, because it appears to uphold historicist theses, whilst it makes little mention of the question of relativism, which it seems to treat offhandedly. Even if Gadamer's presentations on this issue appear far from satisfactory, or coherent, we risk losing our bet.[73] First of all, it is obvious that Gadamer has never recognized that his hermeneutics defended relativism. It is true that his adversaries above all are ready to brandish the spectre of relativism.[74] For Gadamer and Heidegger, relativism is only that, a spectre, a bugbear that intends to create fear by depicting the infamous consequences which are to be upheld by "everything is relative" (hermeneutics says only that we belong to the experience of meaning, that its emergence is unthinkable without us). If everything is relative, everything becomes excusable, and (it is always the example invoked) we can no longer guard ourselves against Hitler. The debate on relativism is often conducted in such an emotive way. In this sense, for Gadamer's hermeneutics, it is only the starting-point. It intends to cause fear.

But hermeneutics suggests that what we need to be afraid of or to distrust is perhaps the form of reflexion which inspires relativism. Gadamer thinks that we can speak of relativism only if we presuppose absolute truth as a possibility, and it owes nothing to history nor language. The accusation of relativism thus presupposes and defends an absolutist knowledge of the truth. This truth claims an absolute perspective (!) which the hermeneutics of facticity deconstructs, given that the very idea of a *fundamentum inconcussum* proceeds from a denial of temporality. If we abandon this absolutism of truth, the charge of relativism loses its *raison d'être*. On the contrary, we learn to see in the historicity of understanding the working mainspring of the truth:

> Historicity no longer means a limiting determination of reason and of its claim to seize the truth; it represents rather a positive condition of the knowledge of the truth. By that, the line of argument for historical relativism loses all real foundation. The demand for a criterion for absolute truth is found to be unmasked as an abstract and metaphysical idol, and loses all methodological meaning.[75]

And to uphold that if everything is relative, everything will be permitted, is to run into the most obvious of contradictions. A knowledge involved, concerned, engaged in history and therefore vulnerable is by this fact a critical knowledge. It demands credible arguments and reasons. The problematic of the circle of understanding allows us to see at what point hermeneutics holds to the idea of adequacy (understood as consonance, where engaged knowledge also speaks) and of coherence. In fact, it is *because* knowledge knows itself to be determined by history that it always remains open to revising its anticipations, and to the horizon of the other. One of the mirages of the idea of absolute truth is to allow us to forget that, for human beings at least, truth remains a matter of vigilance and of horizon.

Knowing whether hermeneutics is itself coherent when it draws attention to the historicity of all understanding is another issue. If we could distinguish two problems, the issue of relativism and that of self-contradiction (pragmatic or performative), we would make progress here. The contradiction consists in maintaining that *all* understanding is dependent on history, as this contention itself claims to be of value in a non-historical way. But does it really claim that this is the case? Gadamer and Heidegger have paid even less attention to this accusation of self-contradiction (it is necessary to state that authors such as Apel and Habermas reactivated it *after* the publication of *Truth and Method*, and in Apel's case, at least afterwards in the name of an ultimate foundation). Gadamer and Heidegger see in it not the fact of a subtle argument, reflectively critical, as it is often presented, but its caricature, that is to say, a reflexion which is surrendered "by surprise" (*Überrumpelungsversuch*), instead of keeping a cap on things themselves, even if they were opposed to transcendental reflexion. The term *Überrumpelung* here is illuminating. It means, in German, a surprise attack, most often cunning and vicious. The person who is attacked from behind while walking in a park is, in German, "*überrumpelt*". Does philosophical reflexion aspire to this sort of argument? Is its task not rather to attack the thing itself, directly and from the front?

The goal of the line of argument of self-contradiction is to show that, if we can at least maintain that the truth carries with it a part of historicity, not everything is relative. But whom do we want to deceive or reassure by that? Does finitude want to escape from its condition of finitude in discovering, thanks to the virtues of reflexion, that its finitude (or its historicity) cannot be upheld without self-contradiction? Fine consolation! If we hold to it, this finitude will become the new "absolute". But this is not an absolute which is of the nature to reassure us about the existence of absolute truth. Is there a contradiction in upholding this "principle" of finitude? No, because it is content to name, to talk of – in our own terms and times – the *condition* in the midst of which is deployed the experience of truth for human beings (because, as Gadamer always says ironically, the gods doubtless have absolute truth). A truth which no longer obeys it is no longer a truth. And this condition is also of value for hermeneutics. It is also a response to its times, a response to a non-historical understanding of truth. The deployment of hermeneutics is itself inscribed in a dialogical context, that which wants to suppress pretensions to an absolute truth. This is why Gadamer tends to assimilate the argument about relativist self-contradiction to a sophistic form. Effectively, he has in view the model of Socratic dialogue, on the back of which there are two contradictory assertions. Gadamer's intention is not, it should be well noted, to deride the possibilities of reflexion, but on the contrary he wishes to sharpen them by recalling that the instruments of reflexion are not sufficient, or become suspect, if we cease to focus on the thing itself. Succumbing to its quest for security, the refuge of reflexion does not see or does not wish to see what historicity means. In effect, it does not perceive that this quest for security rests on a denial of historicity, confirming by that the "historicity" of the latter.

What the anti-relativist argument wants to maintain is the possibility of a universal truth, not dependent on time nor on historical conditions. But hermeneutics does not at all aspire to this sort of certainty. All that hermeneutics wants to recall is that the historical condition of understanding, a condition (in the sense of "human condition", or "predicament" in English) which is still applied to the universal truths of science and of logic, must always be expressed according to the linguistic capacities of an era. But it never occurs to the hermeneutic mind to translate this "condition" by a universal pronouncement, as it knows that every pronouncement, even those of hermeneutics, participates in the same condition (which applies equally to what we have just formulated: it also cannot be understood except in dialogue and response and in a shared linguistic horizon). Gadamer is led to speak of the "hermeneutic *aspect*" in the last chapter of his work by this condition of addition to history and to language. What is universal is not a pronouncement nor a theorem, but an *essential* aspect of meaning, its inscription in an intelligibility circumscribed by history. It was not Gadamer who first talked of a "pretention to universality" – effectively pretentious – but Habermas.

When hermeneutics recalls the historico-linguistic condition of all understanding, it seeks to uncover what it calls, for want of a better phrase, a product of life, which we should not understand in the manner of a logical product of propositions:

> It is one of the prejudices of reflective philosophy that it understands matters that are not at all on the same logical level as standing in propositional relationships. Thus the reflective argument is out of place here. For we are not dealing with relationships between judgments which have to be kept free from contradictions but with life relationships. Our verbal experience of the world has the capacity to embrace the most varied relationships of life.[76]

In this respect, it is not lacking in piquancy that Gadamer, in 1960, explicitly leans on one of Apel's studies, which is a reminder "that the discourse which a person holds about himself must in no case be understood as the assertion which fixes in an objectifying way a being-such, so that the refutation of such pronouncements, in the name of their self-reference and their logical contradictions, is stripped of meaning".[77] The fundamental reason why Gadamer shows reluctance in engaging in this sort of argument also has something to do with the more general distrust towards the free self-possession that often animates the argument of pure reflexion. The philosophy of reflexion presupposes that there could be self-knowledge in the same way as there is knowledge of an object. If knowledge is awakening to the world, can we reify that awakening itself? Can there be awakening of awakening?[78] The metaphor of reflection and of mirrors (and can the anti-relativist argument take into account that its own pronouncements are metaphorical?) is already suspect. It lets it be understood that knowledge's turning back on itself is realizable, as if knowledge can present itself to itself such as it is in itself. But is reflexive knowledge the same as that which reflects on itself? What assures us that the reflected image – in the unthinking "silvering" of the mirror, to take up Rodolphe Gasche's expression – conforms, and can we even talk of assurance in such a game of mirrors? Does the proclaimed transparency not betray a more formidable opaqueness? It could be that knowledge here allows itself to joke, and to soothe, by its own metaphors, as if it were seeking to apply to itself the categories of mastery and of domination that it applied to external nature in objectifying it in the natural sciences. The limit of these metaphors is also that of the philosophy of reflexion.

Gadamer has always distrusted constructions of self-knowledge, and more generally, philosophical constructions. His philosophy owes more to the practice of dialogue (like his contemporaries, his mentors and the great traditional authors) than to the elaboration of theories of pure understanding in the abstract. This corresponds to his conception, more, to his practice of phenomenology: philosophy first of all is a response to phenomena, an insertion into dialogue. Philosophical constructions have always had something artificial in his eyes, "constructed" to be exact. It is true that this philosophical practice is very extensive today, but Gadamer here suspects an instrumentalist distortion of philosophical questioning. True philosophical questions pose themselves to us, and we always arrive a bit too late when we wish to reconstruct problems theoretically *ab ovo*. The problem of relativism, in recent times, is for Gadamer a good example of "problems which are not real questions".[79] He forges from all the pieces a dilemma which exists only if we start from an absolute truth. But the whole of Gadamer's philosophy intends to remind us, with the oracle at Delphi, by which Socrates was authorized, that we are not gods, but human beings. Would we like to charge the oracle at Delphi with relativism?[80] In transforming self-knowledge into a pure knowledge of objects, the philosophy of reflexion succumbs to an instrumentalist conception of knowledge and of philosophy, forgetting the finitude of all knowledge.

Aristotle was perhaps not wrong in reserving this self-seizure of knowledge to divine intelligence, so sovereign that it does not know anything except itself. That is also the danger of the philosophy of reflexion: a thought that listens only to itself. Hermeneutic knowledge, on the contrary, intends to be open to others. And the knowledge which it is a matter of acquiring arises less from an intellectual process than from an experience that overcomes knowlege. Gadamer devoted to this notion of experience one of the most personal chapters of his work,[81] whose crucial importance he often stressed. It is obvious that the experience at issue is not one which the scientist prepares in his laboratory, an experience which allows itself to be objectified, controlled, verified and repeated and which is an essential condition of the exact sciences and of their success. The fundamental hermeneutic experience is of another sort.

Francis Bacon, the great promoter of scientific experience, had foreseen something of it when he spoke of the tendency of the human mind to retain in the memory only what is positive and to forget negative instances.[82] Gadamer willingly recognizes that that is an essential trait of the human mind and that one part of illusion, or even of forgetfulness, remains vital to knowledge. This is the meaning of his rapid allusion to Aeschylus' *Prometheus*: the greatest gift that Prometheus brought to human beings was not fire, but hope (*elpis*), which was given to them when they stopped knowing the date and time of their deaths.[83] Illusion, forgetfulness of death, is essential to life and to creativity. How do we live if we are always thinking of death? We can have a future only if we forget that we do not have one.[84] Life is unlivable without its being partly illusion. We would, however, be wrong to assimilate illusion to a deception or a simple vital lie. We can appeal to the use of the Spanish term *illusion* which could intend to say that we have a goal, a hope, a joy, an ideal, something that makes us live (a use which perhaps also explains the *joie de vivre* of the Spanish[85]). All life needs *illusion*, and faith, ideals, pleasure, happiness have a part in it. Only a Puritan conception of knowledge can reveal nothing other than a lie. Jean-Paul Sartre came close to this phenomenon when he spoke of the "*mauvaise foi*" inherent in all knowledge, but he also missed the mark in still speaking in a Puritan way of a "bad" faith. We can also oppose the Promethean *elpis* to the Heideggerian imperative of a necessary and radical awareness of one's mortality. Certainly there is no *Dasein* without this damned awareness, but the *Dasein* can be invested in projects only if it also forgets the nothingness of its future. Prometheus gave this *elpis*, this hope, to human beings.

But in *Truth and Method*, another important aspect of Aeschylus is emphasized: the *pathei manos*, the idea that we become wise through suffering. Gadamer means by that that true experience is that which surprises us, which knocks us back, which confounds our expectations. This experience leads us to revise our expectations and opens new horizons to us.[86] This negative experience also doubtless happens in science, in the dialectic of trial and error of which the falsificationist Karl Popper has eloquently spoken. Gadamer acknowledges this conception of experience, but thinks that it perhaps stresses too much the voluntarist aspect of experimentation, ignoring the passive and passionate (*leiden-schaftlich*) character of the whole experience of life.[87] The scientist who submits his hypotheses to tests of falsification still remains master of this experience from which he draws results. The reversal which is proper to hermeneutic experience deprives knowledge of such an assurance. It dispossesses it of its certainty to confront it with its essential finitude. As Hegel well saw, the transformation that induces the negativity of true

117

experience brings in a metamorphosis of knowledge itself. It is a new form of knowledge which is conducted by hermeneutic experience: knowledge through an awareness of its own ignorance. True experience thus emerges into a new wisdom: "Thus the negativity of experience has a curiously productive meaning. It is not simply that we see through a deception and hence make a correction, but we acquire a comprehensive knowledge."[88] Its extent resides just in the hold of knowledge over the finitude of knowledge. It is the case of an experience on the part of tragedy which is the lot of the human condition, "an experience . . . always to be acquired, and from it no-one can be exempt".[89] There is a hermeneutic wisdom to this knowledge which allows us, here again, to acquire a horizon (*Horizont gewinnen*). We say that a person who has acquired this magnanimity of horizon is a person of experience.[90]

The person of experience, to whom we attribute wisdom, is not a person who disposes of absolute knowledge or who possesses a mastery of the course of things. On this point, Aristotle delivered the most precious teaching when he placed experience (*empeiria*) at mid-point between isolated perceptions and conceptual universality.[91] This middling position does not mean it is lacking! On the contrary, it closes in on the specific nature of the experience which is to be knowledge that we never stop acquiring. It results from what is common to numerous observations, but it can always be overturned and, what is still more important, it is actualized only in single observations. To bring it back to the order of the concept would be to cut it off from its reference that is constitutive of the order of experience, always concrete, forming and reforming, which remains its only site of actualization. The person who reaches experience from the height of great abstract principles, which are reputed to be of value for every situation, is not a person of experience, nor very wise either. The *empeiria* does not enjoy less of a "universality", which is neither that of a concept nor that of repeated observations. It is the universality of the finitude of experience and the experience of finitude itself.

As there will never be the assurance of a universal and conceptual knowledge, the knowledge of experience will be foreign to all dogmatism. According to Gadamer, hermeneutic experience must lead from one opening to another, to possible experience, of which we can only foresee that it is unforeseeable. Instructed by disappointment, the suffering of its previous experiences, this hermeneutic experience will remain a matter of vigilance and horizon. "Realism", the wisdom of the knowledge of finitude, consists of "hav[ing] insight into the limited degree to which the future is still open to expectation and planning or, even more fundamentally, to have the insight that all the expectation and planning of finite beings is finite and limited."[92]

From a critical perspective, we could wonder whether the finitude proper to the hermeneutic experience *necessarily* leads from one opening to another and to new experiences. Gadamer's reasoning is altogether limpid (because we are finished, we are open), but we can wonder if the finitude of knowledge is not such that it *cannot* open itself to every form of experience. A perspicacious commentator has rightly called it the equivocation of Gadamer's conception of experience.[93] A radicalization of finitude like that promoted by hermeneutics must recognize that a certain closure is also part of human finitude. His insistence on the prejudices of understanding recognizes that it is impossible to be *au fait* with all prejudices. We have seen that hermeneutic knowledge is not to be understood in the sense of objective knowledge, but as an awareness of awakening. If every being-in-the-world is thus sustained by a possibility of awakening, which is finished and at work in history beyond the objective knowledge that can be had of it, it cannot be awakened to all possible ones.

A radical knowledge of the work of history must guard against this *essential* ambiguity of the hermeneutic experience. But this guard also whets its vigilance. If the possibility of mistake can be total, knowledge must open itself still more resolutely to the opportunity represented by dialogue and the perspective of others (which can also be in me, as the best arguments we can bring against our own positions are often those which we suppress in ourselves – whoever has edited a text, however unphilosophical it might be, has had experience of it). In this frame of mind, Gadamer appeals to the example of Platonic dialogue, which has always known that the difference between sophistry and truth is often tenuous. And who can ever be sure of not succumbing to sophistry?

The hermeneutic experience does not emerge in an absolute certainty (whether it is a matter of the certainty of scientific experience or, with Hegel, the experience of absolute knowledge) but in the questioning of all assurance. For this reason, in *Truth and Method*, the dialectical experience of Hegel's knowledge is relayed by the dialogical model of Platonic dialectic, which was developed under the patronage of Socrates and his questioning of all claimed knowledge. Hermeneutic knowledge thus became an art of questioning and of leaving the replies hanging. In the human sciences, the important thing is not always to come to definitive results, but to be able to ask questions. We must also learn to keep certain questions open, because the openness to possible replies is also part of the width of horizon which can form the human sciences. The logic of the human sciences is thus for Gadamer a logic of question. He found a first, but still rudimentary, outline in the logic of question and answer developed by the historian R. G. Collingwood. Collingwood well saw that to understand the course of historical events, we must also reconstitute the question to which the historical action is the reply.[94] The historian who wants to understand what happened must interrogate himself on his questions, the expectations of historical agents, above the known and documented facts. There is however a double naïveté in Collingwood's perspective. The first is to believe that the course of history responds to a conscious plan. In fact, history emerges rather from the order of events, where intentions, causal chains and circumstantial contingency overlap. The second is to believe that we have to transpose ourselves into the questions and the situation of those who contributed to forming the events if we want to understand the facts. Gadamer's conception of application, that the logic of question and response is concrete, has taught us that to understand a question means that we ask it of ourselves. The question which we reconstruct also remains a question which we ask ourselves, even if it is in an attenuated form: "a person says that such and such a question might arise . . .".[95]

But above all, the acuteness of Collingwood's questioning is significant for hermeneutics, because it allows us to go beyond the framework of a hermeneutics of the human sciences. If it is true that we can understand a text only in so far as it is the reply to a question which we still ask ourselves, this also goes for all understanding of language. To understand a discourse, a phrase, a silence, a gesture – all of which emerge from language – is to hear a reply to a question, an urgency, a suffering and a constellation which we must enter if we wish to understand. Thus all understanding is the fact of fusion between what matters in understanding and the person who understands. Gadamer's "directing idea" is that "the fusion of horizons that takes place in understanding is actually the achievement of language".[96]

Language incarnates not only the "object" of understanding – a meaning, whether or not it is linguistic – but also its mode of achievement, its articulation in an understanding that makes sense. But it is a case of an "object" and of an "achievement" which conserve something unfathomable, even disquieting, since the object and the achievement of understanding are so intimately tied to language that it appears impossible to distinguish language about things from the things themselves, and the linguistic effort of the understanding from understanding itself. There is here a redoubled symbiosis since it is at the same time that of language and that of things, but also that of language and that of thought. This non-distinction is only disarming for thought obsessed with objectivity, which would like to be able to distinguish between thought and its articulation in language, and things from their linguistic expression. But it is just this instrumental understanding of language that Gadamer puts into question so as to approach the mystery of "the language which we are". Language is not a tool of which sovereign thought disposes.[97] The last challenge of *Truth and Method* would be to try to think the essential dialogue which we are, with things but also with ourselves, from the moment that we begin to speak. The being is no longer allowed to be distinguished from the language that embraces it. This is the reason for the ontological turning of hermeneutics, following the conducting thread of language.

CHAPTER 5

The Dialogue that We Are

Towards the uncanny nearness of language

"To understand what takes us", to seize what has forever seized us, is how we can resume the paradoxical wager of hermeneutics.[1] The hermeneutics that we have dared to call "projection" focuses on the addition of understanding to a dimension which avoids instrumentalism in that it takes note of our projected being more than it does of our projects. It is so in history, to which we belong much more than it belongs to us. In 1960, Gadamer saw that the most satisfactory way in which a being worked by history could add to its knowledge was through language. This effectiveness of language contributes to "what is the most obscure" (*gehört zum Aller-dunkelsten*), because the linguistic element remains "uncannily near" (*so unheimlich nahe*) for thought.[2] The *unheimlich* is, in the literal sense, what is foreign to us, and what, accordingly, gives us the shivers. But Gadamer's thought is precisely that this *unheimlich* element of language represents our "home". It is in fact in the uncanny nearness, or according to Fruchon's translation, just right, in the "disturbing proximity" of language that we live. Gadamer's hermeneutics, which remains one of "projection", cannot ignore this *Unheimlichkeit,* this disconcerting and immemorial nature of language, but it will never acquire a static mastery of it. How do we master what forever seizes us? In beginning a thought, which can remind us of Heidegger's words, we can at the very most hope "to approach the obscurity of language".[3] Nothing more, but also nothing less.

It is therefore not surprising that Gadamer was later dissatisfied when faced with the developments which he had devoted to language in the last part of his work. He confided to Carsten Dutt that the whole of his work of the previous thirty-five years had from then on been devoted to the deepening of our addition to language.[4] The reflexions of the third section are often of a rudimentary character, but we must above all see here that this is not a fault. In 1960, Gadamer himself admitted that he was only seeking to approach the maddening obscurity of language. This approach to the unapproachable keeps *under this heading* an exemplary character for a hermeneutics of projection that has no ambition other than to recall to knowledge what precedes all thought and makes it possible. In one sense, the more inarticulate and blurred an analysis of language is, the more faithful it is to its object. The last section of *Truth and Method* is a culmination to this chapter.

We must add that, in 1960, in speaking of the linguistic element of all understanding, Gadamer tackled what was largely a philosophical *terra incognita*. We can scarcely imagine what the situation was like in that time, so much has language imposed itself *since*, and in part thanks to hermeneutics, as the absolutely unavoidable, indeed the only, theme of philosophy. It was only in the 1960s that the empire of language imposed itself on reflection, through the undertow of currents so diverse as the Oxford ordinary language philosophy, grammatical structuralism, psycho-analysis (Lacan), deconstruction, hermeneutics, and the last works of Heidegger and Merleau-Ponty. At the end of the 1950s, almost nobody in Germany had read Wittgenstein. Analytic philosophy was imperceptible as such, or was identified with the positivism of the Vienna Circle. Husserl's phenomenology, in spite of its attachment to the theme of meaning, had not focused on language to any extent, nor for that matter had traditional philosophy (a judgement that has had to be modified since, but *because of* the recent inflation in language of contemporary philosophy). Existentialism, that of Sartre above all, which was a dominant force in the 1950s, was not interested in it either. By digging a little, we can unearth exceptions to this forgetfulness of language (Gadamer himself named the little-known works of Richard Hönigswald, Julius Stenzel and Johannes Lohmann), but they recommended them-selves as such only from our own perspective, instructed by the unexpected concealment, suddenly recognized, of language. The only truly notable exception, doubtless important for Gadamer, remains of course that of Heidegger. But we must not forget that his great book on language, *Unterwegs zur Sprache*, was published only in 1959, when the manuscript of *Wahrheit und Methode* was already at the printer. Certainly Gadamer knew, from having occasionally heard them, some of Heidegger's texts, also baffling, on language and poetry. They would certainly have inspired him, and encouraged him in his enterprise, but in a way that is difficult to determine. If several of Gadamer's directions call Heidegger to mind (the ontological direction, "the being which can be understood is language", etc.), it remains that he treats language within the framework of a *hermeneutic* philosophy, that very philosophy which Heidegger had abandoned, or pretended to have left behind, when he turned to the mysteries of language. What Gadamer allows us to see is that the Heideggerian direction was perhaps itself only a radicalization of the previous hermeneutics of the *Geworfenheit*, of "projection", language becoming in a way the "throwing forward" *par excellence* of all presence to being. Gadamer himself speaks of an ontological direction (*Wendung* and not *Kehre*), following the conducting thread of language, a direction that then corresponds, but without realizing it, to the "linguistic turn" of Anglo-Saxon and French philosophy.[5]

We are thus forced to recognize that Gadamer ventured into a still unexplored jungle when he proposed his hermeneutics of language. This is why certain of Gadamer's theses can seem *to us* to lack outline. In some ways, we may feel that, in their generality, they are pushing at open doors. Doubtless this is the case in the first great thesis, according to which language represents both the object and understanding's mode of accomplishment (*Vollzug*). This conception has become so prevalent, and almost too banal, that it is perhaps more urgent today to focus attention, in the name of hermeneutics (we will explain how below), on the *limits* of language. Gadamer was himself harnessed to this task in all his later works.[6]

If we wish to encircle the hermeneutic understanding of language, we must remember the way in which the theme of language was introduced into the general economy of *Truth and Method*, knowledge from the perspective of a dialectic of question and response elaborated within the framework of the hermeneutics of the human sciences. To understand a text or an event is to understand it as a reply to a question. It is the central nerve of hermeneutics, that of application, which finds its concretization in this dialectic: I cannot understand something except by also paying attention to the constellation of questions within which the text that I am interpreting is inscribed, a constellation which I must bring into words, in terms which I can follow. In this, all understanding incorporates an application: indeed, it is nothing other than an application or a translation of meaning.

The understanding–application thus takes the form of a "fusion" of horizons between the interpreter (or his language) and his object (which is also language). This fusion is also described as a dialogical process. This idea of dialogue becomes the true keystone of the third part of *Truth and Method*. Gadamer heavily insists on the similarity that exists between dialogue that takes place between two participants in a conversation, and the dialogue which an interpreter conducts with a text. At the beginning of the third part, Gadamer says that he is leaving the first sort to clarify the second.[7] But in fact, in the web of the book, coming to the wider framework of language is a part of the dialogical model of interpretation in the human sciences. The "dialogical" of question and response was first of all recovered for the human sciences: to interpret a text is first of all to explain yourself to it, to understand it as a reply to questions, but in such a way that it is always the interpreter who makes the text speak, by knowing how to ask his questions. As Gadamer stresses, this does not always mean that the interpreter's perspective is superimposed on the text. He insists on saying that, in fact, the *contrary* happens: the better an interpretation succeeds, the more it is effaced before the text is interpreted. In fact, "no text and no book speaks if it does not speak a language that reaches the other person".[8] Of course Gadamer had trouble in convincing the defenders of the *mens auctoris* that this did not imply any attenuation of the idea of objectivity in the order of interpretation. But we do not see that Gadamer has defended this dialogical conception of interpretation in a line of argument in which he attempted precisely to deal with the *rightness* of the interpretation. Too subjective, or modernizing, an interpretation is just that which super-imposes itself on the text and which is noticed, and disqualified, as such. What interpretation escapes from this broadside? By all evidence, the interpretation which we regard as right (or adequate). But why is it right? Because it makes the text itself speak. But how is such success possible? The text can only speak in the terms, the stresses, the accents, and the tonalities that the interpreter (and the act of reading) lends to it. The essential dialogue with the text operates on this ground of the interpretation's being put into language. We find a parallel in the function of translation: the more the genius of the translator goes unpercieved, the greater the accuracy of the translation.[9] In the same way, every interpretation that aims to give the meaning of a text keeps the lid on the very thing of the text. What is convincing in an interpetation is the well-foundedness of the thing, which makes it worthwhile. If this well-foundedness does not become apparent, the interpretation fails. By contrast, where the well-foundedness imposes itself, each time thanks to a subterranean effort in interpretation and translation, it does not make itself noticed as such. The most successful interpretation is that which effaces itself as an interpretation. The fusion is then total.

According to Gadamer, it is thus always under the (presumed) authority of a thing that the text is interpreted. In this sense, the interpretation is a dialogue and an *account* (*explication*) of the text. The German term *Verständigung* (accord, sometimes rendered as explanation in the translation of the *Complete Works*) well serves Gadamer's ends. To understand (*verstehen*) is primarily to agree (*sich verstehen mit*) with somebody about a thing, an understanding which has the mode of agreement (or of explanation). It is a case of understanding, not the viewpoint of others or their historical situation, but the well-foundedness of the thing itself. We give ourselves up to the detour of a psychological or historicizing interpretation only if the thing itself ceases to be evident. We can thus speak of a relative autonomy of dialogue with respect to its participants. If it is so, those who take part in a dialogue are not so much participants, as those in whom the dialogue participates.[10] The dialogue is thus partly event, a coming-into-being of the thing that escapes from the control of the participants.

To maintain that the linguistic element determines both the *object* and the hermeneutic operation (*Vollzug*) is only to recall that the thing to understand (which is always a meaning in which we can participate) must always be able to articulate itself in an interpretation, or in a meaning in which we fully participate. Gadamer's distinction between the object and the interpretation (already non-hermeneutic terms) appears a little artificial since it is finally about one and the same process: the object becomes such, that is to say the speaking object, only by favour of its transposition into a comprehensible language. Gadamer also explains this unity in speaking about the depths of understanding and interpretation, which the Romantics had already noted: to understand is to be able to articulate the understanding in an interpretation which is put into meaningful language. The term "interpretation" is again distinguished here from that of translation: to interpret a text is to translate it into a text which is intelligible for us. Every interpretation or translation must "reawaken" the meaning of a text in making it speak a meaning to which contemporary knowledge can be awoken.[11] The interpretation or translation that intends to give the meaning of a discourse also partly includes an overexposition of meaning (*Überhellung*), which remains in the service of the meaning of the text itself, always understood as a silently applied meaning.

We could quite rightly object that understanding and interpretation are not necessarily linguistic. This is the case of musical interpretation or of the "understanding" of a picture, which seems to call only for contemplation, or more precisely admiration. Before a musical or pictorial masterpiece, every word is doubtless excessive. Even if Gadamer is sensitive to this powerlessness before works of art[12] in *Truth and Method*, he is nevertheless anxious to speak of a possible linguistic understanding. We note in this respect that Gadamer speaks less of "language" (*Sprache*) than of the "linguistic element" (*Sprachlichkeit*).[13] By that, we understand the virtuality of language, the possibility for understanding of deploying itself in an interpretation that can be followed. Even the musical work and the picture intend to be "followed" if only in their wish to deconstruct all projects of intelligibility. We have seen above that Gadamer speaks in his aesthetics of the "response" that every work of art solicits: art as *Aussage*, a meaningful proposition, exacts a response which is of the order of dialogue. The question is language, in the sense in which a look or a gesture can also be a question or an invitation.

In *Truth and Method*, Gadamer brings up the case of the artist – sculptor or musician – who rejects an interpretation by word or by discourse as secondary and impertinent. But Gadamer thinks that if he can reject it, it is because "he will be unable to deny that his own understanding of a work, expressed in his reproductive interpretation, can itself be understood – i.e. interpreted and justified".[14] In other words, we cannot *refuse* a linguistic interpretation except in the name of another that is at least possible. A successful interpretation is an interpretation that convinces me and that I can follow. This convinced-being, this borne-along being (*Vollzug*) is in the sense which remains the hallmark of understanding, understood as participation in meaning. Is it then absolutely necessary to mention language? Gadamer maintains that it is, so much so that even in the context of these reflexions he evokes for the first time the universality of the linguistic element. Gadamer means by this that all reminders of the *limits* of language still participate in the universality of the linguistic element. What escapes from language is what cannot be said, because no saying can exhaust what wants to be capable of being said. The element of at least the possibility of wanting-to-say, even if it never succeeds, is of value against the actual but always limited possibilities of language. In this way, Gadamer maintains, "language always forestalls any objection to its jurisdiction".[15] But the universality here is always that of "wanting-to-say". The unsayable, the unnameable, everything that is outside language, from the time it is evoked or invoked, even if it has to remain voiceless, is at least capable of being said. Gadamer can maintain that in this sense, and in this sense alone, "the being which can be understood is language". What cannot become language is what cannot be understood, as putting into language is parallel to putting into understanding.

This does not deny, but on the contrary implies, that there are many things which we do not understand (perhaps there is nothing but that). Really, we do not understand a great deal. And perhaps that is after all why we speak. In language, we are "projected" into a network of intelligibility whose vessels are imperceptible to us. There is an inevitable tension in our experience of language. It is certainly the articulation of an intelligibility, but it is made possible only by a work of history which resorts to the order of the unsayable and of the dress rehearsal. The intelligibility which is that of hermeneutic thought thus remains aware of the inherent limits of all intelligibility. Gadamer's thesis is perhaps even clearer in its negative form: the being which cannot be understood is that which is not language. We understand only the being which we can articulate in language. And that is very little. Even what we succeed in stammering is never everything that we would have to be capable of saying. This wishing-to-say of the unsayable, which is in the last instance the unsayable of death or of evil, is perhaps at the heart of the hermeneutics of language. All rigorously hermeneutic understanding of language knows that it is attached to the back of a tiger[16] of incomprehension, untameable.

We might think that this reminder of the limits of language and of intelligibility does not completely conform to the more canonical presentations of Gadamer's hermeneutics, which in fact seem to insist on shelter, familiarity, pride, even the solidity that language has for us. It is true that hermeneutics often presents a conception of language that appears more docile, more reassuring, more "urban". But when they are well understood, the two versions are interlinked. Language presents itself and lives itself entirely in the mode of being-with-itself, of familiarity and bracing intelligibility. There is no doubt about it; we need such language and such urbanity. What would we be without the civilizing influence of language? Language is the most intimate, even the only, being-with-ourselves that we know.[17] But where does this being-with-ourselves come from, if not from a fundamental non-familiarity, from a being's resistance to language? Because finitude is total, it must also forget its dereliction. The refuge of language remains an asylum. Thus the universality of the linguistic dimension in fact flows from the limits of language in the perspective of a hermeneutics of finitude. Gadamer himself has spoken of the uncanny nearness (*so unheimlich nahe*) of language and he was able to write in "The Limits of Language" (1985) that "the *unsatisfying* search for the *mot juste* constitutes life proper, and the essence of language":

> knowledge lives in everybody who speaks when he looks for the *mot juste* – to know the word which can reach the other – but it always knows at the same time that it has not completely found it. The wanting-to-say, the intention, always goes above, or slantwise to, what can be truly encircled by a language or in words which go to rejoin the other.[18]

Why is it so? Because we are not gods, but mortals who never perfectly come to understand one another. "So, here is made manifest an intimate link between the dissatisfaction of the search [for the *mot juste*], of this *desire* (Lacan), and the fact that our own human existence flows in time and before death."[19] If the gods dispose of an absolute transparency, it is because they do not have language.

From Platonic forgetfulness of language
to its Augustinian recall

The supreme principle of philosophical hermeneutics such as I think of it (which is why it is a hermeneutic philosophy) is that we can never fully say what we want to say.[20]

Hermeneutics is part of the dialectic of question and answer in the human sciences so that it can open a way to a dialogical understanding of language. Thus it goes beyond a strictly propositional conception of language, which would limit it to the terms and the structures of proffered, audible and controllable language. If language can be understood only as the reply to a question, it is because a proclamation is never sufficient by itself. A pronouncement necessarily contains unstated presuppositions that it has neither the time, nor the patience, nor the capacity to spell out (or recall), but to which we must force ourselves to listen if we wish to understand what seeks to express itself. In this attention to the unspoken of every discourse, to the question which precedes it and which works in it, there properly resides the hermeneutic understanding of language. In an important article on the universality of the hermeneutic problem (1966), Gadamer explains its great principle when he writes that "The original hermeneutic phenomenon was that there could not be a pronouncement which could not be understood as the reply to a question."[21] By this, hermeneutics intends to oppose itself to an instrumental conception of language which wants to reduce it to the order of real and measurable pronouncements. For Gadamer, such pure pronouncements do not exist. Every pronouncement is motivated by and echoes a question. A logic of pronouncement in Western philosophy could be developed only by an effort of unexpected abstraction, because this logic abstracts from everything which is not explicitly stated in the pronouncement. Gadamer regards this abstraction of the logic of pronouncement as "one of the most fatal decisions of our Western culture".[22] This logic goes best with a calculating and methodical thought that intends to take hold of language, with the pronouncement being the only observable and somewhat tractable element of language. In seeking to approach the linguistic element of our understanding, hermeneutics guards itself against confining the linguistic element to propositional pronouncements alone. It is attentive to the unspoken from which all discourse flows. The element of linguisticity (*Sprachlichkeit*) naturally overflows the framework of what has been said, and everything which is said goes back resolutely to an inexhaustible order of questions, and of distress, so that an instrumental conception would bypass completely the baffling proximity of language for thought.

Thus it is not by chance that language has been forgotten in the Western philosophical tradition: its unseizable "inability to be prethought" threatens the sovereignty of thought. The question of the relationship of thought to language has thus always been supplanted by that of language to the world, and language is swallowed up into the rank of an instrument for the expression of thought. Nominalism, which tends to reduce words to the designation of individual beings to make them signs of an essentially logical or noetic thought, is only the most obvious expression of this. Through its latent nominalism, the whole of Western thought, according to Gadamer, would have succumbed to a forgetfulness of language. Plato and Hegel, who are usually Gadamer's allies, are no exceptions. In fact, Gadamer only knows one exception to the forgetfulness of language: Saint Augustine (which is all the more unexpected because Wittgenstein associated Augustine with an instrumentalist conception of language at the beginning of his *Philosophical Investigations*).

For Gadamer, the great godfather of conjuring with language was Plato. Whoever knows the whole of Gadamer's work will not be at all surprised by the intransigence of the debate with the Platonic conception of language in *Truth and Method*. The dialogical understanding of language that Gadamer intends to develop owes much, if not everything, to Plato and to his putting into perspective the order of pronouncements. The Plato to whom Gadamer is fundamentally the nearest is the one of the *Seventh Letter*, the one who spotted the limits of enunciation because it could always be turned from its original intention and from its primary dialogical horizon. By his dialogical understanding of language, Gadamer equally intended to stress the insufficiency of the discourse put forward, and the logic which held to the tractable order of pronouncements. On this point, Plato is Gadamer's natural ally. But in *Truth and Method*, Gadamer was preoccupied with the Platonic relativization of the order of language. Gadamer was interested less in the *Phaedrus* or in the *Seventh Letter* than in the *Cratylus*, where two contradictory theses on language faced each other. These theses treated the question of knowing whether the designation of words came from convention (*thesei*) or from a natural resemblance to things (*phusei*). What struck Gadamer was the common presupposition in these two theses, in knowing that in both cases the word was understood as a simple name or sign, as if things could be known in themselves before being signified by language. For Gadamer, Plato's clear intention was to show that we cannot attain the truth of things by words. By that, he sought to distance himself from the Sophists, who taught that we can be assured of domination over things by a mastery of words (or rhetoric). For Plato, true knowledge should, on the contrary, seek to liberate itself from the empire of words by being directed to things themselves, that is to say, to the Forms. In saying that, Plato did not necessarily wish to deny that true philosophical thought continued to be deployed in a language, but his essential point was that access to the truth is not given by words themselves, nor their mastery.[23]

It still remains that pure knowledge of the Forms owes nothing essential to language. The order of language is envisaged by Plato only as an exterior and dangerously equivocal aspect of thought.[24] According to Gadamer, Plato did not reflect on the fact that the operation of thought as dialogue (!) of the soul with itself already contained an essential link with language. That is certainly an issue in the *Seventh Letter*, but in 1960, Gadamer did not seem to pay any attention to the dialogical understanding of language that Plato wanted to defend there. He did not speak either of Plato's dialogical art, as he was to do in all his other writings. When he tackled the *Seventh Letter* in *Truth and Method*, it was only to stress that language remains subordinate to the seizure of the One, to the extent that, for Plato, language remains a superfluous moment in knowledge, ordered to the noetic clarity of pure Forms. Gadamer was thus led to a "result" of a singular severity: "Plato's discovery of the ideas conceals the true nature of language even more than the theories of the Sophists."[25] We cannot believe our eyes, the verdict is so harsh. Plato was more of a dissimulator than the Sophists, and Gadamer wrote it!

It is difficult not to see Heidegger's shadow in this whole chapter in *Truth and Method*. Plato appears there, by his logocentric or "Formo-centric" conception of language, as the great precursor of the *characteristica universalis* and of the metaphysics of domination. In reducing language to its instrumental function for thought, he prepared, in terms that are Gadamer's, the understanding of "being as absolutely available objectivity", *"das Sein als die absolut verfügbare Gegenständlichkeit"*.[26] If Gadamer gives so harsh a judgement of Plato, it is because he thinks that his conception of language as a simple exterior sign of thought has sealed the whole of Western thought on language, or rather, that it has prevented the West from embracing the true nature of language and its essential anteriority in relation to language. The title of the chapter in *Truth and Method* devoted to the Western forgetfulness of language speaks of a *Prägung*, of an imprint or a minting of the concept of language which would be maintained throughout the whole history of Western thought. According to Gadamer, the reduction of language to the instrumental order of signs, which always simply refer to Forms, a reduction which consecrated "knowledge being banished to the intellectual sphere", was an "epoch-making decision about thought concerning language".[27] In the aftermath of Platonism, language is used only for the ventilation of thoughts that can be handled without it:

Thought is so independent of the being of words – which thought takes as mere signs through which what is referred to, the idea, the thing, is brought into view – that the word is reduced to a wholly secondary relation to the thing. It is a mere instrument of communication, the bringing forth (*ekpherein*) and uttering (*logos prophorikos*) of what is meant in the medium of the voice.[28]

Western forgetfulness runs in parallel with the secondary (and often injurious) status that is given to it in the order of knowledge. The *logos* of knowledge does not come from the polished texture of language, but from a "logic" which makes the concatenation of ideas such as it is ordered in the intelligible clarity of pure understanding. In the best case, language contents itself with meekly reproducing the course of the logic of thought. In the worst case, it confuses it (in what is called a logical critique of language, by which analytic philosophy is inspired up to the present time). But does this conception of language do justice to its essential anteriority and to the effective exercise of thought itself?

We know that, for Gadamer, the West knows only one single exception to this forgetfulness: Saint Augustine. Gadamer thus devotes a crucial, but difficult, chapter to him. We commonly associate Augustine with an instrumental conception of language; with a certain accuracy, after all. His *De Magistro*, for example, is a dialogue on the *inconvenience* of language for thought, a theme strongly reminiscent of Plato. Besides, Gadamer is much less interested in Augustine's writings on language than in his reflections on the idea of the Trinity, of which the least that can be said is that it is not a matter of a natural, or particularly limpid, departure for a philosophy of language. Further, in *Truth and Method*, Gadamer almost never cites the texts of Augustine that have inspired him, contenting himself with a rapid, and vague enough, allusion to chapters 10–15 of Book XV of *De Trinitate*.[29] In fact, the author most frequently cited and used by Gadamer in this chapter is Thomas Aquinas!

What made Gadamer so enthusiastic about Augustine? First of all, and in a very general way, it was Christian (and not just Augustinian) thought on the Incarnation. Gadamer thinks that the Incarnation concerns thought that has nothing Greek about it, as it is not about embodiment in the Greek, and Platonic, sense of the term, where a spiritual being, a soul, inhabits a body which is fundamentally foreign to it. In fact, this Gnostic idea of embodiment gives well enough the Platonic and instrumental conception of language according to which the material sign reflects a strictly spiritual and by its essence independent thought of the accidental materiality of the sign. This is why the materiality of language, the linguistic exteriorization of thought, cannot seriously be taken into consideration in such thought about embodiment.[30] The mystery of the Incarnation means that we must think differently about the relationship between spirit and matter. The Incarnation of the Son does not represent a diminution for God. It remains the essential and saving manifestation for us. For Christian thought, the Incarnation does not mean a loss, as it is the true and only revelation of the divine. In this context, Gadamer is of course not interested in the immediately theological framework of Christian reflection. What captivates him is the rehabilitation of the Incarnation as such, and of the *materiality* of meaning for a philosophical understanding of language. Whilst depending on terminology which is still Greek, Christian thought about the Incarnation achieves a dimension that is still closed to Greek thought, and that allows us for the first time to think of language in its essentially historical and consequential character. Gadamer thinks that Christian thought has also succeeded in disengaging events from the language of the spiritual idealty of thought, thus leading to the discovery by philosophical thought of language as an autonomous theme.[31]

Augustine was also inspired by the model of language in approaching the mystery of the Incarnation. Gadamer did the opposite: he was inspired by the Christian model of the Incarnation to think again about the consequential character of language. Augustine first of all began from the Stoic distinction between the external *logos* and the internal *logos* (*logos prophorikos* and *endiathetos*). With the Stoics, the internal *logos* meant above all the work of reflexion that *precedes* the linguistic exteriorization of thought, a reflexive capacity which characterizes humankind as such. In their reflections on language, the Stoics stressed above all the internal *logos*, the uttered word always being thought of as a secondary process to the simple exteriorization of mental language. The Augustinian understanding of language and of the Incarnation insists more on the singularity of the external *logos*. For Christian thought, in effect, it cannot be a matter of a secondary and inessential manifestation. The materiality of incarnate meaning thus becomes significant for itself. This is what first fascinated Gadamer.

Christian thought knew two great manifestations of this exteriorization of the word: creation, which was produced by virtue of the word of God, and the act of salvation, which is represented by the birth of the Son. Gadamer is interested only in the linguistic consequences of this re-evaluation, indeed of this totally new thought about the Incarnation, because it is not Platonic. The first consequence concerns the essential *identity* of the internal and external words in the process of incarnation. For the Gadamerian hermeneutics of language, this identity means that the pure act of thought cannot be distinguished from its exteriorization and its linguistic manifestation. The materiality of language stops appearing from then on as an imperfect manifestation of thought, to become its only true place of actualization. In this sense, Augustine (or more generally, Christian thought about the Incarnation) represents for Gadamer a passionate exception to the Western forgetfulness of language. For us, as for the Incarnation of God, the exteriorization of the word is not a secondary act, posterior to the achievement of knowledge, but on the contrary blends with the formation of thought itself.[32] The identity that interests Gadamer here is thus that of thought and of the internal word, which can never be deployed except in language:

> This is more than a mere metaphor, for the human relationship between thought and speech corresponds, despite its imperfections, to the divine relationship of the Trinity. The inner mental word is just as consubstantial with thought as is God the Son with God the Father.[33]

The second consequence treats the consequential and processive character of the Incarnation. The Incarnation does not allow itself to be reduced to an event that would be a strictly spiritual affair. In hermeneutic terms, language's becoming flesh is an intrinsic part of meaning, of the meaning which can be understood, shared and communicated. Finished beings such as ourselves participate in the event of meaning only through the multiform materiality of its manifestations and its images, a diffusion that does not come from the order of logical sequence. Thought does not exist except in this carnal, incarnate immersion. In Gadamer's terms, language is not formed by a reflexive mental act.[34] This reflexive act, if we can possibly distinguish it as such, would have to be produced outside language, in the bosom of pure thought. But it is the realm of pure thought that the Augustinian conception has made problematic in recalling that meaning for us is always an incarnate meaning. For Gadamer, thought is no longer allowed to think outside language. The materiality of language is the deal, the place, indeed the "placing" in which all thought can and must be deployed.

The last and most important consequence is that this necessary materiality of language does not mean that thought is reduced to the order of uttered enunciations. As in Christian thought about the Incarnation, the external manifestation of the *logos* continues to go back to an "internal word", a "thought" which spoken language never exhausts, but which will never be accessible in a definitive and objective way. Gadamer wonders what this internal word consists of. All that we can say is that it represents "the thing thought to the very end", but this terminal thought is for us only a limiting concept. If we wish to seize the finitude which is always that of thought expressed in words, it is not absolutely indispensable. Words are always only a very imperfect, and dangerous, manifestation of the thought that seeks to express itself. The terms which we employ always have something contingent and partial; they are words that come to us and that never succeed in embracing everything which we would like to be able to say, nor everything which it is necessary to say, to avoid misunderstanding. The Platonic and Gnostic mistake was to think that the perfection of thought is to be found in a purely noetic elsewhere, in a *logos endiathetos* that would only be pure thought and which would have nothing to do with the sinister thickness of language. In other words, we must preserve the difference (indeed, the *différance*) of the internal word, but keep well in view that it is never realized or reached once and for all. The internal word continues to represent, to "incarnate", what we seek to understand in thought that is risked in words, but its articulation necessarily remains devoted to linguistic expression, imperfect and stammering. It remains that its aim is indispensable to the understanding of the external word. We can understand what is said only in seeking to hear what is not said, that is to say the question or the constellation of questions to which what is uttered resorts. But the unsaid is still part of the space of language, of linguisiticity (of the *Sprachlichkeit*) to the extent to which we seek to understand it, even if it goes back to what can never completely be said. Nothing can ever be as it should be. What Augustine verifies is that the universality of the linguistic condition runs parallel to the limits of language.

If we were previously allowed to discover the materiality of language from the analogy between the divine process of incarnation and the necessarily linguistic expression of our thought, this time it is the *difference* between the Word of God and the human word which is illuminating for hermeneutics. The *logos* incarnate corresponds to the divine essence. It incarnates exactly its full and integral manifestation. *This* unity of essence (*homoousia*) between the exteriorization of the *logos* and the internal word does not correspond to our experience of language. Unlike the Word of God, no words can be the perfect expression of our minds.[35] Such imperfection does not come from language as such, as Platonism thought, but from the finitude of thought itself. The human mind is not pure presence itself, pure *noesis noesos*. On the contrary, its thought progresses following the rhythm of the words that give it body. Augustinian thought about the Incarnation invites us to consider this debt of thought to the polished and constantly renewed deal of language.

In his Augustinian reflections on language, Gadamer thus stresses two aspects which are not contradictory but complementary: there is, on the one hand, the possible identity of essence between thought, because there can be no thought capable of being thought without the element of language. But, on the other hand, we cannot say of expressly uttered language (of the *logos prophorikos*) that it is the perfect expression of thought, that is to say, of what we want to say, or of what we must say, to be understood adequately. I think that Gadamer perhaps insisted more on the first point in *Truth and Method*, whereas in his last works, it is the irreducibility of the internal word, of what intends to be said, to the uttered discourse which seems to be of more importance. If, in *Truth and Method,* he maintains that the linguistic element of language continues to integrate in its bosom all the objections which we could raise against its universality, he freely recognizes in his more recent works that "the supreme principle of philosophical hermeneutics . . . is that we can never fully say what we intend to say".[36] Doubtless we must not speak of an evolution in Gadamer's thought, but of a difference in accent, because these two aspects go together. But it was Augustine who allows us to think of this essential solidarity.

The conceptualization and the universality of rhetoric

Gadamer thus owes an enormous amount to this Augustinian insight. It obliges us to think of human finitude from its essential relation to language: thought is essentially put into language, even if the effective utterance of language cannot exhaust what we want to say. This thought of finitude leads Gadamer to question the logical prejudices that have dominated our conception of language since Plato. Hermeneutics thus pays more attention to materiality and what can be called the unvarying incarnation of meaning. Gadamer's thought is directed towards an understanding of rhetoric. We must however rid ourselves of a pejorative conception of rhetoric, brought about precisely by too logical an understanding of language and of rationality. The only rationality that is accessible to us is that which can be articulated in language. This rhetorical rationality is rooted in an already constituted, and practised, meaning, which is addressed to individuals who are not pure beings of reason. That does not mean that all rationality can be reduced to simple effects of meaning. A logical prejudice alone allows us to enter such a skimpy conception of rhetoric. We should fight against this logical reduction of meaning in the name of a rationality which is always our own. The rhetorical meaning is always one which must be debated and which we must try to defend by argument and by reason. Even the idea of argumentation – often asserted today by thoughts hostile to rhetoric and hermeneutics – presupposes that it does not stand up by itself and that we must make it the object of an eloquent defence, susceptible of attracting adherence and convincing souls. We do not engage in argument except about what does not stand up by itself, or what cannot be the object of a mathematical demonstration. In mathematics, there are no arguments: instead, there are proofs. In all other areas of our knowledge and practices, we must engage in argument because truth and justice do not have this evidence. This meaning which must be defended every time does not allow itself to be thought without rhetoric, that is to say without language, language which is incarnated each time and which can thus communicate with others.

Gadamer approached this rhetorical conception of language and of rationality when he dealt with the problem of conceptualization (*Begriffs-bildung*) in *Truth and Method*. He sought to oppose the phantom of a total self-sufficiency of thought in the order of the formation of concepts. The true place of thought is never that of pure conceptual explanation. To this logical construction of thought, Gadamer opposed the idea that the true process of thought is realized in an explanation in words (*Explikation im Wort*).[37] Gadamer is guided here by the Augustinian theme of the Incarnation. Thought succumbs to a logical illusion when it thinks that its work arises from a strictly conceptual process. Thought is first and foremost the seeking of words to say what is intended to be said and heard, everything that must be taken into account when we try to embrace something. Such a work of conceptual formation (*Bildung*) is achieved by the act of speech when it passes from one word or one image to another to deploy its thoughts about something. In this orientation on the thing, the true effort of the speech that thinks or the thought that speaks arises less from the act of subsuming than from the seizing of resemblances. This search by language corresponds to what Gadamer calls the essential metaphoricity of language and thought:

> The genius of verbal consciousness consists in being able to express these similarities. This is its fundamental metaphorical nature, and it is important to see that to regard the metaphorical use of a word as not its real sense is the prejudice of a theory of logic that is alien to language.[38]

Each word is never anything but figurative, an incarnation of meaning in a formula which can be understood, shared and always deepened: "at the beginning of generic logic stands the advance work of language itself".[39]

Gadamer holds that this performance of language, which we can call "rhetorical", is valuable, and not the ideal of logical demonstration which is so universally imposed in the wake of Aristotelian logic (even if, as Gadamer and many others have stated, Aristotle himself followed this logic much less than the genius of language in his own scientific enquiries).

> The consequence of accepting the ideal of logical proof as a yardstick, however, is that the Aristotelian critique has robbed the logical achievement of language of its scientific legitimacy. That achievement is recognised only from the point of view of rhetoric and is understood there as the artistic device of metaphor ... What originally constituted the basis of the life of language and its logical productivity, the spontaneous and inventive seeking out of similarities by means of which it is possible to order things, is now marginalized and instrumentalized into a rhetorical figure called metaphor.[40]

For thought that aspires to be pure logic, or forgets its historical basis, metaphor and rhetoric can appear only as deficient modes of knowledge: metaphor is the figure of style of a thought that does not yet have clarity of concept, and rhetoric is the artifice to which we have recourse when a restraining proof is not available.

In these two reductions, Gadamer denounces the same Platonizing prejudice, that is to say the forgetfulness of language as the crucible of all proofs, of all clarity, and of rationality. In *Truth and Method*, Gadamer is still content with protesting against the reduction of metaphor to the order of rhetoric and against too instrumental a conception of rhetoric. But after 1960, Gadamer developed a more ambitious conception of rhetoric. He even ended by associating the universality of hermeneutics with that of rhetoric.[41] This universal conception of rhetoric was doubtless presupposed in the impetus of thought in 1960, when rhetorical tradition made valuable incursions, but its real deployment became perceptible only in his later articles, notably in "Classical and Philosophical Hermeneutics" (1968), "Rhetoric, Hermeneutics and the Critique of Ideologies" (1971), "Hermeneutics and Rhetoric" (1976) and numerous recent interviews. Gadamer appealed to rhetoric because it was a case of a tradition of thought that has also defended the legitimacy of a human rationality inspired by the real life of language without following the exclusive model of logical demonstration.

> How can theoretical reflexion in understanding not be inspired by rhetoric, which has forever been the only thing to become the advocate of a pretension to truth which defends the legitimacy of verisimilitude, of the *eikos* [*verisimile*], and of what convinces

common reason against the the pretensions of science to certainty and demonstration? To convince and be convinced of something, without possessing proof, represents the goal and the measure as much of the art of understanding and interpretation as of the art of eloquence and of conviction. And this vast field of luminous and commonly-recognised convictions has not been shrunk little by little by the progress of science, which is capable of being extensive, but this field still spreads to each new knowledge sought, to claim it and adapt it. The ubiquity of rhetoric is limitless.[42]

We can understand that this rhetorical inspiration provoked Habermas's critique of ideologies. Besides, rhetoric has played a determining role in the debate which set up Habermas and hermeneutics in opposition, as is witnessed by the title of Gadamer's reply, "Rhetoric, Hermeneutics and the Critique of Ideologies", which of course also alluded to the pompous rhetoric of social emancipation then deployed by Habermas. At bottom, Habermas maintained that the rhetorical conviction produced by understanding or by dialogue could rest on a "pseudo-communication",[43] that is to say, on fallacious arguments or those in which rationality is strictly strategic. Against a conviction that is again only rhetorical, Habermas was concerned to oppose the understanding that is tied "to the principle of rational discourse according to which the truth will be guaranteed *only* by a consensus which would be established in idealised conditions of an unlimited communication, protected from all domination, and could be permanently upheld".[44] True understanding would be stripped of rhetoric, but it could be achieved only in such an ideal situation: "Truth is the singular constraint which forces us to a universal recognition without constraint; such recognition is tied to an ideal situation for words, that is to say, to a form of life allowing a universal incomprehension without constraint."[45] But this is another way of saying that this non-rhetorical truth will *never* be achieved, which does not get us very far.

Habermas can depreciate rhetoric only in the name of an ideal rationality, which is never that of the human world. Do we have to wait for the Last Judgement to know the truth? In the meantime, perhaps Habermas's devaluing of rhetoric should be put into question, in the name of a more reasonable conception of rationality. This was the meaning of Gadamer's reply:

If rhetoric is also addressed to assumptions, as has always been clear, it does not for all that mean to say that it comes out of the domain of the reasonable (*Vernunftigen*). Vico was right to say that what came out of it was autonomous value, which is that of the *copia*, of the richness of viewpoints. I find it to be frighteningly unreal that one attributes to rhetoric, as does Habermas, a constricting character which we must overtake, to the profit of unconstrained rational dialogue. We thus underestimate not only the danger of an eloquent manipulation and the tutelage of reason, but also the opportunities for the accord due to eloquence, on which rests social life. All social practice – and *a fortiori* that which intends to be revolutionary – is inconceivable without the function of rhetoric ... To see only a simple technique or an instrument of social manipulation in rhetoric is to give in to a skimpy meaning of it. Really, it is an essential overturning of all reasonable behaviour.[46]

A set logical purpose in favour of demonstrative proof leads us to associate rhetoric with a sordid manipulation of minds that cheapens rational arguments. Every rational argument, to the extent of being an *argument* intended to be convincing, is unthinkable without rhetoric. An argument presumed rational must also convince us that it is rational, that is to say that reasons work in its favour. If Habermas's critique has a foundation of truth, it is because it is right to recall that there is a heuristic distinction to be made between a fallacious conviction, possibly obtained by constraint, and one which rests on "good" argument. But this distinction is still part of rhetoric, adequately understood. What is a good argument, in fact, if not one susceptible of convincing a vigilant awareness, which has been sufficiently instructed by rhetoric to be wary of obvious arguments that do not take account of the relevant aspects of the thing to be understood? It is then up to a more sustained or substantial argument to defend this relevance. But to speak of relevance and substance is to recognize the universality of rhetoric without which human rationality is nothing but a dream.

The universality of rhetoric thus results in a hermeneutics of vigilance. We cannot be content with sighing, alongside ambient postmodernism, that if everything is only rhetorical, reason itself is only a dream. Because certain arguments are more credible, more consistent, more solid than others, the idea of a "communicative" reason must be preserved and practised. We deliberately speak here of "communicative" reason. In recent translations, notably of Habermas, the preference has been to speak of a "communicational"[47] rationality. The term is not only very heavy; it is also deliberately coined. We forget above all that the term *kommunikativ*, which we intend to translate, is a foreign word in German, as it has itself been borrowed from the Romance languages: it is the exact German transliteration of the term "communicatif". Why be so stubborn as to make it unrecognizable in repatriating it to its original language?

Hermeneutic rationality is communicative in the precise sense in which it lives in the communication and the convictions which are shared by those who understand, and who understand themselves. The reason of arguments is credible because it proceeds from conviction. But this rationality is not that of the Last Judgement, but what can convince us *hic et nunc* and in the bosom of which we always debate about reasons that speak (!) in favour of pretensions to validity. No other rationality is given to us. To recognize with the oracle at Delphi that we are not gods is to recognize the limiting character of that incarnation, each time rhetorical, of rationality and of meaning. In default of an absolute foundation (the only one which would be non-rhetorical), "we are constrained to turn to each other to lend ourselves certainty without authority, without any strength other than that conferred by the accord of the speakers".[48] And nothing prevents critical reason itself from succumbing to sophist arguments or "common places". But the possibility that sophistry infiltrates even where it is not suspected cannot be set aside by a hermeneutics of facticity. Whence its singular and insurpassable vigilance.

Gadamer has conscientiously applied this vigilance to what he calls the history of concepts, the *Begriffsgeschichte*. A hermeneutics that takes over the debt of all conceptualization towards the rhetorical work of language must recognize that no philosophical concept drops straight from the skies of pure understanding. Before they were scholastic constructions, notions first sprang from the life of a language. The basic idea of *Begriffsgeschichte* is that the relevance of a language cannot be detached from the urgency that gave it birth in the life of a language, and in the contexts of discussion where it has been employed since. In so far as it is an exercise in vigilance and probity, the memory of the history of concepts makes us rediscover, in order to understand and to share them, the original experiences that presided at their introduction and in the use of concepts which have become so prevalent that they have become the instruments of calculating thought. Gadamer developed this conception of *Begriffsgeschichte*, which is rather reminiscent of the Heideggerian destruction, only after *Truth and Method*, in his important essay programme of 1970, "The History of Concepts as Philosophy".[49] But he also contributed to its institutionalization by participating in the setting up of an encyclopaedia (*Historisches Wörterbuch der Philosophie*, edited by Joachim Ritter since 1970) and a review (*Archiv für Begriffsgeschichte*) specifically devoted to the history of concepts. Through the history of concepts, the knowledge of the work of history is concretized in vigilance over the work of language.

Conclusion

The truth of the word

> Tis but thy name that is my enemy; – Thou art thyself, though, not
>   a Montague
> What's Montague? It is nor hand nor foot,
> Nor arm, nor face, nor any other part
> Belonging to a man. O, be some other name!
> What's in a name? That which we call a rose
> By any other name would smell as sweet.
>
> Shakespeare, Romeo and Juliet

In the hope of approaching its uncanny nearness, Gadamer first spoke of an anteriority of language to thought. To think is to try to explain yourself in words. We are awoken by language to thought, but still earlier, to the presence of things. Gadamer eventually speaks of a contemporaneity of language to thought, rather than of an anteriority. The anteriority of language is not reduced to a vision or a schematization of reality by the mind, since the world is present through language, and we are present to the world. The past anterior of the language is really a present indicative.

Guillaume de Humboldt was right in saying that language represents a vision of the world. But for Gadamer, that is not enough: it is *the world itself* which is language speaking for us, to the extent that we cannot distinguish the world itself, the linguistic sense from an "*en soi*" which would be more world than what is articulated in words. In seeing the world's setting in language as a mental capacity (*Geistekraft*) and a process of formalization, Humboldt remained the prisoner of a subjectivist metaphysics on the powers of understanding.[1] Gadamer was opposed to this conception of language, which was still too formalist, because he felt that it was a new instrumental view of thought *vis-à-vis* language: in modelling the diversity of experience on different linguistic forms, each language reveals a different "take" on reality (a conception of language as a scheme of thought, or as a "symbolic theme", which is also that of Cassirer). In Gadamer's eyes, this idea of language as a "take" or a "vision" of the world does not do justice to the full *presence* of the world in language:

> Nevertheless this concept of language constitutes an abstraction that has to be reversed for our purpose. *Verbal form and traditionary content cannot be separated in the hermeneutic experience.* If every language is a view of the world, it is so not primarily because it is a particular type of language (in the way that linguists view language) but because of what is said or handed down in this language.[2]

For Gadamer, language is not a "take" on reality, nor its putting into linguistic form; it is the world which is most world. It can perhaps be objected that it is a question only of the human world, but Gadamer's reply is that the world is never anything but human. Following Heidegger, he insists that people alone are distinguished by their capacity to inhabit a world. This primordial inhabitation is in all aspects language.

Gadamer also tried to approach this revelatory power of language by speaking of the "truth of the word" (*Wort*[3]). He makes a furtive allusion to it in *Truth and Method*, where the expression is encircled by speech marks, as if Gadamer had astounded himself by the boldness of his own formula. But there are always these most risky expressions, those of which we are the least sure, which render best what thought seeks. After the last edition of the work, in 1986, he nevertheless came back to the charge, with the allusion being followed by a new note where he referred to a forthcoming article, "Von der Wahrheit des Wortes".[4] Gadamer allowed this article to mature for a long time. He presented the theme for the first time in May 1971, and from 1972, in the Postface to the third edition of *Truth and Method*, he announced an imminent publication on it.[5] The text appeared only in 1993 in volume 8 of his *Works*, devoted to aesthetics and poetry. When in 1997 I edited his *Lesebuch*, which reassembled some of his most important articles, Gadamer strongly advised me to retain this text, ancient and recent at the same time.

The *Wort* of which Gadamer speaks is not the "word" understood as a linguistic entity (the plural form of this in German is *Wörter*), but the word which seizes us, which makes sense, which speaks (the plural in German is *Wörte*). This meaning of *Wort*, which is a faint echo of the Greek *logos*, is often rendered in French by "parole" [or in English by "word" – trans.].

The best way of rendering the meaning is to talk, with Gadamer, of a *truth* of the word, of a word that is revelatory of being, in the "subjective" sense of the genitive, because the being, before all reflexive awareness, reveals itself. Gadamer's essential intuition is that the truth of the word precedes all instrumentalism of awareness *vis-à-vis* language. In his 1993 article, Gadamer above all developed this power of the "truth" of the word by declaring it poetic, but it is intended to be applied to every linguistic manifestation, which is never the manifestation of an *"en-soi"* put into language, but the manifestation of the world itself (still in the subjective sense of the genitive). Gadamer writes: "What language is as language and what we seek (to think of) as the truth of the word is not seizable if we leave the self-declared forms of communication in language. On the contrary, these forms of communication cannot be seized in their possibilities except in the poetic way of speaking."[6] What is revelatory of poetic speech is the world itself, a world which is present to itself *as* world by the "there" that carries our presence into the world. In relaying these reflections on the work of art, which has no being except in its presenta- tion (*Darstellung*), Gadamer says that the world has no being for us except in the "there" of language. He speaks here of a "valency of being of the word", of the *"Seinsvalenz des Wortes"*.[7] Poetic discourse lives on this presence of being in the word, but it also recalls us to the "there" itself, which is our awakening to being, and to the marvel of this awakening: "The universal 'there' of being in the word is the marvel of language, and the highest possibility of speech consists in capturing this proximity to being, to reassemble the being which disappears and escapes. It is a case of proximity, of presence, not of this or that, but of the possibility of everything."[8] The truth of the word holds to this universal "'there' of being in the word". It is the upholder, the safeguard, of proximity, *"das Halten der Nähe."*[9]

To Shakespeare's famous question "What's in a name?", Gadamer would be tempted to reply, everything! The word preserves the "there" of the word, which condenses its essence. And Shakespeare would probably be in agreement. Is it by chance that Juliet herself evokes the example of the rose when she seeks precisely to speak of her forbidden love for Romeo? The name of the rose is never only a name – it speaks of beauty, of love (right up to the borders of kitsch, which is that of the rose and of the power of its name) – and its perfume would not be so sweet if it were called otherwise. The unfolding of Shakespeare's play also confirms this "truth of the word". What prevents Juliet from marrying Romeo is precisely his name, Montague. It is all very well to say that Montague is only a name and it is not real. But the curse of the name ends by causing their deaths. The word is the truth of the being.

But what is dwelt on in the "there" of language is not only the presence of the thing: it is always also its absence, the being which escapes and disappears. The "there" is woven from presence and absence, like all awakening. To be awoken to being, to a "there", is at the same time to be closed to other possibilities. This conception of the *Dasein* was already Heidegger's. Gadamer always saw in this thought of "there", in the game of light and of recovery, the directing idea of Heidegger's hermeneutics of facticity, his recall of the immemorial character of all presence to being.[10] The marvel of marvels is not that *something* is there, but that there is a "there", that the "there" is revealed to human beings whilst remaining hidden.[11] The hermeneutics of language is the thought of the "there" where the being is revealed and escapes at the same time.

The speculative truth of language

Such a thought thus does not reduce the "there" of language to that of expressed pronouncements. Gadamer insists that the concept of pronouncement "is in the most extreme opposition to the essence of the hermeneutic experience and to the linguistic character of human experience in general".[12] No pronouncement can exhaust what is seeking to be said. The "universal 'there' of the being in the word" is not that of language effectively spoken, codified, registered, fixed, but that which is aware of the limits of all pronouncements to say what can be said. Gadamer is thus opposed to the logic of the pronouncement or of the proposition (*Aussage*). Gadamer finds the caricature of the *Aussage* in the deposition or the declaration (German again speaks here of *Aussage*) made at the time of an interrogatory examination. We must reply to questions, but without knowing why they are asked. The declarations made there have the talent of reappearing in incriminating contexts very different from those in which they were proffered. Their repetitions are also a good example of the violence which is done to language when it is reduced to the sphere of pronouncements which have been uttered.

Every discourse, as we have found with Augustine, goes back to an unsaid to which we must be able to listen if we want to understand what is said. Augustine speaks here of the internal word. If the internal word of a human thought is explained only in thought, the external word still never exhausts what wants to be said, the wishing-to-be-shouted of the internal word. This return of the said to the unsaid, of the finite order of the discourse to the infinity of wishing-to-say, corresponds to what Gadamer calls in *Truth and Method* the *speculative* achievement of language.

"*Speculative*" according to Gadamer comes from *speculum*, "mirror", and evokes that "truth of the word" that is able to allow the resonance of a meaning that goes beyond what is said. To say everything remains in the order of the infinity of wishing-to-say, of everything which has to be said to allow a discourse to be heard. The successful discourse is that which succeeds in making itself heard in this way, speculatively. We must cite in this respect rather a long passage from *Truth and Method*, because one pronouncement alone does not succeed in giving this speculative truth of the word, recognized from 1960 onwards:

> Language itself has something speculative about it in a quite different sense – not only in the sense Hegel intends, as an instinct-ive pre-figuring of logical reflection – but, rather, as the realization of meaning, as the event of speech, of mediation, of coming to an understanding. Such a realisation is speculative in that the finite possibilities of the word are oriented toward the sense intended as toward the infinite. A person who has something to say seeks and finds the words to make himself intelligible to the other person. This does not mean that he makes "statements". Anyone who has experienced an interrogation – even if only as a witness – knows what it is to make a statement and how little it is a statement of what one means. In a statement the horizon of meaning of what is to be said is concealed by methodological exactness; what remains is the "pure" sense of the statements. That is what goes on record. But meaning thus reduced to what is stated is always distorted meaning. To say what one means, on the other hand – to make oneself understood – means to hold what is said together with an infinity of what is not said in one unified meaning and to ensure that it is understood in this way.[13]

The privilege of the pronouncement or of the proposition in Western logic is that of its availability. Its tangibility and its ability to be mastered are all that language offers. Certainly, logic also admits that language proceeds from presuppositions which are never stated in the pronounce-ment itself. This is why it attempts to derive truth from the pro-nouncement of other, more universal, propositions. Hermeneutics seeks to think otherwise of the truth of the word, the "there" of language. We must seek to hear, in the finite terms of language, the infinity of wishing-to-be-said, because what we must hear is never only the logico-semantics of the discourse uttered, but language which is looking for itself. In another notable anticipation of the thought of the "truth of the word", *Truth and Method* speaks of the "dialectic of the word", that "which assigns to every word an internal dimension of multiplication": "every word, in so far as it is an event of the moment, also gives presence to the unsaid to which it is related, in replying and in making a sign . . . every human speech is finite, in the sense that it carries in itself an infinity of meaning to be developed and interpreted".[14]

If this is so, language ceases to represent captivity for the human mind. The hermeneutic thesis about the linguistic condition of all understanding reminds us that we dispose of a certain freedom in relation to language, a freedom which is not instrumental. We know that everything can be said otherwise, and often better, if we want to come to the meaning which stammers in pronouncements. The hermeneutic understanding of language is to take at its word the word which seeks to be said. We must always have recourse to other words to understand the having-to-say of the word. Habermas well rendered Gadamer's thought when he spoke here of the essential "porousness" of human language, to describe its capacity to open itself to new horizons and to put into question the limits of its own pronouncements.[15] All that has been said can be explained in a different way, in the name of the sayable of which the first pronouncement is only the first expression. To possess a language is in a way to be able to rise above it, to enlarge our horizons whilst remaining in the horizon of possible sayings. This freedom allows us to question ourselves once again, and to escape from conditions that are too particularizing. Human language is thus characterized by a perpetual self-transcendence: it always goes beyond itself by the very fact that it is language. What cannot be transcended is the horizon of understanding itself, and of the possibility of turning it into language. But it is always possible to understand oneself in another way, and to raise oneself above established understanding. It is the hermeneutic promise of universality.

The universal aspect of hermeneutics: the universality of aspect or of finitude

Despite appearances, the theme of hermeneutic universality has a modest enough meaning in *Truth and Method*. In fact, it is only a matter of the universality of an *aspect*, that is to say – if we can risk saying it – of the addition (better, of the "there") of the understanding. The understanding carries the meaning intended to the tradition which it interprets and renews, to the foreign discourse which it translates, in a word, to the language which it speaks, which is as much that of things as that of thought. We are always "there" where things, thoughts, moods, experiences, happen, in a "there" that resists objectivation, because we must be "there" to understand. The universal aspect of hermeneutics holds to what can be called the universality of the aspect: everything presents itself to us under an aspect, because it concerns us and we participate in its manifestation. The aspect of a thing is what is called in Greek its *eidos*. So, according to Gadamer, Plato was inspired by language when he wanted to understand the true essence of things. To turn to the Forms, which is the subject of the *Phaedo*, means for hermeneutics that it is in the *logoi*, in language, that the true being of things is revealed to us. We must only free this turning towards the *logoi* from the instrumental and noetic conception of knowledge which the *Cratylus* imposes on it.

In stressing the universality of the hermeneutic aspect, Gadamer's fundamental idea is to mark the limits of objectivizing thought, which seeks to gain a hold on the being, for the purpose of domination. So that there is no mistake, this objectivation is indispensable in science. But science has acquired an authority and a monopoly so uncontested in our civilization that we have come to think that all knowledge, all relationship to being, resorts to objectivation. Gadamer judges to be unilateral not science as such, or even the method, but this evolution of Western civilization. It makes us forget that the reign of the objectivable is immensely restrained in the field of our experience. But the limits of objectivizing knowledge are not those of hermeneutic vigilance. The fields of art, of history, of the human sciences, of ethical knowledge, of philosophy and, in the last instance, of language itself intend to show that the immersion of the interpreter in the sense that concerns him is not prejudicial to the rightness, the adequacy of understanding, but is its essential condition. To close your eyes to this "hermeneutic aspect" of meaning is to succumb to the fetishism of modern science and to the sham of objectivity. It is to lack the essential "there" of understanding and to reject the vigilance which is necessarily incumbent on the being located in time.

Gadamer has successfully made this hermeneutic aspect emerge for the human sciences. When he speaks of a "universalization" of hermeneutics, Gadamer does so to indicate that we have gone beyond the problematic of the human sciences, towards a more universal theme which under this title concerns philosophy.[16] In very general terms, this theme treats of the universality of understanding and of language for human experience. This thesis of the universality of hermeneutics had been introduced at the very beginning of the third section of *Truth and Method*. It concerns the linguistic character of the object (*Gegenstand*) and of the hermeneutic achievement. But we have seen that the essential hermeneutic achievement is, in fact, the search for language, for a "to-say" which always exceeds the actualized possibilities of saying. It is this excess of having-to-say over saying that is at the heart of achievement and the hermeneutic object. At its roots, this thought is one of finitude, of the finitude of language, of meaning and of understanding.

The universal aspect of hermeneutics is thus that of finitude. Banal, do we say? Perhaps, but it could be that the greatest truths of philosophy (there are few of them) are thus very banal. But this appeal to finitude is important if we wish to counter the propensity of understanding to let itself be seduced by the sham of infinity that makes it forget its finitude. The objectivation of modern science is one of the forms of this forgetfulness of finitude. The knowledge of objectivation specifically intends to obliterate the "there" of all understanding and all awakening to being in the name of a dominating and certain knowledge, which is certain because it is dominating. It would be foolish to want to object to this model of knowing, where it is legitimate. It is however necessary to contest its universalization when it distorts ways of knowing and experience where the finitude of the "there" is constitutive of the meaning to be understood, and of the vigilance that its penetration demands. With Gadamer, this is the meaning of the appeal to finitude.

Hermeneutics as metaphysics of finitude

The last pages of *Truth and Method* announce this universal thought of finitude, but in such dizzying developments that they have disconcerted many. Gadamer in effect maintains that hermeneutics, freed at last from the yoke of the human sciences, leads us to the horizon of the questions of classical metaphysics ("*führt uns in die Problemdimension der Klassischen Metaphysik zurück*"[17]). Here he first of all thinks, and this can be surprising, of the medieval doctrine of transcendentals. What attracts him to this doctrine is that it complies with the integration of knowledge into a domain of being which passes over the possibilities of control and objectivation of understanding.

> As was to be expected, this involves us in a number of questions with which philosophy has long been familiar. In metaphysics *belonging* refers to the transcendental relationship between being and truth, and it conceives knowledge as an element of being itself and not primarily as an activity of the subject. That knowledge is incorporated in being is the presupposition of all classical and mediaeval thought.[18]

We must see that Gadamer does not intend to reactivate for its own sake the medieval doctrine of transcendentals in the name of an *ontologia perennis*, but to recall that this integration of the understanding with what is understood is first of all the fact of human finitude. Above what it believes itself to be, understanding is itself insertion into being, the proof being that it is itself more being than knowledge. Modern nominalism cancelled this finitude in separating the knowing subject from his world, which thus became infinitely disposable and capable of being mastered. To the infinity of this instrumentalism of the subject, Gadamer opposes the finitude of the addition of understanding in such a way that it would have been glimpsed in the medieval metaphysics of the "transcendentals", where knowledge is not a matter of domination, but of participation in being and in truth.

In another surprise, Gadamer discloses that the most elegant witness to these metaphysical thoughts of the finitude of all understanding is the concept of the Beautiful in Plato.[19] We could speak of a late, but deserved, rehabilitation of Plato after the severe debate with the *Cratylus,* where Plato had in a Heideggerian manner been depicted as the great precursor of the instrumentalist thought of the domination of being. The Form of the Beautiful allows us to discover the Plato who has always mattered most to Gadamer, the thinker about finitude, that is to say of the participation of understanding in a meaning which goes beyond it. According to Gadamer, "in the Platonic tradition was formed the conceptual vocabulary which is needed for thought of the finitude of human existence".[20] We can say that Gadamer invokes this Plato of finitude in all his works after *Truth and Method*, against the Heideggerian reading which makes the forgetfulness of being and finitude begin with Plato. In 1960, Gadamer remained with his rather sharp allusions, which deserve to be overcome.

The doctrine of the Beautiful first allows Gadamer to attach the "metaphysics" of the insertion of understanding in being to the horizon of reflections on the truth of art which opened *Truth and Method*. Gadamer there showed that presentation – reception or understanding – could not be detached from the pretensions to truth of a work of art. Presentation is not external to art it is essential to what it has to say. It is the same with the Beautiful. The Beautiful is always what illuminates us, what ravishes us, what looks at us. The distinction between knowledge and the work arrives too late when it is a matter of embracing what is beautiful. In the same way that the work of art carries us into its game, understanding belongs to the being of what it understands. It is a part of it. It is the objectivizing distinction between the understanding and what is understood, between the work and the Beautiful, which misses the essential, the addition of understanding to a "there". Presentation does not emerge from an attitude of subjectivity, but from the being-to-be-understood.

By this very fact, the hermeneutic concept of truth is illuminated. Gadamer takes it from the rhetorical tradition of the *illuminatio*. What is true in itself, what is safe in all respects, is what arises from an infinite knowledge. The only example accessible to us is that of mathematics. Every other truth emerges for us from what is illuminating, probable, and from what demands, by this fact, a vigilance of knowledge. Gadamer rehabilitates this concept of the *probable* in the name of human finitude:

> This concept . . . belongs to the tradition of rhetoric. The *eikos*, the verisimilar, the "probable" . . . the "evident", belong in a series of things that defend their rightness against the truth and certainty of what is proved and known . . . Indeed, just as the beautiful is a kind of experience that stands out like an enchantment and an adventure within the whole of our experience and presents a special task of hermeneutical integration, what is evident is always something surprising as well, like a new light being turned on, expanding the range of what we can take into consideration. The hermeneutical experience belongs in this sphere because it too is the event of a genuine experience. This is in fact always the case when something speaks to us from tradition: there is something evident about what is said, though that does not imply it is, in every detail, secured, judged, and decided. The tradition asserts its own truth in being understood, and disturbs the horizon that had, until then, surrounded us. It is a real experience in the sense we have shown. The event of the beautiful and the hermeneutical process both presuppose the finiteness of human life.[21]

Gadamer's difficult idea is that the light which illuminates us in this way arises from the being such as is forever put into language. This ontological co-addition of being can be understood in the language that the Platonic doctrine of the Beautiful helps us to embrace, to the extent to which it implies human finitude. The Beautiful, as transcendental, as Form, goes back to an "order of being" of which what is understood is also a part. Gadamer observes that it is not by chance that beauty was first perceived as an order of things before it was understood as the object of artistic production and feeling. If natural beauty has ceased to be the paradigm of modern aesthetics, it is because reality itself has been ontologically reduced to a shapeless mass ruled by the mechanical laws.[22] Beauty then becomes a particularity of the human mind, a feeling, a game without bite on reality. The Beautiful is at the limit of what the artist produces, when he himself adopts an attitude of production in the face of a reality deprived of meaning: he himself becomes a creator, creator of a beauty that would not have being without him. This aesthetic thought, as we have seen, participates in mechanical thought, which has objectivated the real in an unformed mass, from which the subject is exiled. To recall that the Beautiful meant for Plato and the transcendental philosophy of the Middle Ages an essential trait of being is, for Gadamer, to take back the instrumentalism of modern thought, which cuts off understanding from meaning, from the being who challenges it.

The Platonic Form of the Beautiful stresses at the same time the *transcendence* of what illuminates us, the transcendence of the Form and its incarnation, its manifestation on the territory of finitude. Plato in fact said in the *Philebus*, to which Gadamer had devoted his first book in 1931 and to which he returned at the end of *Truth and Method*, that the Form of the Good, which to us cannot be seized, takes refuge in the Beautiful, where it can be contemplated. The essence of beauty is to manifest itself, to illuminate, to shine. The Beautiful thus expresses the necessary manifestation of the Form in the sensible, whilst preserving its transcendence, since beauty is detached from the mediocrity which surrounds us. In Gadamer's terms, there is a separation (*chorismos*) between the Form, the Beautiful, and the sensible, but at the same time here it is abolished.[23]

The Beautiful is thus the being which "shines" at the centre of the sensible, the *ekphanestaton*, what has most lustre. This idea of lustre of course emerges from being, but human intelligence is also implied in its lustre, because to shine is always to shine for, to appear to. The understanding that is clarified is so first of all by the light of being, so much and so well that it becomes impossible to distinguish in a precise manner the source of the light in which being and understanding bathe at the same time. We must repeat that Gadamer does not intend to revive just as it was a Platonic metaphysics of being in itself that would be pure light. Nothing is more contrary to our experience of finitude than the idea of a being that would be such! Rather, he is inspired by the metaphysics of light in thinking of the immemorial anteriority of light that surrounds being and understanding in relation to all reflective intervention in knowledge. This original co-addition of the understanding and the being understood is achieved in Gadamer in the name of a hermeneutic radicalization of finitude.

This co-addition is first of all for him the fact of language, of our linguistic – and, by that, finished – experience of the world. In fact, the "light", which makes things clear and intelligible, – things! – is always that of the word, "*das Licht des Wortes*".[24] Gadamer's idea is that the light of language is always what proceeds from things such as we experience them. In fact, we tend to see in language an intelligible rendering of a reality which would be by itself indifferent to this intervention, even to an invention of our minds.

The metaphysics of light helps us to think of a solidarity in some way "pre-instrumental" of being and the word.

The light that causes everything to emerge in such a way that it is evident and comprehensible in itself is the light of the word. Thus the close relationship that exists between the shining forth (*Vorscheinen*) of the beautiful and the evidentness (*das Einleuchtende*) of the understandable is based on the metaphysics of light. This was precisely the relation that guided our hermeneutical inquiry.[25]

Language is thus captured by being, and vice-versa.

This thought that being is incarnated as language is also one which Augustine put forward in his commentary on Genesis. We must note that God "spoke" for the first time only when he had created light. In fact the truth of the word allows things to be distinguished as such.[26] Being is always detached on the horizon of possible understanding, which is that of possible language.

Gadamer's difficult developments could have created the impression that his hermeneutics is oriented towards a project of total understanding. The references to the Platonic metaphysics of light (!) could have confirmed this feeling. In fact, Gadamer intends to prepare, not new thoughts about infinity, but a metaphysics of finitude. The language that allows us to understand being, to find ourselves in it, is not an instrument at our disposal. It is the light, in itself incomprehensible, to the favour of which the being is given. "Light" is not a synonym for "integral intelligibility". In fact, there is no light except in the midst of an essential obscurity. The excess of light is itself a source of blindness to the extent to which its superexposition comes about, always at the expense of what remains in the shade. It is the injustice of all discourse, of all understanding. The language that we have, or that holds us, is never the last word on being. As is underlined by the title of the last section of Gadamer's work, "Language as horizon of hermeneutic ontology", language is for us nothing but the horizon of being. What is a horizon? What allows us to see, whilst at the same time also indicating the *limit* of what we are to see. But the horizon also moves with us. We can enlarge our horizon, find other words, better silences to say the whole being that would like to be able to be said, but there is no horizon to think of the horizon as such. To accuse hermeneutics of remaining at the horizon of language is to lead into an instrumental concept of language and of human experience. Only one instrumental – or divine, which amounts to the same thing – thought can hope to go beyond the horizon of a language that is at least possible. Hermeneutics is a thought about finitude and, through that, about language. We bitterly resent the limits of language, but we will never transcend them. This knowledge of the limit is one of our mortality, always present, but deferred.

But the horizon of language which cannot be overtaken can at least be enlarged. To raise ourselves above our particularities or our too unilateral conceptions always remains possible, and to be wished. Finitude is thus invited to a constant exercise of judgement and vigilance. The universality accorded to this finitude worked by history is also that of the vigilance which it inspires.

Notes

Introduction

1. The year 1900 was significant for hermeneutics. Besides the death of Nietzsche, the publication of Freud's *Interpretation of Dreams* and Gadamer's birth, it was also the year Husserl's *Logical Investigations* appeared, which launched the phenomenological movement, and Dilthey's essay "The Emergence of Hermeneutics", which marked the beginning of philosophy's interest in the history of hermeneutics.

2. See Gadamer, "Autoprésentation", *La Philosophie Herméneutique* [*PH*] (Paris: PUF, 1996), 28 (*GW* 2, 498).

3. On the works of Hönigswald, see the collection edited by W. Schmied-Kowarzik, *Erkennen-Monas-Sprache*, Internationales Richard-Hönigswald-Symposion (Kassel, 1995), (Würzburg: Königshausen & Neumann, 1997) (with a letter of 1919 from Hönigswald to Gadamer).

4. See the interview with Gadamer in the *Gadamer-Lesebuch* (Tübingen: Mohr, 1997), 281.

5. See Hans-Georg Gadamer, *Philosophische Lehrjahre* (Frankfurt: Klostermann, 1977), 17.

6. See the author's article, "Gadamer vor Heidegger", *Internationale Zeitschrift für Philosophie,* 1996, 197–226.

7. As Gadamer was to learn from his other great teacher at Marburg, Nicolai Hartmann (see Gadamer, "Die Griechen unsere Lehrer", *Internationale Zeitschrift für Philosophie,* 1994, 139). Paul Natorp also expressed his satisfaction with Gadamer's thesis in a letter of 30 November 1922 to Edmund Husserl (see Husserl, *Briefwechsel,* (Dordrecht, Boston, London, 1994), vol. V, 161).

8. Martin Heidegger, *Interprétations Phénoménologiques d'Aristotle*, preceded by Hans-Georg Gadamer, "A Youthful Theological Essay", trans. Jean-François Courtine (Mauzevin: Trans-Europ-Repress, 1992).

9. In the 1957 conferences on the problem of historical knowledge, which can be considered as the first public version of the ideas in *Truth and Method*, Gadamer devoted a whole chapter to the impact of Heidegger's "Hermeneutics of Facticity" on the human sciences. See *Le Problème de la Conscience Historique* [*PCH*] (Paris: Editions du Seuil, 1996), 49–71.

10. See *Praktische Wissen* (1930), *GW* 5, 230–48. The inaugural lecture of 23 February 1929 was on philosophical ethics (of which there appeared a new version in 1985 in *GW* 7, 396–406). The last work which Gadamer had published is an edition of Book VI of the *Nikomachische Ethik* (*Nichomachean Ethics*), *Buch VI* (Frankfurt: Klostermann, 1998).

11. For these five courses, see Gadamer, *GW* **10**, 4. For the list of Heidegger's courses during this semester, see T. Kiesel, *The Genesis of Heidegger's "Being and Time"* (Berkeley, CA: University of California Press, 1993), 463, and Heidegger's letter to Jaspers of 14 July 1923 (*Martin Heidegger–Karl Jaspers Briefwechsel* (Frankfurt: Klostermann, 1990), 41), where Heidegger mentions only one lecture and three seminars, perhaps forgetting the colloquium with Ebbinghaus.
12. See *GW* **10**, 21.
13. Heidegger's letter to Jaspers, 14 July 1923.
14. Gadamer, "Zur Systemidee in der Philosophie", *Festschrift für Paul Natorp zum Siebzigsten Geburtstag* (Berlin: De Gruyter, 1924), 55–75.
15. Gadamer, "Metaphysik der Erkenntnis, Zu dem Gleichnämigen Buch von Nicolai Hartmann", *Logos* **12**, (1923–4), 340–59.
16. See Gadamer, "Autoprésentation", *PH*, 17.
17. See Heidegger, *Einführung in die Phänomenologische Forschung, GA*, vol. 17 (Frankfurt: Klostermann, 1994). In his letter to Jaspers on 14 July 1923, Heidegger was already expressing hostile opinions about Husserl.
18. "Der Aristotelische Protreptikos und die entwicklungsgeschichtliche Betrachtung der Aristotelischen Ethik", *Hermes* **63** (1928), 138–64, now in *GW* **5**, 164–86.
19. See the author's study "Gadamer on Humanism", *Sources of Hermeneutics* (Albany, NY: SUNY Press, 1995), 111–23.
20. The author goes into detail on all these historical and political issues in his biography of Gadamer, *Hans-Georg Gadamer: Eine Biographie* (Tübingen: Mohr Siebeck, 1999).
21. *Über die Ursprünglichkeit der Wissenschaft* (Leipzig: Verlag, 1947); *Über die Ursprünglichkeit der Philosohie: Zwei Vorträge* (Berlin: Chronos-Verlag, 1948). In contrast to Heidegger, Gadamer has frequently answered questions put to him about his attitude to Nazism. See *TPHGG*.
22. Found in several volumes of Dilthey's *Gesammelte Schriften* (Stuttgart, 1957–60) [trans].
23. *PH*, 29.
24. See *GW* **10**, 199.
25. *Ibid.*
26. See especially "La Vérité dans les Sciences Humaines" (1953), *PH* 1996, 63–71, and "Qu'est-ce que la Vérité?"(1955), in *AC*, 39–56.
27. See Rudolf Bultmann, "The Problem of Hermeneutics", *Zeitschrift für Theologie und Kirche* **47** (1950), 47–69, and also in *Glauben und Verstehen*, vol. II (Tübingen: Mohr, 1952), 211–35. The Japanese interpreter Etsuro Makita thinks that this article by Bultmann caused Gadamer to take up hermeneutics.
28. Pierre Fruchon suggests another interpretation in his *L'Herméneutique de Gadamer*, stressing Gadamer's interpretation of Plato. This is an essential key, but despite the title of his book, Fruchon neglected the whole of Gadamer's hermeneutics in *Truth and Method*, together with the debates and literature that it generated, and also Gadamer's debt to Heidegger.
29. A similar project has already been undertaken by Joel Weinsheimer in his book *Gadamer's Hermeneutics: A Reading of* Truth and Method (New Haven, CT: Yale University Press, 1985). Our two projects differ only on a minor point: whereas Weinsheimer insists on the links between Gadamer and the recent trends in epistemology (Popper, Kuhn), we insist on the distance between hermeneutics and epistemology. The epistemological trends that Weinsheimer considers themselves question the evidence of classical epistemology. But we will see that Gadamer's perspective is still more radical.

Chapter 1: The Problem of Method and the Project of a Hermeneutics of the Human Sciences

1. *Angst* is a common term amongst existentialists, and can roughly be translated as *terror*, *fear*, *dread*, or *anguish* [trans.].
2. It is expressed in the alliteration of the letters "s", "l", "g" and "f" in the first two verses of Rilke's poem, which remind us that everything we throw and project ourselves is preceded by "as long as". The gain is that the time can be measured, but by the yardstick of the present, it can only be venial. The poem is from Rilke's posthumous publications. Gadamer has not cited the last eleven verses, perhaps because they are less optimistic.
3. See K. Kerenyl, "Theos: 'Gott' auf Griechisch" in K. Kerenyl, *Antike Religion* (Munich, Vienna, 1971), 207–17, a theme evoked by Gadamer in his book *Der Anfang der Philosophie* (Stuttgart: Reclam, 1996), 126.
4. See *GW* 2, 447.
5. See *GW* 10, 75, *GW* 1, 3, and *TM*, xxiii, where the programme of the work is set out in the following formulation:

   Even though in the following, I shall demonstrate how much there is of *event* in all *understanding*, and how little the traditions in which we stand are weakened by modern historical consciousness, it is not my intention to make prescriptions for the sciences or the conduct of life, but to try to correct false thinking about what they are.

6. See *GW* 2, 438.
7. *GW* 8, 373–99.
8. See the interview in the *Gadamer-Lesebuch* (Tübingen: Mohr Siebeck, 1997), 294.
9. *PH*, 48, *GW* 2, 498.
10. See the self critical essay, *GW* 2, 10–11.
11. See *GW* 2, 247; *GW* 2, 11; *GW* 4, 346–7; *GW* 8, 377.
12. See Heidegger, *Sein und Zeit*, 143.
13. The example is from Gadamer, in an interview from *Lesebuch*, 1997, 283.
14. *GW* 1, 9; *TM*, 4.
15. Gadamer was interested in Herder's theme from 1941. See "Herder and his Theories of History", *Regards sur l'histoire* (Paris: Sorlot, 1941), 7–36. For the German version, see *Volk und Geschicte im Denken Herders* (Frankfurt: Klostermann, 1942), reprinted in *GW* 4, 318–35. The humanist theme of education would be taken up again one year later in *Platos Staat der Erziehung*, 1942, *GW* 5, which itself deepened the ideas of the 1933 article, "Plato and Poetry" (*GW* 5, 187–211). On the context of the publication of these writings, see Gadamer's *La Philosophie Herméneutique*, trans. J. Grondin (Paris: PUF, 1996), 26 ff. (*GW* 2, 490).
16. *GW* 1, 16; *TM*, 10.
17. Conference held in Heidelberg on 7 July 1995, under the title "What is General Formation Today?"(*Was ist Allgemeine Bildung Heute?*). Gadamer has always been preoccupied by this topic.
18. *WM*, *GW* 1, 18–23; *TM*, 12–15.
19. *WM*, *GW* 1, 13; *TM*, 8.
20. In Grondin, "*sens commun*" [trans]. See *GW* 1, 23; *TM*, 19.
21. Grondin, "*lieux communs*" [trans].
22. See the author's article "Hermeneutik", *Historisches Wörterbuch der Rhetorik,* vol. III, (Tübingen: Mohr, 1996), 1350–74.
23. *WM*, *GW* 1, 29; *TM*, 20–22.
24. *WM*, *GW* 1, 28; *TM*, 22–3.
25. On this subject, see R. Makkrecl's essay, "Kant, Dilthey and the Idea of a Critique of

Historical Judgment", *Dilthey-Jahrbuch* (10), 1996, 61–79. In his book *Imagination and Interpretation in Kant: The Hermeneutical Import of the* Critique of Judgement (Chicago, IL: University of Chicago Press, 1990) Makkreel had already shown that the distinction between explanation in the natural sciences and understanding in social sciences stemmed from the Kantian distinction of determining judgements (which subsume the particular under the universal, or under a law) and reflecting judgements (which start from the particular and try to understand its significance within a totality). If the methodologists of the nineteenth century did not themselves notice, it was because Kant was primarily for them the author of the *Critique of Pure Reason*, understood as a discourse on the method of the pure sciences.

26. *WM, GW* 1, 46; *TM*, 41.
27. *WM, GW* 1, 47; *TM*, 41.
28. *WM, GW* 1, 47; *TM*, 41–2.
29. *WM, GW* 1, 50ff.; *TM*, 44ff.
30. *WM, GW* 1, 56; *TM*, 50–1.
31. *WM, GW* 1, 57; *TM*, 51.
32. *WM, GW* 1, 65; *TM*, 59–60.
33. This work has not been translated into English, but the title means, "Lived Experience and Poetry" [trans].
34. *WM, GW* 1, 70; *TM*, 64.
35. *WM, GW* 1, 82; *TM*, 76.
36. *WM GW* 1, 88; *TM*, 83.
37. See *WM GW* 1, 90; *TM*, 85.
38. *WM GW* 1, 145; *TM*, 140.
39. *WM GW* 1, 145.
40. *WM GW* 1, 95; *TM*, 89–90.
41. *WM GW* 1, 93; *TM*, 87.

Chapter 2: Truth after Art

1. *WM, GW* 1, 111; *TM*, 105–6.
2. *WM, GW* 1, 115; *TM*, 109.
3. See "Le mot et l'image – 'autant de vérité, autant d'être'"(1992), *PH*, 194 ff. (*GW* 8, 379).
4. Gadamer often established a link between the German word for poetry, *Dichtung*, and the diktat which it embodies.
5. On this important conception of an "eminent text" in Gadamer, see "Aesthetic Experience and Religious Experience", *AC* II, 295 ff. (*GW* 8, 145), and "Der 'eminente' Text und seine Wahrheit", *GW* 8, 286–95.
6. See "L'Europe et l'oikouménè", *PH*, 243 (*GW* 10, 283).
7. On the response that is evoked by music, see "L'Europe et l'oikouménè", *PH*, 243 ff., and "Musik und Zeit", *GW* 8, 362–5.
8. See *GW* 9, 462.
9. See especially *Über das Lesen von Bauten und Bildern, GW* 8, 331–9.
10. On the crucial importance of this notion of "interior ear" for Gadamer's last theory of aesthetics, see the author's article, "Das Innerte Ort: Distanz und Selbstreflexion in der Hermeneutik", *Denken der Individualität: Festschrift für Josef Simon zum 65 Geburtstag* (Berlin: De Gruyter, 1995), 325–34.
11. The idea of emanation is brought up (*WM, GW* 1, 145; *TM*, 140) to note the ontological valency which a painting confers on what it represents. The being of what is represented becomes manifested as such. Presentation (*Darstellung*) is not uniquely raised by performance arts such as music and poetry (*WM, GW* 1, 142; *TM*, 138), but

constitutes the essence of the production of truth which constitutes art.

12. The term "transformation" has nothing to do with Nietzsche's "transmutation of values" (*Umwertung*). To avoid this misunderstanding, what follows will use the terms "transfiguration" or "metamorphosis".

13. On the application of this hermeneutic notion of the world to art, see P. Ricoeur, *La Critique et la Conviction* (Calmann-Levy, 1995), 262ff.

14. *WM, GW* 1, 116–17; *TM*, 111.

15. See Heidegger, "The Origin of the Work of Art" in Krell (London: Routledge, 1993).

16. *GW* 3, 249–61.

17. *GW* 1, 118; *TM*, 113.

18. *GW* 8, 383.

19. *WM, GW* 1, 120–1; *TM*, 115. See also *GW* 8, 25–36, 80–5.

20. This concept of the Christian *kerygma* later led Bultmann to the demythologization of the Christian message: we must purge the Christian message of its mythological elements in order to return to the *Sache*, to the issue of predication or of the Christian *kerygma*. On the coherence of the development in Bultmann's thought, see Wohlfahrt Pannenberg's illuminating presentation of the history of Protestant theology of the last two centuries, *Problemgeschichte der neuren evangelischen Theologie in Deutschland* (Göttingen: Vandenhoeck and Ruprecht-UTB, 1996), 208.

21. *GW* 1, 21; *TM*, 16.

22. *Glauben und Verstehen*, Vol. 1 (Tübingen: Mohr, 1980, eighth impression), 26–37.

23. The German term *Anspruch* also means a claim (to validity, to truth), or a request. But the request is always to someone. Theology thus speaks here of address. Perhaps we also think of the legal meaning of "appeal". J.-L. Marion has proposed a brilliant phenomenological description of the term in *Réduction et Donation* (Paris: PUF, 1989), 278ff., 297ff.

24. These are the last words of the introductory essay of *Kunst als Aussage* (*GW* 8, 8), *AC* II, 149.

25. See *GW* 1, 134; *TM*, 129.

26. *WM, GW* 1, 137; *TM*, 132–3. We will see that, for Gadamer, the example of tragedy is not only decisive for the understanding of art, but it impregnates the whole of his concept of the hermeneutics of experience (*Erfahrung*) which puts into question the abstraction of scientific experimentation in the name of the *test* and of tragic *suffering*. See *WM, GW* 1, 362; *TM*, 357–8.

27. *GW* 1, 142; *TM*, 137–8.

28. See *GW* 1, 147; *TM*, 142.

29. *WM, GW* 1, 149; *TM*, 144–5.

30. *GW* 1, 153; *TM*, 148.

31. *GW* 1, 151; *TM*, 146.

32. See especially "The Word and the Image – 'so much truth, so much being'", *GW* 8, 395 ff., and *Über das Lesen von Bauten und Bildern* (1979), *GW* 8, 331–8.

33. *GW* 1, 165; *TM*, 160.

34. *GW* 1, 166; *TM*, 160–1. In the few pages on literature in *Truth and Method*, Gadamer seems to want to put into question the essential difference that there can be between great literature and all other forms of writing (*GW* 1, 168; *TM*, 163), a surprising thesis because the conception of the "eminent text" which Gadamer later developed rests precisely on this distinction. This thesis can only be understood in its strategic place in the economy of his work: placed at the very end of the first part of his aesthetics, it already serves as to prepare the transition towards hermeneutics which, in the Diltheyan way, ranges over all the "manifestations of life fixed in writing". If any *writing* exacts an effort in understanding and deciphering, literature in a wide sense can be emblematic of the transition from aesthetics to hermeneutics, as it announces the universalization of the language dimension. The conception of the eminent text later

allowed thoughts of the difference of the literary text, which seems to be effaced in *Truth and Method*, where the work seeks to reject the absolutization of aesthetic difference.

35. On the links between hermeneutics and literary theory, see J. Weinsheimer, *Philosophical Hermeneutics and Literary Theory* (New Haven, CT: Yale University Press, 1991).
36. See *WM, GW* 1, 148; *TM*, 143 (*Seinsvorgang*).
37. See *GW* 8, 239, and *GW* 2, 7.
38. T. Adorno, *Ästhetische Theorie* (Frankfurt: Suhrkamp, 1970), 185.

Chapter 3: The Destruction of Prejudices in Nineteenth-Century Aesthetics and Epistemology

1. For Dilthey and historicism, see F. Rodi, *Erkenntnis des Erkannten: Zur Hermeneutik des 19 und 20 Jahrhunderts* (Frankfurt: Suhrkamp, 1990); T. Nenon, "Hermeneutical Truth and the Structure of Human Experience", *Dilthey-Jahrbuch* 8 (1992–3). For Schleiermacher, see M. Frank, *Das Individuelle Allgemeine: Textstrukturierung und Interpretation nach Schleiermacher* (Frankfurt: Suhrkamp, 1977). In the author's book on *L'Universalité de l'herméneutique* (Paris: PUF, 1993), he prefers to insist on what in Schleiermacher and Dilthey prepares for the radicalization of hermeneutics.
2. See "Entre Phénoménologie et Dialectique: Essai d'autocritique", *AC II*, 16 (*GW* 2, 7) and his more recent essays on Dilthey in *GW* 4, 406–47.
3. *WM, GW* 1, 178; *TM*, 173. For a fuller presentation of the history of hermeneutics, which is a little less tied to the concern to oppose his own systematic contribution to it, we can turn to the essay, "Herméneutique Classique et Philosophique" (1968), *PH*, 85–118.
4. *WM, GW* 1, 182; *TM*, 179.
5. *WM, GW* 1, 183; *TM*, 180.
6. *WM, GW* 1, 184; *TM*, 180.
7. *WM, GW* 1, 189; *TM*, 184–5.
8. *WM, GW* 1, 195; *TM*, 192.
9. F. Schleiermacher, *Hermeneutik und Kritik,* ed. M. Frank (Frankfurt: Suhrkamp, 1977), 321.
10. See "Exkurs VI: Zum Begriff des Ausdrucks", *GW* 2, 384–6, particularly 386. "There is no doubt that the critique of the psychologisation of 'expression' is the focus of the *whole* of my enquiry, and that it is at the *basis* of my critique of 'the art of the lived' and of the hermeneutics of Romanticism."
11. On the universality of the concept of expression in Dilthey and Misch, see the author's article, "Georg Misch und die Universalität der Hermeneutik: Logik oder Rhetorik?" *Dilthey-Jahrbuch* 11 (1997–8), 48–63.
12. *GW* 2, 384.
13. *GW* 2, 385.
14. *GW* 2, 384.
15. *WM, GW* 1, 191; *TM*, 187–8.
16. R. Bubner, *Geschichtsprozesse und Handlungsnormen* (Frankfurt: Suhrkamp, 1984), 75–8.
17. But Gadamer remarked that in so far as the historical school takes account of the success and the efficacy which transforms facts into historical events, it is not completely exempt from teleology (*WM, GW* 1, 207; *TM*, 203). The idea of progress in the order of "ethical powers" in Droysen confirms it.
18. *WM, GW* 1, 215; *TM*, 210.
19. *WM, GW* 1, 201; *TM*, 198.
20. *WM, GW* 1, 216; *TM*, 212.

21. *WM, GW* 1, 221; *TM*, 217.
22. *WM, GW* 1, 221; *TM*, 217.
23. *WM, GW* 1, 219; *TM*, 215.
24. *WM, GW* 1, 237; *TM*, 233.
25. *WM, GW* 1, 202; *TM*, 198.
26. "Das Problem Diltheys: Zwischen Romantik und Positivismus", *GW* 4, 406–24. On Dilthey's latent Cartesianism, see Heidegger's summer semester course on Fichte, *GA* 28, 137.
27. See R. Aron, *La Philosophie Critique de l'histoire* (1938) (Paris: Julliard, 1987). See also G. Gusdorf, *Introduction aux Sciences Humaines: Essai Critique sur leurs Origines et leur Développement,* University of Strasburg, 1960.
28. "Origines et Développement de l'herméneutique", in W. Dilthey, *Le Monde de l'Esprit*, vol. 1 (Paris: Aubier), 332–3.
29. *Ibid.*, 319.
30. "La Vérité dans les Sciences Humaines" (1953), *PH*, 63–72, and "Qu'est-ce que la Vérité?" (1955), *AC* II, 39–56.
31. *PCH* (Paris: Nauwelaerts, 1963), re-edited (Paris: Editions du Seuil, 1996) where the conferences are dated 1958 in error.
32. See Gadamer, "Wahrheit und Methode: der Anfang der Urfassung", *Dilthey-Jahrbuch* 8 (1992–3), 131–42. The German text often corresponds to the French text of the first Louvain conference (1996, 28ff.). Gadamer thus used the first edition of *Truth and Method* to edit his conference speeches.
33. See *PCH*, 1966, Preface, 14.
34. *WM, GW* 1, 239; *TM*, 235.
35. See *WM, GW* 1, 307: *Geschichtlichsein heisst, nie in Sichwissen Aufgehen.* On the epistemological reductionism of the problem of historicity in Dilthey, see Heidegger, *GA* 27, 350.
36. See *WM, GW* 1, 242; *TM*, 237. See also *PCH*, 45.
37. See "Die Kehre des Weges" (1985), published for the first time in 1995 in *GW* 10, 71.
38. *WM, GW* 1, 262; *TM*, 258.
39. Where his third conference was entitled, "Martin Heidegger and the Significance of his 'Hermeneutics of Facticity' for the Human Sciences". See also the little-known course by Gadamer, *Lectures on Philosophical Hermeneutics* (Pretoria: Van Schaik's Boekhandel, 1982), 5.
40. This was the thesis of the author's first dialogue with Gadamer in *Hermeneutische Wahrheit? Zum Wahrheitsbegriff Hans-Georg Gadamers* (Königstein, 1982), (second edition, Weinheim: Belz-Athenäum, 1994).
41. In the final edition of *WM* (1986) Gadamer returns to it in a note to the title of his chapter devoted to Heidegger.
42. See notably T. Kisiel, *The Genesis of Heidegger's* Being and Time (Berkeley, CA: University of California Press, 1993).
43. *WM, GW* 1, 238; *TM*, 233–4.
44. See F. Rodi, *Erkenntnis des Erkannten: Zur Hermeneutik des 19 und 20 Jahrhunderts* (Frankfurt: Suhrkamp, 1990), 103.
45. See *PCH*, 49.
46. Husserl, *Die Krisis der Europäischer Wissenschaften* (The Hague: Nijhoff, 1954).
47. *WM, GW* 1, 252; *TM*, 248. On the concept of the lived world, which inspired Gadamer to develop his conception of the hermeneutic experience, see *WM, GW* 1, 253; *TM*, 248–9 and the texts devoted to the *movement* of phenomenology in *GW* 3, 105–71.
48. *WM, GW* 1, 261; *TM*, 256–7.
49. On the meaning of Heideggerian hermeneutics, see the author's article "L'herméneutique dans *Sein und Zeit*", in J.-F. Courtine (ed.), *Heidegger 1919–1929: De l'herméneutique de la Facticité à la Métaphysique du Dasein* (Paris: Vrin, 1996),

179–92. On the "projection" (*Geworfenheit*) which Heidegger subversively finds behind the idea of *subjectum,* see GA **28**, 116ff.

50. See Heidegger, *Being and Time,* section 31, *SZ*, 143; *WM, GW* **1**, 264; *TM*, 260.
51. *WM, GW* **1**, 264; *TM*, 260.
52. *WM, GW* **1**, 265 (*PCH*, 53); *TM*, 261.
53. *WM, GW* **1**, 266; *TM*, 262.
54. *WM, GW* **1**, 267; *TM*, 262.
55. *WM, GW* **1**, 264; *TM*, 259.
56. *WM, GW* **1**, 268; *TM*, 263. We note that in the same chapter Gadamer reproaches Heidegger for not "completely escap[ing] the problematic of transcendental reflection" (*WM, GW* **1**, 260; *TM*, 255). Gadamer here thinks of the transcendental in the neo-Kantian sense of an epistemological foundation. As we see, it is the medieval and transcendental meaning which Gadamer uses to the very end of the book.

Chapter 4: Vigilance and Horizon in Hermeneutics

1. *WM, GW* **1**, 268; *TM*, 264.
2. *SZ*, 153, 314.
3. *WM, GW* **1**, 366; *TM*, 266–7.
4. *WM, GW* **1**, 268; *TM*, 264.
5. *WM, GW* **1**, 296; *TM*, 291. See also *PCH*, 74:

> There is now the question of determining more precisely the structure of the understanding which is at the basis of hermeneutics; it is, as we have seen, something like a "dimension" of tradition. At this stage, a traditional hermeneutic "rule" comes to our aid. It was formulated for the first time by Romantic hermeneutics but its origins go back to ancient rhetoric. It is concerned with the circular relationship between the whole and its parts: the meaning anticipated thanks to the whole is understood through its parts, but it is in the light of the whole that the parts take on their clarifying function.

6. *WM, GW* **1**, 296; *TM*, 291: "The harmony of all the details with the whole is the criterion of correct understanding."
7. *PCH*, 84.
8. See O. Marquard, *Abschied vom Prinzipellen* (Stuttgart: Reclam, 1981). Gadamer has always seen a misunderstanding of his intentions (see *WM, GW* **1**, 317; *GW* **2**, 233 and the interview in the *Gadamer-Lesebuch* 1997, 282).
9. See *WM, GW* **1**, 271; *TM*, 266; *PCH*, 77; "Of the circle of understanding", *PH*, 76.
10. See *WM, GW* **1**, 299; *TM*, 293.
11. See on this subject Gadamer's reply to Apel (and to Heidegger!) in *TPHGG*, 95:

> Apel describes what disturbs him in my thought, namely, the "strange primacy of the past over the future". This, however, must astonish me. The future which we do not know is supposed to take primacy over the past? Is it not the past which has stamped us permanently through its effective history? If we seek to illuminate this history, we may be able to make ourselves conscious of and overcome some of the prejudices which have determined us.

12. *WM* **1**, 181–2.
13. See Gadamer's precision in the interview in the *Gadamer-Lesebuch*, 1997, 285.
14. See *WM, GW* **1**, 274; *TM*, 269:

> a person trying to understand a text is prepared for it to tell him something. That is why a hermeneutically trained consciousness must be, from the start, sensitive

to the text's alterity. But this kind of sensitivity involves neither "neutrality" with respect to content nor the extinction of one's self, but the foregrounding and appropriation of one's own fore-meanings and prejudices. The important thing is to be aware of one's own bias, so that the text can present itself in all its otherness and thus assert its own truth against one's own fore-meanings.

15. See *WM*, *GW* 1, 301; *TM*, 295. Gadamer later radicalized this idea. See on this topic the interview in the *Gadamer-Lesebuch*, 1997, 285: "What properly characterises our prejudices is that we are not aware of them!"

16. *GW* 1, 281; *TM*, 276–7.

17. *GW* 1, 281; *TM*, 277.

18. *GW* 1, 304; *TM*, 298. See also "Of the circle of understanding" (*GW* 2, 64). See also the more detailed analysis of Gadamer's solution in the author's "The Hermeneutic Horizon of Contemporary Thought", *PH*, 206–9.

19. *WM*, *GW* 1, 295; *TM*, 291–3.

20. See, for what follows, *WM*, *GW* 1, 280; *TM*, 276.

21. *WM*, *GW* 1, 280: (in reply to the pretensions of historicism to be a radicalization of the Enlightenment): "It is at this precise point that the attempt to construct a philosophical hermeneutics must intervene in a critical way."

22. In French, "un 'travail' de l'histoire" [trans.].

23. To justify this translation, I return to the 1981 article, "Le Travail de l'histoire et le Problème de la Vérité en Herméneutique", reprinted in *L'Horizon herméneutique de la pensée contemporaine*, 213–33. More recently, I have also profited from the illuminating unpublished thesis of Phillipe Treguer, "Le Concept de Vérité dans l'hermeneutique Philosophique de H.-G. Gadamer", Department of Philosophy, Caen University, 1996.

24. See *WM*, *GW* 1, 298; *TM*, 294.

25. *WM*, *GW* 1, 295; *TM*, 290.

26. *GW* 2, 10–11.

27. Gadamer focuses uniquely on the idea of an integrated historical Enlightenment, which is not always recognized by those who see in his philosophy a "critique of the Luminaries". See his reply to David Detmer ("Gadamer's Critique of the Enlightenment") in *TPHGG*, 287:

> It is extremely astonishing to me that my project of a philosophical hermeneutics as well as some other such projects are being discussed under the title "Critique of Enlightenment" and not with reference to the idealist concept of the "completed enlightenment" which was coined by Fichte. For what matters to us can only be the question whether a completed enlightenment which would dissolve all human predisposition and societal prejudices is an intelligible claim.

28. Gadamer devoted a long section to this notion of "source" in an appendix to *Truth and Method* (*GW* 2, 383–5).

29. On the theme of immemorial history in Heidegger's and Gadamer's hermeneutics of "projection", see *GW* 2, 103; *3*, 236; *2*, 334; *10*, 64.

30. See Hegel, *Phenomenology of Spirit*, trans. A. V. Miller (Oxford: Oxford University Press, 1977). On this reading of Hegel, see Heidegger's first course in Freiburg in the winter semester, 1928–9: *GA 27*, 317.

31. *WM* 1, 307.

32. The idea is evidently not Gadamer's own. We find it, for example, in the experience of the mixture of knowledge and Habit, almost always given a capital letter (as is Time!) in Marcel Proust. Gadamer's merit is to have taken from it a philosophical "wisdom" ("knowledge"); even to have recalled that all philosophy perhaps proceeds from wisdom in life, which is a matter of serenity and of responsibility.

33. Heidegger, *Hermeneutik der Faktizität, GA* **63**, 7.
34. *GA* **63**, 15.
35. In the *Republic* it is the state of watchfulness (*hupar*) which distinguishes the guardians from the state of sleep or of dreaming (*onar*), which is that of most mortals.
36. WM, *GW* **1**, 312; *TM*, 307. The original text speaks here, in still more epistemological terms, of the "task" (*Aufgabe*) of the knowledge of the work of history. It is a matter of a correction which, exceptionally, has not been signalled by quotation marks in the edition of the *GW*. We note nevertheless that the term "vigilance" is found in the early Gadamer, where it represents an essential determinism in practical knowledge which proceeds from the Socratic knowledge of one's own ignorance. See on this topic Gadamer's 1930 article on "Practical Knowledge" (*GW* **5**, 238).
37. *GW* **1**, 311; *TM*, 306.
38. See *WM*, *GW* **1**, 285; *TM*, 281.
39. *WM*, *GW* **1**, 286; *TM*, 281.
40. *WM*, *GW* **1**, 285; *TM*, 280.
41. *Ibid*.
42. *WM*, *GW* **1**, 292; *TM*, 287. On this point see Grondin, "Canonicity and Hermeneutic Philosophy", *Théologiques* (1), 1993, 9–23.
43. *WM*, *GW* **1**, 292; *TM*, 287.
44. *WM*, *GW* **1**, 292–3; *TM*, 287–8.
45. *WM*, *GW* **1**, 295; *TM*, 290.
46. *WM*, *GW* **1**, 310; *TM*, 305. On the fusion of horizons in the interpretation of poetry, see "Texte et Interprétation" (*GW* **2**, 351), where it is confirmed that it is less the idea of a controlled fusion than the event of fusion that matters most to Gadamer.
47. Both would probably be plural in English [trans.].
48. See Gadamer's interview with the *Suddeutsche Zeitung* of 10–11 February 1990. See also *Über die Verborgenheit der Gesundheit* (Frankfurt: Suhrkamp, 1993), 109; *Das Erbe Europas* (Frankfurt: Suhrkamp, 1989).
49. *WM*, *GW* **1**, 312; *TM*, 307.
50. *WM*, *GW* **1**, 313; *TM*, 308.
51. Also in English [trans.].
52. *WM*, *GW* **1**, 313. We should note that the very term *subtilitas applicandi* is not textually found in the pietist J. J. Rambach, as Gadamer claims when he affirms that he would have added (*GW* **1**, 313) *subtilitas applicandi* to *subtilitas intelligendi* and *subtilitas explicandi*. In the end, Gadamer is right. From page 2 of his *Institutiones Hermeneuticae Sacrae* (1723), Rambach defined the practical work of sacred hermeneutics by saying that it was a matter of understanding (*investigandum*) the meaning of the Scriptures, of explaining it to others (*aliis exponendum*), and of being able to apply it with wisdom (*sapienter applicandum*). This element of application is entirely proper to pietist hermeneutics and it can be added effectively to the subtleties of understanding (here, *investigare*) and explanation (here, *exponere*). The idea according to which pietism would have added the "*sapienter applicare*" to the *subtilitates intelligendi* and *applicandi* are clearly expressed by Friedrich Lucke, the first editor of Schleiermacher's hermeneutics (F. Schleiermacher, *Hermeneutik und Kritik,* ed. M. Frank, Suhrkamp: Frankfurt, 1997, 99), where Lucke deplores the resurgence of the idea in recent authors (a value judgement behind which we can hear Schleiermacher himself). Citing Ernesti in Latin, Lucke writes, "Unde in bono interprete esse debet, subtilitas intelligendi et subtilitas explicandi." Earlier, in his *Institutiones Hermen. Sacrae*, Rambach added a third element, the *sapienter applicare,* an element that more recent authors have had the misfortune to emphasize once again. It is very probably Lucke's text of 1838 that led Gadamer to coin the term *subtilitas applicandi* and to apply it retrospectively to Rambach. In *Truth and Method*, Gadamer (who edited a later text by Rambach in the collection that he compiled with Gottfried

Boehm, *Seminar: Philosophische Hermeneutik* (Frankfurt: Suhrkamp, 1977), 62–8, but in which the *subtilitas applicandi* is also absent) said that his acquaintance with Rambach's treatise was founded on the summary written by Morus (in his *Super Hermeneutica Novi Testamenti Acroases Academicae*, Leipzig, 1797), but Morus's text which he cites does not mention the *subtilitas applicandi* either. Lucke was therefore his true source and, in the last analysis, Rambach's thought itself, well rendered by Lucke. See on this topic I. M. Feher's article, "Hermeneutik und Philologie: Verständnis der Sachen, Verständnis des Textes", forthcoming.

53. See *PH*, 43–62. But we would be wrong to refer to precise texts, as it is such a preponderant model for the whole of Gadamer's hermeneutics. It is also one of his earliest concerns, as his first texts on *Plato's Dialektische Ethik* and the essay on Aristotle's practical wisdom in the *Protreptique* reveal.

54. The issue of knowing whether Gadamer is eventually closer to Aristotle than to Plato is too hotly debated to be treated within the limits of the present work. It appears clear, as is attested by the great volume 7 of his *Works, Plato in Dialogue,* that Gadamer has always been closer to Plato, preferring from afar the dialogical achievement of his thought to the work of Aristotle's concept, and also the allusive irony of his Socratic style to the demonstrative certainties of the Stagirite. But in *Truth and Method*, he is curiously more critical than elsewhere of Plato (in the third part, he severely attacks his instrumental conception of language) and often prefers to follow Aristotle's model. Did he have the feeling of following in Heidegger's shadow, as he later so candidly confessed (see *GW* 2, 491)?

55. The opposition between Kant and Aristotle has been noted particularly in an important article of 1963, "On the Possibility of Philosophical Ethics" (*GW* 4, 175–88), which played a large part in the rediscovery of Aristotle's ethical actuality and in what has been called in Germany "the rehabilitation of practical philosophy". As the debates that have ensued have had a tendency to contrast Kant's universalism with Aristotle's relativism, Gadamer has insisted more in his recent works on their solidarity, notably in "Aristotle and the Ethics of Imperative", *GW* 7, 381–95, where Kant, read through Gerhard Krüger, appears as a critic of the ethical Enlightenment, and Aristotle's inheritor in the tradition of practical philosophy.

56. On *this* solidarity, often reiterated, with Kant, see *GW* 3, 336. See also Gadamer's reply to K. O. Apel in *TPHGG*, 97: "The doctrine of the inseparability of *ethos* and *phronesis* remains fundamental. This holds for Plato's ideal republic as well as for the ethics and politics of Aristotle, and even for a Kant who has been correctly understood." See particularly "Aristoteles und die Imperativische Ethik", *GW* 7, 387ff.

57. *WM, GW* 1, 319; *TM*, 314.

58. *WM, GW* 1, 322; *TM*, 317.

59. *WM, GW* 1, 307; *TM*, 303–4.

60. *WM, GW* 1, 327; *TM*, 322.

61. *GW* 4, 180.

62. On Betti, see "Hermeneutics as a Rigorous Science According to Emilio Betti", in *L'Horizon herméneutique de la pensée contemporaine*, 155–77.

63. *WM, GW* 1, 332; *TM*, 327.

64. *WM, GW* 1; *TM*, 327.

65. *WM, GW* 1, 333; *TM*, 327.

66. *WM, GW* 1, 338; *TM*, 332.

67. *WM, GW* 1, 334; *TM*, 329.

68. *WM, GW* 1, 344; *TM*, 339.

69. *WM, GW* 1, 346; *TM*, 340.

70. *TPHGG*, 385.

71. See P. Ricoeur, *Temps et Récit*, vol. 3 (Paris: Seuil, 1985), 280ff. It seems that Ricoeur is the closest to Gadamer's questions and to the hermeneutic tradition in this chapter. The

use of the term "hermeneutics" in Ricoeur owes astonishingly little to the German Romantic tradition of Gadamer, Heidegger, Dilthey, Droysen, Boeck and Schleiermacher. This tradition is almost never referred to in the great works of hermeneutics that he published soon after that of Gadamer, *De l'interprétation* (1965), and *Le Conflit des Interprétations* (1969). This only shows that it is possible to enter hermeneutics from different horizons. It is still the case that it is the experience of the interpretation of objective meaning in Biblical writings (or in great symbols) that Ricoeur afterwards universalized and confronted with other practices of interpretation (essentially with the hermeneutics of suspicion, of Freud and of structuralism). He only relatively late entered the dialogue with the hermeneutic tradition, but he conducted it from the perspective which he had so magisterially used in his writings of the 1960s. In his book *La Métaphore vive* of 1975 (p. 12), he excused himself for the growing injustice that he felt for not having paid attention to this tradition. He engaged with it in his hermeneutics course given in Louvain in 1971, which led to the recapitulation of the history of hermeneutics in *Du Texte à l'Action: Essais d'herméneutiques II* (1986), which took up important articles of the 1970s. His reattachment to the mainstream of hermeneutics was delayed, and is necessarily marked by the perspective developed in the 1960s, which accounts for the persistent – almost "Cartesian" (according to Gadamer's rather severe critique) priority given to objectivations and to the necessity to submit them to a structural or semiotic explanation that has the intention of decoding meaning in abstracting from the intrinsic meaning. But his whole hermeneutics ends in dismissing the objectivism of meaning. Ricoeur finally rejoins what represents the point of departure of the hermeneutics of "projection" and its Romantic tradition through a long detour on objectivism: the critique of the wish to dominate inherent in the very concept of objectivation. Whether it is a matter of biblical hermeneutics or of phenomenology (where the same objectivism is at work), Ricoeur in effect starts with the primacy of objectivation and later pays attention to the hermeneutic approaches of suspicion and of confidence. Hermeneutics holds this concept of donation and of objectivity to be problematic. In this sense, hermeneutics remains outside the opposition between suspicion and confidence. All understanding oscillates between these two expectations.

72. *WM*, *GW* 1, 348; *TM*, 342.
73. See "Herméneutique et Rélativisme", 192–211.
74. See the recent and cutting debate led by K. O. Apel, "Regulative Ideas or Truth-Happening? An Attempt to Answer the Question of the Conditions of the Possibility of Valid Understanding", *TPHGG*, 67–94.
75. *GW* 2, 103. See also Heidegger, *GA* 27, 314.
76. *WM*, *GW* 1, 452; *TM*, 448. For a defence of hermeneutics against the charge of relativism inspired by Davidson, see D. C. Hoy, "Post-Cartesian Interpretation: Hans-Georg Gadamer and Donald Davidson", *TPHGG*, 111–28.
77. *WM*, *GW* 1, 425*n*.
78. On this experience of limits of reflexion, see also R. Brague, *Aristote et la Question du Monde* (Paris: PUF, 1988), 17. Brague, like Gadamer, reads Aristotle through Heidegger.
79. *WM*, *GW* 1, 383; *TM*, 375–6 (where Gadamer criticizes the abstract conception of the history of "problems").
80 *TPHGG*, 385.
81. *Ibid.*, 235.
82. *WM*, *GW* 1, 355; *TM*, 349.
83. *GW* 4, 167. On Prometheus and the importance of forgetfulness for human culture (and sanity!) see, more recently, Gadamer, *Über die Verborgenheit der Gesundheit* (Frankfurt: Suhrkamp, 1994), 88, 193–4. Gadamer had already arranged an important conference on "Prometheus and the Tragedy of Culture" in 1944 (in Dresden!), in *GW* 9, 150–61.

84. *Über die Verborgenheit der Gesundheit*, 88.
85. An example taken from the Larousse French–Spanish dictionary: *Qué illusión ir esta noche al teatro*, which means, "How enjoyable it is to go to the theatre". A small treatise has also been devoted to the genius of the Spanish language: Julian Marias, *Breve Tradato de la Illusión* (Madrid: Alianza Editorial, 1984, 1990).
86. See *WM, GW* 1, 359–60; *TM*, 356–7.
87. *WM, GW* 1, 359; *TM*, 353.
88. *WM, GW* 1; *TM*, 353.
89. *WM, GW* 1, 361; *TM*, 356.
90. *WM, GW* 1, 359, 377; *TM*, 354, 373–4.
91. *WM, GW* 1, 373; *TM*, 364–5.
92. *WM, GW* 1, 363; *TM*, 357.
93. See C. von Bormann, "Die Zweideutigkeit der Hermeneutischen Erfahrung", *Hermeneutik und Ideologikritik* (Frankfurt: Suhrkamp, 1971), 83–119. Gadamer recognized its pertinence in *GW* 2, 256.
94. *WM, GW* 1, 376; *TM*, 372.
95. *WM, GW* 1, 381; *TM*, 375.
96. *WM, GW* 1, 383; *TM*, 378.
97. *WM, GW* 1, 384; *TM*, 379.

Chapter 5: The Dialogue that We Are

1. *WM, GW* 2, 108.
2. *WM, GW* 1, 383; *TM*, 378.
3. *WM, GW* 1.
4. See particularly the interview with C. Dutt, *Hans-Georg Gadamer im Gespräch* (Heidelberg: Carl Winter Verlag, 1993), 36, and that in the *Gadamer-Lesebuch*, 282. In this sense, we must understand the express and insistent references in the last edition of *Truth and Method* (*WM, GW* 1, 447, 465) on the issue of language.
5. Gadamer underlines this in a note added to the edition of 1986 (*WM, GW* 1, 421; *TM*, 417–18), a valuable note but more or less happily placed in the body of the text. The reference to the text of Themistius which we expected here is given in the previous note. There is thus room for suspecting a typographical mistake (the text for notes 38 and 39 seems to have intervened).
6. See particularly *GW* 8, 350–61, where there are four texts "on the limits of language" (*an den Grenzen der Sprache*). I have for my own modest part heavily stressed these limits of language, but in the name of what I believe to be the hermeneutic understanding of language. See particularly *L'Horizon herméneutique de la pensée contemporaine* (Paris: Vrin, 1993), 253–69: more recently, "L'universalité de l'herméneutique et les limites du langage", *Laval Théologique et Philosophique* 53 (1997), 181–94, and "La Définition Derridienne de la Déconstruction: Contribution au Rapprochement de L'Herméneutique et de la Deconstruction", *Archives de Philosophie* 62 (1999), 5–16, 1998.
7. *WM, GW* 1, 387; *TM*, 383–4.
8. *WM, GW* 1, 401; *TM*, 397.
9. Because here again, "the interpreter does not know that he intervenes himself and that he introduces his own concepts into the interpretation" (*WM, GW* 1, 407; *TM*, 403).
10. *WM, GW* 1.
11. On this idea of interpretation and translation as a reawakening (*Wiedererweckung*) of meaning, see *WM, GW* 1, 392, 416; *TM*, 388, 412.
12. See *GW* 1, 405, *TM*, 401: "We must rightly understand the fundamental priority of language . . . Indeed, language often seems ill suited to express what we feel. In the face of the overwhelming presence of works of art, the task of expressing in words what

they say to us seems like an infinite and hopeless undertaking . . . but this does not alter the fundamental priority of language." On silent admiration before a work of art which is still a linguistic form, see also *GW* 2, 185.

13. On this linguistic element which cannot but recognize the limits of effective or propositional language, see the interview in the *Gadamer-Lesebuch*, 289.

14. GW 1, 403; *TM*, 400.

15. *GW* 1, 405; *TM*, 401.

16. Following Nietzsche's famous metaphor, taken up by Michel Foucault in *Les Mots et les Choses* (Paris: Gallimard, 1966), 333.

17. See *GW* 2, 198, and *GW* 3, 236: "Is language not always language with-oneself (*Heimat*) and the realisation of familiarity with the world?" It is true that we could give numerous simlar texts against the interpretation (or "superexposition") proposed here. But why insist so much on speaking of familiarity and of country (*Heimat*) if not on the basis of an essential expatriation (*Heimatlösigkeit*) and non-familiarity that we can call "finitude"? Gadamer recognizes it in the conclusion of "Von der Wahrheit des Wortes", *GW* 8, 56: "But who is at home with a language?" See also *GW* 8, 78: "Our fundamental experience so far as we are temporal beings consists just in that everything is stripped to us, that all the contents of our lives go away, becoming more and more pale until they are lost in the most faded memory, and they can no longer throw out anything except a quasi-unreal light." This *fundamental* experience is that of Gadamer's hermeneutics of language. On the links between the familiarity of language and the immemorial working of our finitude, see finally *GW* 3, 236: "Certainly, this freedom is not acquired in the sense of an absolute transparency or of a being-with-ourselves which is no longer threatened by anything. But in the same way that the thought of the immemorial preserves what is proper to it, in knowing the being-with-ourselves (*Heimat*), the immemorial nature of our finitude is achieved in the incessant placing in language of our *Dasein*, from top to bottom, in birth and death."

18. *GW* 8, 361.

19. *Ibid*. On Lacan and Gadamer, see Claus von Bormann, "Unglückliche Begegnungen: Gadamers Philosophische Hermeneutik und Lacans Psychoanalytische Theorie der Deutung", *Dilthey-Jahrbuch* 8 (1992–3), 11–56.

20. *GW* 10, 274. See *TPHGG*, 496: "In this lies the real problem which really came to my full attention only through Heidegger and which found expression in the Scholastic distinction of *actus signatus* and *actus exercitus*. It concerns the fact that not everything which one knows and can know in effect is sayable in a thematic assertion."

21. *GW* 2, 226. On the relativization of propositional language which that introduces, see "L'universalisation de l'herméneutique chez Gadamer", in *L'Horizon herméneutique de la pensée contemporaine*, 235–51.

22. *GW* 2, 193.

23. *WM*, *GW* 1, 411; *TM*, 407.

24. *Ibid*.

25. *WM*, *GW* 1, 412; *TM*, 408.

26. *WM*, *GW* 1, 418; *TM*, 414.

27. *WM*, *GW* 1, 418; *TM*, 413–4.

28. *Ibid*.

29. In *L'Universalité de l'herméneutique* and elsewhere, I have returned to Augustine's texts in the hope of clarifying, and to a certain extent deepening, Gadamer's thought. I have demonstrated elements of Augustine's thought which perhaps were not those that Gadamer had in mind. I have since profited much from the critical remarks of D. Kaegi, "Was heisst und zu welchem Ende studiert man philosophische Hermeneutik?", *Philosophische Rundschau* 41, 1994, 128.

30. Contempt for the body also explains the hostility of pagan, particularly Platonic, philosophy to the mystery of the Incarnation, judged unworthy of divinity. See on this

topic the very fine book by Pierre Hadot, *Plotin ou la simplicité du regard* (Paris: Gallimard, Folio collection, 1997), 26.

31. *WM, GW* 1, 423; *TM*, 419.
32. *WM, GW* 1, 428; *TM*, 423–4.
33. *WM, GW* 1, 425; *TM*, 421.
34. *WM, GW* 1, 430; *TM*, 425.
35. *WM, GW* 1, 429; *TM*, 424.
36. *GW* 10, 274.
37. *WM, GW* 1, 432; *TM*, 428.
38. *WM, GW* 1, 433; *TM*, 429.
39. *WM, GW* 1, 435; *TM*, 431.
40. *WM, GW* 1, 436; *TM*, 432.
41. See *GW* 2, 111, 289, 291, 305. On the intimate links that allowed Gadamer to think that rhetoric and hermeneutics have a common universality, see the article "Hermeneutik", *Historisches Wörterbuch der Rhetorik*, vol. 3, 1350–74. See also *Rhetoric and Hermeneutics in our Times*, ed. Michael J. Hyde and Walter Jost (New Haven, CT: Yale University Press, 1997).
42. *GW* 2, 236–7. Gadamer makes this claim here particularly about the conception of rhetoric defended by G. B. Vico, *De Nostri Temporis Studiorum Ratione* (Godesberg, 1947). On the universality of rhetoric, see the interview of the *Gadamer-Lesebuch*, 284, 291, and *GW* 2, 467.
43. See Habermas, "La Prétention à l'universalité de l'herméneutique", *Logique des Sciences Sociales et Autres Essais* (Paris: PUF, 1987), 268.
44. *Ibid.*, 269.
45. *Ibid.*, 270.
46. *GW* 2, 467.
47. In French, "communicationnelle" [trans.].
48. R. Brague, "Le Récit du Commencement: Une Aporie de la Raison Grecque", in J.-F. Mattei (ed.), *La Naissance de la Raison en Grèce* (Paris: PUF, 1989), 31.
49. *GW* 2, 77–91. For the foundation of the dictionary and the review devoted to the history of concepts, see also Gadamer, *Philosophische Lehrjahre*, 183. Gadamer's most recent works are concentrated on the intimate link between the concept and the life of a language. The last cycle of conferences, which he gave in Naples in January 1997, was entitled, "From the Concept to the Word". To get an idea of the final orientation of his thought, which prolongs the rhetorical thrust of his hermeneutics of 1960, see the conference "Vom Wort zum Begriff", *Gadamer-Lesebuch*, 1997, 100–110, and the last pages of the 1992 article, "Towards a Phenomenology of Ritual and Language", *GW* 8, 400–440 (especially 426ff., "Towards the Concept").

Conclusion

1. *WM, GW* 1, 444; *TM*, 440.
2. *WM, GW* 1, 445; *TM*, 441.
3. *WM, GW* 1, 443; *TM*, 441.
4. *WM, GW* 1, 443. The article appeared only seven years later. See *GW* 8, 37–57. this text should not be confused with the article of the same title published in the Jahresgabe der Martin-Heidegger-Gesellschaft in 1988, reprinted in 1993 in *GW* 9 under the new title, "Poetry and Thought in the Mirror of Hölderlin's *Andenken*". The fact that there are two different texts, both with the same title, announced a long time before, is all the more revelatory of the persistence of the theme in Gadamer's works.
5. *GW* 2, 475.
6. *GW* 8, 53.

7. *GW* 8, 54.
8. *GW* 8, 55.
9. *GW* 8, 56.
10. See *GW* 10, 64ff.
11. *Ibid.*
12. *WM, GW* 1, 472; *TM*, 469.
13. *WM, GW* 1, 472–3; *TM*, 469.
14. *WM, GW* 1, 462; *TM*, 458.
15. Habermas, *Zur Logik der Sozialwissenschaften* (Frankfurt: Suhrkamp, 1970).
16. See *WM, GW* 1, 478–9; *TM*, 474.
17. *WM, GW* 1, 464; *TM*, 460.
18. *WM, GW* 1, 462; *TM*, 458.
19. *WM, GW* 1, 481; *TM*, 477. The idea of a metaphysics of finitude occasionally comes up in Gadamer's work (see *Philosophische Lehrjahre* in a text which dates from 1949). In his *Lectures on Philosophical Hermeneutics* (Pretoria: Van Schaik's Boekhandel, 1982), 29, Gadamer sees in it the consequence of his hermeneutic philosophy.
20. *WM, GW* 1, 490; *TM*, 486–7.
21. *WM, GW* 1, 489; *TM*, 485–6.
22. *WM, GW* 1, 483; *TM*, 479–80.
23. *WM, GW* 1, 485; *TM*, 481.
24. *WM, GW* 1, 487; *TM*, 483.
25. *Ibid.*
26. *Ibid.* This simultaneity of the Word of God and the creation of things also fascinated Franz Rosenzweig in his analysis of the first chapter of Genesis in *Der Stern der Erlösung* (1921), section 139 (Frankfurt: Suhrkamp, 1988), 168.

Bibliography

For a complete bibliography of Gadamer's work until 1994 see Etsuro Makita, *Gadamer-Bibliographie* (Frankfurt: Peter Lang, 1995). For recent work on hermeneutics and Gadamer see J. M. Aguirre-Ora, "Bibliografia de y sobre Hans-Georg Gadamer", *Scriptorium Victoriense* **39** (1992), 300–45; H. Volat-Shapiro, "Gadamer and Hermeneutics: A Bibliography", in H. Silverman (ed.), *Gadamer and Hermeneutics* (London: Routledge, 1991); M. Ferraris, *Storia dell'Ermeneutica* (Milan: Bompiani, 1988); J. C. Petit, "Répertoire bibliographique sur l'herméneutique", *Recherches et théories* **27**, UQAM, 1984.

Hans-Georg Gadamer: *Gesammelte Werke*, vols I–X (Tübingen: Mohr, 1985–95):
  I *Hermeneutik I: Wahrheit und Methode: Grundzüge einer philosophischen Hermeneutik* (1986, second edition, 1990).
  II *Hermeneutik II: Wahrheit und Methode. Ergänzungen – Register* (1986, second edition, 1993).
  III *Neuere Philosophie I: Hegel–Husserl–Heidegger* (1987).
  IV *Neure Philosophie II: Probleme – Gestalten* (1987).
  V *Griechische Philosophie I* (1985).
  VI *Griechische Philosophie II* (1985).
  VII *Griechische Philosophie III: Plato im Dialog* (1991).
  VIII *Ästhetik und Poetik I: Kunst als Aussage* (1993).
  IX *Ästhetik und Poetik II: Hermeneutik im Vollzug* (1993).
  X *Hermeneutik im Rückblick* (1995).

Aguirre-Ora, J. M., *Raison critique ou raison herméneutique? Une analyse de la controverse entre Habermas et Gadamer* (Paris: Éditions du Cerf, 1988)
Albert, H., *Kritik der reinen Hermeneutik* (Tübingen: Mohr, 1994).
Apel, K. O., "Regulative Ideas or Truth-Happening? An Attempt to Answer the Question of the Conditions of the Possibility of Valid Understanding", in *The Philosophy of Hans-Georg Gadamer* (La Salle, IL: Open Court, 1997), 67–94.
Bernasconi, R., "Bridging the Abyss: Heidegger and Gadamer", *Research in Phenomenology* **16** (1986), 1–24.
Bernstein, R. J., *Beyond Objectivism and Relativism: Science, Hermeneutics and Praxis* (Philadelphia, PA: University of Pennsylvania Press, 1988).

173

Bouveresse, J., *Herméneutique et Linguistique* (Paris: Éditions de l'Éclat, 1991).

Castelli, E. (ed.), *Démythologisation et idéologie* (Paris: Aubier, 1973).

Da Re, A., *L'ermeneutica di Gadamer e la filosofia pratica* (Rimini: Magglioli, 1982).

Davey, N., "Habermas' Contribution to Hermeneutic Theory", *Journal of the British Society for Phenomenology* 16 (1985), 109–31.

Davey, N., "Hermeneutics, Language and Science: Gadamer's Distinction between Discursive and Propositional Language", *Journal of the British Society for Phenomenology* 24 (1993), 250–65.

Depew, D. J., "The Habermas–Gadamer Debate in Hegelian Perspective", *Philosophy & Social Criticism* 8 (1981), 425–46.

Di Censo, J., *Hermeneutics and the Disclosure of Truth: A Study in the Work of Heidegger, Gadamer and Ricoeur* (Charlottesville, VA: University Press of Virginia, 1990).

Dostal, R. (ed.), *The Cambridge Companion to Gadamer* (Cambridge: Cambridge University Press, 2001).

Dostal, R., "The World Never Lost: The Hermeneutics of Trust", *Philosophy and Phenomenological Research* 47 (1987), 413–34.

Ferraris, M., *Storia dell'ermeneutica* (Milan: Bompiani, 1988).

Ferry, J.-M., *Habermas: L'éthique de la communication* (Paris: PUF, 1987).

Figal, G. (ed.), *Begegnungen mit Hans-Georg Gadamer* (Stuttgart: Reclam, 2000).

Figal, G., Grondin, J., Schmidt, D. (eds), *Hermeneutische Wege* (Tübingen: Mohr, 2000).

Fleury, P., "Lumières et Tradition: J. Habermas face à H.-G. Gadamer", in *Comprendre et interpréter: Le paradigme herméneutique de la raison*, ed. J. Greisch (Paris: Beauchesne, 1993), 343–60.

Fruchon, P., "Herméneutique, langage et ontologie: Un discernement du platonisme chez H.-G. Gadamer", *Archives de Philosophie* 36 (1973), 529–68; 37 (1974), 223–42, 353–75, 533–71.

Fruchon, P., *L'Herméneutique de Gadamer: platonisme et modernité* (Paris: Éditions du Cerf, 1994).

Gens, J.-C., "La réévaluation par Gadamer du concept piétiste d'application", *L'Art du comprendre*, no. 4, February 1996, 24–37.

Giddens, A., "Habermas' Critique of Hermeneutics", in A. Giddens, *Studies in Social and Political Theory* (London: Hutchinson, 1977), 135–64.

Giurlanda, "Habermas' Critique of Gadamer: Does it Stand Up?", *International Philosophical Quarterly* 27 (1987), 33–41.

Greisch, J. (ed.), *Comprendre et interpréter: La paradigme herméneutique de la raison* (Paris: Beauchesne, 1993)

Greisch, J., *Herméneutique et grammatologie* (Paris: Éditions du CNRS, 1977).

Greisch, J., *L'Âge herméneutique de la raison* (Paris: Éditions du Cerf, 1985).

Grondin, J., *Hans-Georg Gadamer: Eine Biographie* (Tübingen: Mohr, 1999).

Grondin, J., *Hermeneutische Wahrheit? Zum Wahrheitsbegriff Hans-Georg Gadamers* (Königstein: Forum Academicum, 1982; second edition, Weinheim: Belz-Athäneum, 1994).

Grondin, J., *L'Universalité de l'herméneutique* (Paris: PUF, 1993).

Grondin, J., *L'Horizon herméneutique de la pensée contemporaine* (Paris: Vrin, 1993).

Grondin, J., "La définition derridienne de la déconstruction: Contribution au rapprochement de l'herméneutique et de la déconstruction", *Archives de Philosophie* 62 (1999), 5–16.

Grondin, J., *Sources of Hermeneutics* (Albany, NY: SUNY Press, 1995).

Guillemot, J.-L., "L'évolution de la critique de l'herméneutique chez Habermas", *Eidos* XI (1983), 55–75.

Habermas, J., *Logique de sciences sociales et autres essais* (Paris: PUF, 1987).

Hahn, L. E. (ed.), *The Philosophy of Hans-Georg Gadamer* (La Salle, IL: Open Court, 1997).

Hollinger, R. (ed.), *Hermeneutics and Praxis* (Notre Dame, IN: University of Notre Dame Press, 1985).

How, A. R., "Dialogue as Productive Limitation in Social Theory: The Habermas–Derrida Debate", *Journal of the British Society for Phenomenology* 11 (1980), 131–43.

How, A. R., "A Case of Creative Misreading: Habermas's Evaluation of Gadamer's Hermeneutics", *Journal of the British Society for Phenomenology* 16 (1985), 132–44.

Ingram, D., "The Historical Genesis of the Gadamer–Habermas Controversy", *Auslegung: A Journal of Philosophy* 10 (1983), 86–151.

Janicaud, D., *La Phénoménologie éclatée* (Paris: Éditions de l'Éclat, 1998).

Jay, M., "Should Intellectual History Take a Linguistic Turn? Reflections on the Habermas–Gadamer Debate", in D. La Capra & S. L. Kaplan (eds), *Modern European Intellectual History* (Ithaca, NY: Cornell University Press, 1982).

Kelley, M., "The Gadamer–Habermas Debate Revisted: The Question of Ethics", *Philosophy & Social Criticism* 14 (1988), 369–90.

Kisiel, T., "Ideology Critique and Phenomenology: The Current Debate in German Philosophy", *Philosophy Today* 14 (1970), 151–60.

Kisiel, T., "The Happening of Tradition: The Hermeneutics of Gadamer and Heidegger", *Man and World* 2 (1969), 358–85.

Krajewski, B., (ed.), *Gadamer at 100* (Berkeley, CA: University of California Press, 2000).

Kusch, M., *Language as Calculus vs. Language as Universal Medium: A Study in Husserl, Heidegger and Gadamer* (Dordrecht: Kluwer, 1989).

Langlois, L., "La signification éthique de l'expérience herméneutique dans *Vérité et méthode*", *Laval Théologique et Philosophique* 53 (1997), 69–87.

MacIntyre, A., "Contexts of Interpretation: Reflections on Hans-Georg Gadamer's *Truth and Method*", *Boston University Journal* 24 (1976), 41–6.

Marchildon, R., "À propos de la conception herméneutique de la vérité", *Laval Thélogique et Philosophique* 53 (1997), 141–50.

Mendelson, J., "The Habermas–Gadamer Debate", *New German Critique* 18 (1979), 44–73.

Michelfelder, D. & Palmer, R. E. (eds), *Dialogue and Deconstruction: The Gadamer–Derrida Encounter* (Albany, NY: SUNY Press, 1989).

Misgeld, D., "Discourse and Conversation: The Theory of Communicative Competence and Hermeneutics in the Light of the Debate between Habermas and Gadamer", *Cultural Hermeneutics* 4 (1976-7), 321–44.

Misgeld, D. & Nicholson, G. (eds), *Hans-Georg Gadamer on Education, Poetry, and History* (Albany, NY: SUNY Press, 1992).

Moratalla, A. D., *El arte de poder no tener razón: La hermenéutica dialógica de H.-G. Gadamer* (Salamanca: Publicaciones Universidad Pontifica de Salamanca, 1991).

Palmer, R. E., *Hermeneutics: Interpretation Theory in Schleiermacher, Dilthey, Heidegger and Gadamer* (Evanston, IL: Northwestern University Press, 1969).

Renaud, F., "Gadamer, lecteur de Platon", *Études Phénoménologiques* 26 (1997), 33–57.

Ricoeur, P., *Du texte à l'action: Essais d'herméneutique II* (Paris: Éditions du Seuil, 1986).

Ricoeur, P., "Herméneutique et critique des idéologies", *Du texte à l'action*, 1988, 333–77.

Ricoeur, P., Temps et récit (Paris: Éditions du Seuil, 1985).

Ricoeur, P., & Gadamer, H.-G., "The Conflict of Interpretations", in R. Buzina & B. Wilshire, *Phenomenology: Dialogues and Bridges* (Albany, NY: SUNY Press, 1982), 299–320.

Ripanti, G., *Gadamer* (Assise: Citadella Editions, 1978).

Risser, J., *Hermeneutics and the Voice of the Other: Re-reading Gadamer's Philosophical Hermeneutics* (Albany, NY: SUNY Press, 1997).

Sansonetti, G., *Il pensiero di Hans-Georg Gadamer* (Brescia: Morcelliana, 1988).

Schapiro, G. & Sica, A. (eds), *Hermeneutics: Questions and Prospects* (Amherst, MA: University of Massachusetts Press, 1984).

Schmidt, L. K., *The Epistemology of Hans-Georg Gadamer: An Analysis of the Legitimization of Vorurteile* (Frankfurt: Peter Lang, 1987).

Schmidt, L. K. (ed.), *The Specter of Relativism: Truth, Dialogue, and Phronesis in Philosophical Hermeneutics* (Evanston, IL: Northwestern University Press, 1995).

Smith, P. C., "The Ethical Dimension of Gadamer's Hermeneutical Theory", *Research in Phenomenology* **18** (1988), 75–92.

Silverman, H. (ed.), *Gadamer and Hermeneutics* (London: Routledge, 1991).

Smith, P. C., *Hermeneutics and Human Finitude: Towards an Ethical Theory of Understanding* (New York: Fordham University Press, 1991).

Teichert, D., *Erfahrung, Erinnerung, Erkenntnis: Untersuchungen zum Wahrheitsbegriff der Hermeneutik Gadamers* (Stuttgart: Metzler, 1991).

Thérien, C., "Gadamer et la phénoménologie du dialogue", *Laval Théologique et Philosophique* **53** (1997), 167–80.

Thiselton, A. C., *The Two Horizons: New Testament Hermeneutics and Philosophical Description with Special Reference to Heidegger, Bultmann, Gadamer and Wittgenstein* (Exeter: Paternoster Press, 1980)

Vattimo, G., *Au-delà de l'interpretation* (Paris: Éditions Universitaires de Boeck, 1997).

Wachterhauser, B. (ed.), *Hermeneutics and Modern Philosophy* (Albany, NY: SUNY Press, 1986).

Wachterhauser, B. (ed.), *Hermeneutics and Truth* (Evanston, IL: Northwestern University Press, 1994).

Warncke, G., *Gadamer: Herméneutique, tradition et raison* (Paris: Éditions Universitaires de Boeck, 1991).

Weinsheimer, J., *Gadamer's Hermeneutics: A Reading of* Truth and Method (New Haven, CT: Yale University Press, 1985).

Weinsheimer, J., Wright, K., Grondin, J., three essays on the theme "Gadamer and the Truth of Art" in *Encyclopedia of Aesthetics*, vol. II, ed. M. Kelly (New York: Oxford University Press, 1998), 261–71.

Wiehl, R. (ed.), *Die antike Philosophie in ihrer Bedeutung für die Gegenwart: Kolloquium zu Ehren des 80. Geburtstages von Hans-Georg Gadamer* (Heidelberg: Carl Winter Verlag, 1980).

Wright, K. (ed.), *Festivals of Interpretation: Essays on Hans-Georg Gadamer's Work* (Albany, NY: SUNY Press, 1990).

Index